D1564006

"Getting along with others is a basic key to success—and happiness. When people are high on this dimension (termed *political skill* by the authors), all doors (opportunities) are open; when they are low, the opposite may be true—important routes to success are closed. Political skill is invaluable in many different contexts, from building a career in an organization, to starting a new company and making it a success. The authors are outstanding researchers and true experts concerning political skill, so this new edition is certain to be even more informative and more valuable than the first edition. A 'must read' for people in many different fields."

—Robert A. Baron, Regents Professor,
Oklahoma State University

"Political Skill at Work is both thoroughly researched and splendidly readable. If you enjoy reading about workplace politics, and want to know more about how to navigate the political environment with political skill, you will love this book."

—Gerhard Blickle, Professor of Psychology,
University of Bonn, Germany

"So, you think office politics is about self-interest and dirty tricks? Think again. Political skill can lead to positive outcomes for you and your organization, such as improving your job performance, influence, reputation, and career prospects. Don't complain when others play politics. Become a master politician yourself. This new edition of *Political Skill at Work* uses fascinating examples and robust evidence to make the case. Want to start playing the politics game? You already are."

—David A. Buchanan, Emeritus Professor of Organizational
Behaviour, Cranfield University School of Management

POLITICAL SKILL
AT WORK

How to Influence, Motivate, and Win Support

Revised Edition

GERALD R. FERRIS

PAMELA L. PERREWÉ

B. PARKER ELLEN III

CHARN P. McALLISTER

DARREN C. TREADWAY

NICHOLAS BREALEY
PUBLISHING

BOSTON • LONDON

First published in 2005 by Davies-Black Publishing
This second edition published in 2020 by Nicholas Brealey Publishing
An imprint of John Murray Press

An Hachette UK company

24   23   22   21   20   1   2   3   4   5   6   7   8   9   10

A CIP catalogue record for this title is available from the British Library

Library of Congress Control Number: 2019957539

ISBN 978-1-52937-466-7
US eBook ISBN 978-0-89106-339-1
UK eBook ISBN 978-1-47364-406-9

Printed and bound in the United States of America.

John Murray Press policy is to use papers that are natural, renewable, and
recyclable products and made from wood grown in sustainable forests.
The logging and manufacturing processes are expected to conform to the
environmental regulations of the country of origin.

John Murray Press Ltd   Nicholas Brealey Publishing
Carmelite House   Hachette Book Group
50 Victoria Embankment   53 State Street
London EC4Y 0DZ   Boston, MA 02109, USA
Tel: 020 3122 6000   Tel: (617) 263 1834

www.nbuspublishing.com

CONTENTS

PART III: POLITICAL SKILL IN SPECIFIC CONTEXTS

Revised Edition Authors

Gerald R. Ferris, Ph.D.
Florida State University

Pamela L. Perrewé, Ph.D.
Florida State University

B. Parker Ellen III, Ph.D.
Northeastern University

Charn P. McAllister, Ph.D.
Northern Arizona University

Darren C. Treadway, Ph.D.
Daemen College

ABOUT THE AUTHORS

Gerald R. Ferris, PhD, is the Marie Krafft Professor of Management, Professor of Psychology, and Professor of Sports Management at Florida State University. Prior to accepting this chaired position, he held the Robert M. Hearin Chair of Business Administration and was Professor of Management and Acting Associate Dean for Faculty and Research in the School of Business Administration at the University of Mississippi From 1999 to 2000, and before that he served as Professor of Labor and Industrial Relations, of Business Administration, and of Psychology at the University of Illinois at Urbana-Champaign From 1989 to 1999 and as the Director of the Center for Human Resource Management at the University of Illinois From 1991 to 1996. Ferris received a PhD in Business Administration from the University of Illinois at Urbana-Champaign. He has research interests in the areas of interpersonal and political influence in organizations, performance evaluation, and strategic human resources management. Ferris is the author of over 275 articles published in such scholarly journals as the *Journal of Applied Psychology, Organizational Behavior and Human Decision Processes, Personnel Psychology, Academy of Management Journal,* and *Academy of Management Review,* and such applied journals as the *Academy of Management Executive,*

Human Resource Management, Human Resource Planning, and *Organizational Dynamics.* Ferris served as editor of the annual series *Research in Personnel and Human Resources Management* from its origin in 1981 until 2003. He has authored or edited nearly 40 books, including *Political Skill at Work* (Davies-Black, Nicholas Brealey); *Human Resources Management: Perspectives, Context, Functions, and Outcomes* (Prentice-Hall); *Handbook of Human Resource Management* (Blackwell); *Strategy and Human Resources Management* (South-Western); and *Method & Analysis in Organizational Research* (Reston). Ferris has consulted on a variety of human resources topics with companies, including ARCO, Borg-Warner, Eli Lilly, Motorola, and PPG, and he has taught in management development programs and lectured in Austria, Greece, Hong Kong, Japan, Singapore, and Taiwan, in addition to various US universities. Professor Ferris's work on influence at work has been the focus of considerable general interest as well. He has been interviewed on national television on *CBS This Morning* (by Charles Osgood); on radio stations for call-in programs in most major cities in the United States as well as the BBC in London and stations in Tokyo, Singapore, and New Zealand; and his work has been written up in major US newspapers from coast to coast. Ferris has been the recipient of a number of distinctions and honors. In 2001, he was the recipient of the Heneman Career Achievement Award, and in 2010 he received the Thomas A. Mahoney Mentoring Award, both from the Human Resources Division of the Academy of Management.

Pamela L. Perrewé, PhD, is the Robert O. Lawton Distinguished Professor, the Haywood and Betty Taylor Eminent Scholar of Business Administration, Professor of Sports Management, and Distinguished Research Professor at Florida State University. She received her bachelor's degree in psychology from Purdue University and her master's and PhD degrees in Management from the University of Nebraska. Dr. Perrewé primarily teaches courses in Organizational Behavior and Human Resource Management and has taught at the undergraduate, graduate, and PhD levels. She has served on approximately 100 doctoral dissertation committees and has chaired over 20 of these dissertation committees. She has been awarded the Developing Scholar Award, University Teaching Award, and Graduate Mentoring Award at Florida State University. Dr. Perrewé has focused her research interests in the areas of job stress, coping, organizational politics, emotion, and social influence. Dr. Perrewé has published over 40 books and book chapters and over 140 articles in journals such as *Academy of Management Journal, Journal of Management, Journal of Applied Psychology, Organizational Behavior and Human Decision Processes, Journal of Organizational Behavior, Journal of Occupational Health Psychology,* and *Personnel Psychology.* She has served as a member of the Editorial Review Board for *Academy of Management Journal, Journal of Occupational Health Psychology, Human Resource Management Review,* and *Leadership and Organizational Studies.* She has fellow status with the Southern Management Association, the Society for Industrial and Organizational Psychology, the Association for Psychological Science, and the American Psychological Association. Further, she is the lead editor of an annual research series entitled *Research in Occupational Stress and Well-Being,* published by Emerald Publishing. Finally, Dr. Perrewé is the Faculty Athletics Representative for Florida State University, and she is the liaison to the Atlantic Coast Conference and the National Collegiate Athletic Association.

B. Parker Ellen III, PhD, is an Assistant Professor of Management and Organizational Development in the D'Amore-McKim School of Business at Northeastern University. He received a Bachelor's in Civil Engineering from Auburn University, a Master's in Managerial Sciences from Georgia State University, and a PhD in Organizational Behavior and Human Resource Management from Florida State University. Professor Ellen's research centers on social influence in organizations (primarily organizational politics and leadership) and has been published in a number of highly regarded academic outlets, including *Journal of Management, Journal of Management Studies, Journal of Organizational Behavior, The Leadership Quarterly,* and *Annual Review of Organizational Psychology and Organizational Behavior.* His work has been recognized with several awards, including a top-rated submission at the Society for Industrial and Organizational Psychology annual conference and the 2014 Meredith P. Crawford Fellowship from the Human Resources Research Organization. He currently serves on the Editorial Board of *Journal of Organizational Behavior.* Prior to academia, Professor Ellen spent nine years in the consulting engineering industry, serving in a number of project, office, regional, and firm-wide management roles for a privately held organization with more than 50 offices across the United States. In addition to his primary management responsibilities, he spent the final two years of his professional career codirecting the firm-wide training program for midcareer professionals.

Charn P. McAllister, PhD, is an Assistant Professor of Management in the W.A. Franke College of Business at Northern Arizona University. He received his bachelor's degree in Engineering Psychology from the United States Military Academy at West Point, his master's in Humanities from American Military University, and his PhD from Florida State University. Dr. McAllister's research interests include political skill, interpersonal mistreatment, and stress. His research has been published in journals, including *Journal of Applied Psychology, Personnel Psychology, Journal of Management, Journal of Organizational Behavior, Journal of Business Ethics,* and *Military Psychology.* Additionally, he has published work in the *Harvard Business Review* (HBR.org) and various news outlets. Prior to his time in academia, Dr. McAllister served as an officer in the US Army. After training as an OH-58D Kiowa Warrior pilot, he served in various leadership positions from platoon leader to Air Cavalry Troop Commander and deployed twice in support of Operation Iraqi Freedom.

Darren C. Treadway, PhD, is currently a Visiting Professor of Business at Daemen College. He received a PhD from Florida State University and an MBA from Virginia Tech. Dr. Treadway's research interests include social influence processes in organizations, with particular reference to organizational politics, political skill, workplace bullying, and leadership. He has published over 45 articles in leading journals such as *Journal of Applied Psychology, Journal of Management, The Leadership Quarterly, Journal of Organizational Behavior,* and *Human Relations.* Dr. Treadway serves as Associate Editor of *Frontiers on Psychology: Organizational Psychology* and on the Editorial Board of *Journal of Organizational Behavior* and *The Journal of Leadership and Organizational Studies.* His research has been awarded the *Journal of Management* Best Paper Award and has twice been recognized by Emerald Publishing with a Citation of Excellence. Prior to his employment, Dr. Treadway was on faculty at the University of Mississippi and the University at Buffalo, where he was twice named the Researcher of the Year and his cumulative contributions earned him the University at Buffalo Exceptional Scholar Award.

Introduction: Politics Is Not a Dirty Word

If you ask people why they didn't get a job or promotion they wanted, you shouldn't be surprised to hear something along the lines of, "It was a political decision." The specific translation of their response may vary depending upon the circumstances, but the core message remains the same. For example, they could mean that the boss was playing favorites in the team by promoting the person closest to them, or that they gave the job to an old college buddy despite a lack of qualifications. Regardless, what they're trying to communicate is that they feel the decision was unfair. They believe someone got a job or promotion that wasn't deserved, and, on top of that, it was at the expense of someone who did deserve it (usually, the person you asked). So when people say a decision was political, they're usually trying to communicate that something didn't go their way and that they don't think it was fair.

You might have said, or at least thought, something like this at times during your career as well. This labeling of situations that don't go our way as political is a natural reaction, referred to in psychology as an "attribution." Through quite a few experiments and research studies over several decades, results have shown that people tend to make external attributions (that is, assign blame to things outside their control) when bad things happen and internal attributions (that is, take credit based on personal triumph) when good things happen. So when "Tom" gets promoted over others, it's because he worked hard and has valuable skills, but if others get promoted over Tom, he's likely to claim it wasn't fair, that it was "just politics."

The use of politics doesn't just stop at descriptions of things that are deemed unfair, though. Often, people use the term to describe situations where intentional manipulation has taken place, where they or others were taken advantage of through nefarious actions. In fact, if you conduct an online image search for the term "office politics," you'll notice among the top results several that depict people in professional attire backstabbing, gossiping, and fighting. Not surprisingly, then, many people aren't fond of organizational politics. In fact, when the topic is mentioned, people often visibly cringe because they view it as something decidedly negative and potentially immoral. Is this true? Not always.

Organizational politics actually is a neutral concept. The root of the word for politics comes from the Greek word *polis*, which means that politics refers to things of or for the community. In fact, one of Merriam-Webster's definitions of *politics* is "the total complex of relations between people living in society." Given this, organizational politics is, at its core, simply a term that captures the complexities of social interaction in organizations, without any value ascribed. However, just like power (a closely related concept) or money, organizational politics can be used in positive or negative ways.

The examples of organizational politics to advance self-interest at the expense of others at work are those with which we're all too familiar. This use of organizational politics captures those instances when people gossip about others at work, intentionally trying to damage a colleague's reputation and hinder their success in the organization. It also includes the strategic use of information, such as withholding knowledge that would be important or beneficial to others, as well as manipulating facts during conversations in efforts to intentionally deceive. In essence, the negative use of organizational politics represents all the ways people attempt to stack the deck to ensure that they, or those in their inner circle, get ahead while others are held back.

But organizational politics is much more than just a negative means to desired ends. It also can be and often is used to facilitate outcomes that are generally positive for others, even the collective. In government, nonprofit, and industry organizations, great leaders often *must* rely on politics to get things accomplished, especially the really hard stuff. One prominent example of this was during the Cuban Missile Crisis. Although most people understand this historical event through a geopolitical lens and view it as a diplomatic triumph in the traditional sense of the political arena, what has been documented in the book (and later in the movie) *Thirteen Days* shows how President John F. Kennedy adeptly navigated the internal organizational politics of his own administration to resolve a standoff over the deployment of Soviet missiles in Cuba. Throughout the nearly two-week period, President Kennedy's advisors fought with each other, and the president, about how to handle the crisis. In addition to enduring the deceit of an adversarial foreign power in the Soviet Union, President Kennedy had to ensure against being manipulated by his cabinet to avoid catapulting the world into a nuclear war. In the end, he and those in his inner circle were able to wield their influence in a manner that avoided a catastrophic end.

Perhaps you don't envision yourself needing to sidestep an actual nuclear conflict, but rather just an analogous one in your own career. Surviving at work often requires navigating organizational politics. Take F. Ross Johnson, the infamous former CEO of RJR Nabisco who likely wouldn't have had the chance to set in motion the largest leveraged buyout in Wall Street history had he not been able to prevail in the political arena at Standard Brands. Johnson was second in command at the company, but his boss wanted him out. Things culminated in a contentious meeting of the Standard Brands board of directors in Manhattan. His career was on the line, but as Bryan Burrough and John Helyar wrote in *Barbarians at the Gate*, "...when it came to corporate politics, no one was ready to count out Ross Johnson. He seemed to have a knack for survival." Johnson survived the attack and emerged from the meeting victorious. His boss, Henry Weigl, was removed as CEO, with Johnson installed as his replacement.

These are just two of countless examples. More recently, politicians, like former president Bill Clinton, emerged relatively unscathed from the most serious of national scandals, and before fraud ultimately caught up to her, Elizabeth Holmes survived a board coup in the early days of Theranos to replace her as CEO. We relish stories like these—politicians and executives, who now have achieved the fame, recognition, and deference of rock stars, playing to crowds like virtuoso musicians in efforts to meet their own agendas. But this doesn't just happen at the highest level of government or in corporate boardrooms. It happens throughout organizations. In fact, in a landmark study in an electric company in the early 1900s, researchers found evidence of an "informal organization," in many ways distinct from the formal organizational hierarchy, that dictated the ways things unfolded at work extending all the way to the shop floor.

At this point, it's doubtless that many of you are excited about the possibility of prevailing in the political arena, but we recognize that likely many of you are starting to get turned off. Despite our description of politics as a neutral phenomenon that can get used to facilitate both good and bad outcomes, you're tempted to put the book down because you "don't like playing politics." We understand, but we want to make sure you know that you actually are already playing. You see, most of us work for a living, and almost all of us who work for a living do so in organizations, whether large or small business; educational institutions; or local, state, or national government. And politics are ubiquitous in all types of organizations—regardless of type, size, or age. That's right. From start-ups to centuries-old Fortune 500 firms, politics are a fact of organizational life.

This reality extends to all forms and structures as well. Organizations of all types have experienced monumental changes in the past few decades. Downsizing, restructuring and redesign, mergers and acquisitions, and other changes represent major shifts that have dramatically altered the ways workplaces function. Political maneuvering is rampant during these shifts, but even when "the dust settles" and multilevel bureaucracy and the associated formal policies, systems, and features that went along with such traditional forms of organizing are replaced with flatter structures and open environments, politics are a key factor. In fact, in these new organizational forms, the interactions required among work team members, supervisors, and subordinates, as well as between employees and clients, increases, which arguably makes politics even more prevalent.

Thus, regardless of your work situation, politics is a part of organizational life. As Sherlock Holmes says, "The game is afoot!" You are in it. You actually can't choose not to play. You can only choose how to act. You need to be able to influence others to follow your ideas, decisions, and new programs of action. In fact, even if you are self-employed, you deal with customers and other individuals in ways that require influence. But, how? Do you force people to comply with your wishes or interests? Threaten them? Intimidate them? Some people certainly try, but research and practice have shown that this is not an effective long-term strategy (and often it's one that backfires even in the short term). Instead, you need to develop a style of interaction that allows you to read and interpret situations and exhibit just the right kind of behavior that will make others do what you want—and do so *willingly*, as if it was their own idea.

This last part is the key to effectively surviving and thriving through organizational politics. Those most adept are the ones able to influence others in such a way that what they are doing goes almost undetected. People might recognize them as influential, but, somehow, they can never tell when they are being influenced. These master organizational politicians have the capacity to understand what behaviors and activities to demonstrate in particular situations at work, but also how to transmit or execute such behaviors in genuine, sincere, and convincing ways that result in successful influence attempts, or "getting their way." Further, they are those who somehow are always well positioned—in the proper place, at the right time, and in a stance on a particular issue that allows them to succeed.

This book aims to help you become one of those people. It is a "how to" as well as a "what to" book, in that it informs you about "what" things you should do in certain situations but also "how" to execute those behaviors in ways that are effective and result in successful influence. Bookstores are full of books on "winning at office politics" that tell you what things to say and do. The reason the readers of those books do not turn into overnight successes (or even long-term successes) is that it takes more than simply knowing what to do; you have to execute the "what" in convincing ways or understand the "how" of influence. To know both what and how to influence others at work, therefore, takes *political skill.*

The chapters that follow are about the nature of political skill and the roles it plays in your ability to influence others and, therefore, in your own personal job and career success. In them, you will learn to understand, realize, enhance, and use political skill at work. Indeed, the title contains an intentional double meaning, as this book will describe both political skill at work (i.e., in the organizations) and the characterization of political skill at work (i.e., the way political skill operates and how it results in personal and organizational effectiveness).

The book is organized into three parts and twelve chapters. Part I introduces you to political skill. It explains its nature in detail, outlines its dimensions, distinguishes it from other related concepts, and describes how it is measured (including an opportunity to assess your own level of political skill). Then it describes how political skill works and what makes it so essential to successful influence. Next, it addresses whether we can train or develop political skill in people. Finally, it discusses the role of political will, the motivation to put your political skill to work.

Part II deals more specifically with how you can use political skill for self-improvement and increased effectiveness in the workplace. The chapters in this section address the role of political skill in getting hired, maximizing job performance and career success, enhancing your reputation, and coping with stress to facilitate health and well-being.

Part III focuses on political skill in more "advanced" circumstances. These chapters show how political skill can build extensive and influential networks, how it enhances negotiation outcomes (for both parties!), and its role in digital interactions. We close with a chapter on how political skill helps organizations, not just individuals, realize greater effectiveness through leadership and team performance.

As with most books, we've put some thought into the organization of the chapters. They're ordered to orient you to political skill before showing you what it can do. Thus, our intent is for readers to progress through the chapters in order. However, we recognize that you might have picked it up for a specific purpose. Perhaps you have an interview coming up for your dream job. We still recommend reading chapter 1 first so that you understand the nature of political skill, but after that you might want to jump to chapter 5 to look at some of the specifics regarding how political skill can help you get the job. Or, you might be agonizing over how to negotiate a raise or preferred work arrangement with your boss. If so, you might want to read chapter 10 a little sooner. Perhaps you're so overwhelmed at work that you are just trying to get through the next day, too stressed to think about advancing. Well, jump ahead to chapter 8. Finally, maybe you made it this far, but you're still skeptical. You can't imagine politics being used for anything other than selfish gain. If that's the case, we hope you'll start with chapter 12 to learn how political skill makes leaders *and* their teams and organizations more effective.

Regardless of how you move through the book, we believe

you'll find value in every chapter, regardless of your work situation or career stage. We've tried to include a variety of examples to make the content accessible to everyone. However, we're still academics, so we've included research highlights at the end of the chapters to give you a sense of the science behind our claims. (That's right, we didn't just make this up!) Additionally, we really want this book to help you advance your career. To that end, we've created a website to accompany the book (politicalskillatwork.com). On it, you'll be able to take the Political Skill Inventory to assess your political skill, access some of the latest research, and find out ways to develop your influence ability.

With that, we invite you to let us share with you what we have learned about political skill over nearly 30 years of research in a number of different organizations, with people from many different occupations, in countries all over the world. We have found political skill to be a fascinating concept that we believe can help you excel at work and look forward to showing just what it can do for you. Again, politics doesn't have to be dirty, and despite some of the examples mentioned, political skill is more than just something you can use to get out of trouble, or to get away with self-serving efforts to increase your own personal wealth at the expense of others. Of course, these are misuses. However, we regard political skill as an effective characteristic that can contribute to good things happening for individuals *and* the organizations in which they work.

PART I

UNDERSTANDING POLITICAL SKILL

1

SURVIVING AND THRIVING IN THE POLITICAL ARENA

In 1979, Tom Wolfe published the culmination of his extensive research on US pilots involved in the research and development of rocket-powered aircraft. Wolfe's conclusion was that these pilots, who not only accepted but excelled in jobs fraught with risk, were distinguished from others by their possession of certain characteristics both required for and reinforced by their working environments. Together, the characteristics, described as a combination of confidence and skill, gave the pilots something that enabled them to succeed, the essence of which is captured in the phrase Wolfe coined as the title of his book—*The Right Stuff*.

Although the typical job doesn't require the same type or level of danger as being the first to climb aboard a rocket-powered vessel, the political nature of organizations is such that surviving and thriving within them does require a special set of skills. Indeed, organizations can be viewed as political arenas, where informal negotiation and bargaining, deal making, favor doing, quid pro quo interactions, and coalition and alliance building characterize the way things really get done. Similar to Wolfe's description of the test pilots, we argue that those who excel in the political arena at work possess the right stuff for professional success. Yes, job performance and career success are determined in part by intelligence and effort, but it is clear that, more often than not, something else is required to advance within an organization or a particular field.

Some have referred to this something else or organizational right stuff as interpersonal style, savvy, or street smarts. However, these are typically more abstract concepts with imprecise descriptions, built largely on anecdotes rather than a body of scientific research. As a result, some people come to believe and purport that, when it comes to success in workplace politics, you either have *it* or you don't. For those who want to improve their ability to influence others and advance in their careers, this view is problematic. If what is needed to gain and wield influence at work is abstract and our understanding of it imprecise, then we can't identify its components, we can't actually measure or detect it beyond notions of "I know it when I see it," and most important we can't practice or develop it in ourselves or others to help facilitate career success. Fortunately, this is not the case. As described in the introduction, our research, as well as that of many others over the past several decades, demonstrates that political skill is the so-called right stuff that facilitates success at work, and that it can be developed.

What Is Political Skill?

Political skill was first introduced to the management and organizational behavior literature in the early 1980s when two organizational theorists (Jeff Pfeffer and Henry Mintzberg) mentioned it, independently, in their treatises on power in organizations. Both Pfeffer and Mintzberg identified political skill as necessary for success in organizations.[1] But we can trace the origin of political skill back to the interestingly similar, yet parallel, work of psychologist E. L. Thorndike and entrepreneur Dale Carnegie, who both worked in New York in the early 1900s. Thorndike introduced the concept of social intelligence, which referred to understanding people and acting on that knowledge in influential ways. Carnegie, through his still famous courses on interpersonal effectiveness, taught people fundamental principles of how to work with and through others. Both the scientific and applied work of these four men established the foundational idea that success is linked to social and interpersonal competence.

Interestingly, though, more systematic research on political skill, including efforts to formally define it and develop survey instruments for measuring it and its effects, didn't occur until the late 1990s. This period of dormancy for the concept likely was due in part to people's tendency to have a negative reaction to anything with a "political" label. However, over the past two decades, people have begun to understand the value of political skill, and research on the construct has increased exponentially as the concept has gained greater acceptance. As a result, we now have a fairly robust understanding of what political skill is and how it facilitates interpersonal success.

Definition

Political skill is defined as the ability to effectively understand others at work and to use that knowledge to influence others to act in ways that enhances one's personal and/or organizational objectives. As such, it is often referred to as an adeptness in both reading and reacting, as politically skilled individuals combine an ability to comprehend social situations with the capacity to adjust their behavior to match the varying situational demands encountered when dealing with others. Perhaps more important, political skill enables individuals to exercise selected behaviors in a manner that appears to be sincere, inspires support, and engenders trust, such that they can effectively influence and shape the responses of others.

For example, imagine a meeting at work where the boss has assembled a number of her subordinates around a conference table. She explains to the group that sales have been lagging, and that this is to be a brainstorming session to come up with an approach to marketing the group's flagship product. After some initial discussion, several members of the team begin to offer alternatives to the current strategy. Although not overtly dismissive of the ideas being suggested, the boss rather quickly manages to poke holes in the ideas being presented, listing a number of reasons why the approach won't work and ultimately rejecting each alternative approach. A politically skilled member of the group observes the first couple of these iterations and quickly comes to a conclusion: the boss doesn't really want a new approach. Perhaps this is because she was the driving force behind the existing marketing strategy. Instead of offering an idea that is a complete departure from this existing approach, the politically skilled member of the team suggests that rather than "throw the baby out with the bathwater," the group focus instead on tweaking the existing strategy. The boss suddenly seems to perk up, smiles at the politically skilled subordinate with a "great idea!" and redirects the group to start offering suggestions in this vein.

In the scenario just described, the politically skilled subordinate has observed the boss's comments (and likely body language as well) and determined that despite what she said, the boss doesn't really seem to want to change course. As a result, the subordinate decides the best course of action is to suggest a less drastic change in strategy, maintaining some portions of the current approach, which clearly scores points with the boss. Beyond simply understanding what is happening in the situation, though, politically skilled individuals exude a sense of personal security and calm self-confidence that attracts others and gives them a feeling of comfort. This self-confidence doesn't go so far as to be perceived as arrogance, which allows politically skilled individuals to always maintain proper balance and perspective. Thus, we suggest that people high in political skill not only know precisely *what* to do or say in different social situations at work, but they know *how* to do or say it in a manner that disguises any ulterior, self-serving motives. Returning to the example above, we would argue that this ability to appear sincere enabled the politically skilled subordinate to make the suggestion to stay true to the current course of action without seeming like they were kissing up to the boss.

How Political Skill Differs from Other Concepts

The description of people with the abilities described above as having "street smarts" likens political skill to a form of intelligence. In fact, some might argue that competencies like political skill are simply a function of intelligence. However, research has shown that political skill is independent from intelligence or cognitive ability. Although intelligence certainly aids in success at work and doesn't hurt when you're trying to influence someone, the possession of political skill, or its effective use, does not depend on having a high IQ. In fact, it is possible to possess modest or even below-average intelligence and still be very politically skilled. In terms of its derivation, we believe there are aspects of political skill that are dispositional or inherited, but we see other aspects that can be developed or shaped through a combination of formal and informal training and developmental experiences (see chapter 3).

Additionally, the ability to understand others and control one's actions makes political skill similar in concept to emotional intelligence, another social effectiveness construct that has received considerable attention in the popular, business, and research press in the past two decades, primarily as a function of Daniel Goleman's (1995, 1998)[2] best-selling books. Emotional intelligence focuses predominantly on the emotion-based aspects of interpersonal effectiveness, influence, and control. Conversely, political skill incorporates knowledge and skill that go beyond emotions. Therefore, particularly because of Goleman's broad characterization of emotional intelligence (which has led some to suggest that Goleman regards emotional intelligence as including everything except cognitive ability or intelligence),[3] it is related to political skill but represents a distinct construct.

In fact, several research studies have examined the relationship between the two and found that although they are positively correlated, they should not be considered completely overlapping or redundant concepts.[4] Even more pertinent to your success at work, however, is the research that has shown political skill out-performs emotional intelligence when predicting effectiveness at work.

Further, political skill is somewhat related to certain personality traits and with other related constructs that purport to measure social effectiveness or interpersonal sensitivity. For example, research has shown that political skill is related positively to concepts like self-monitoring (i.e., the tendency to alter one's behavior to match that of others), agreeableness (i.e., the tendency and desire to promote and create harmony among groups), and conscientiousness (i.e., a focus on goal striving and accomplishment). However, as with emotional intelligence, research has shown political skill to be a distinct concept, capable of predicting success at work beyond these traits and characteristics.

Finally, it is important to note that political skill is different from social skill, because, on the surface, some people might see the two concepts as appearing to be very similar. Social skill generally is regarded as competencies in communication and the ease, comfort, and connectedness with which individuals interact with others. Political skill, as we have seen, involves going beyond mere ease and facility of interaction to include *managing* these interactions with others in influential ways that lead to individual and organizational goal accomplishment.

Dimensions of Political Skill

In the opening discussion of this chapter, we likened political skill to a sort of organizational "right stuff." That analogy was made in part because conceptualizations of having the "right stuff" consider success as derived from a combination of characteristics. Thus, to really understand what political skill is and how it helps people succeed at work, we need to consider its components—that is, the individual elements that together make up the construct. We've hinted at these parts so far, as we have described the ability to read and understand people as well as the capacity to act on that knowledge in influential ways. However, there are other key aspects of political skill that are critical to its makeup and need to be represented in a complete description of the concept. To date, we have identified four key facets of political skill. These facets, also referred to as dimensions, are social astuteness, networking ability, interpersonal influence, and apparent sincerity.

Social astuteness. We begin with the ability to understand interpersonal situations. Politically skilled individuals are astute observers of others and are keenly attuned to social situations. Beyond that, they are able to comprehend social interactions and accurately interpret their behavior, as well as that of others, in social settings. This is due to their strong powers of discernment and high self-awareness. This quality of interpersonal sensitivity is referred to as social astuteness and is central to political skill in that it allows for a deeper understanding of the social fabric at work. Although this seems like a straightforward quality of observation, it is much more than that.

Socially astute individuals go beyond just cataloging what they see. Instead, they integrate this new information from their observations with existing knowledge from prior interactions to make better and deeper sense of the present situation. One way to understand this richer level of social comprehension is to draw a parallel from the 1999 movie *The Matrix*. In this film, many individuals just saw what appeared to be there, but others were able to see beyond what was presented, to the very core of the situation, which gave them a greater understanding of what was happening around them. Similarly, politically skilled individuals are able to see within the organizational "matrix" to understand the intricacies of the social situation, including potentially hidden agendas. Think back to our example of the politically skilled subordinate who was able to decipher why the boss was rejecting new ideas.

This individual was able to integrate the new information from observing the boss at the meeting with prior information (i.e., the boss championed the existing strategy) to understand what was happening better than her colleagues did. Not surprisingly, with this ability to decipher interactions at work, socially astute individuals often are seen as ingenious, even clever, in dealing with others.

Networking ability. Although political skill is a characteristic that can facilitate individual success at work, it is rarely possible for individuals to succeed alone. Thus, connections, friendships, alliances, and coalitions are critical for individuals to navigate organizational politics. In this vein, organizational scholars have argued that "to pursue political action, it is inevitable that actors in the organization align themselves with others"[5] and that having connections and allies is important for developing and exercising influence.[6] In fact, it has been argued that "executives need to build good networks—both informal advice networks and formal coalitions—for influencing political decisions."[7] Given this, networking ability is an important aspect of political skill.

Indeed, politically skilled individuals are good at developing and leveraging diverse networks of contacts. People in these networks tend to hold assets seen as valuable and necessary for successful personal and organizational functioning. The politically skilled seem to naturally understand who these powerful people are, are able to facilitate interactions with them, and are particularly good at fostering relationships they can draw on later, when needed. Masters of the quid pro quo, they are often highly skilled negotiators and deal makers and are adept at conflict management. They know when to call on others for favors, are perceived as willing to reciprocate, and inspire commitment and personal obligation from those around them. Furthermore, individuals high in networking ability ensure they are well positioned in order to both create and take advantage of opportunities. Thus, politically skilled individuals enjoy a favorable social identity among those in their network, resulting in significant and tangible benefits, such as gaining favorable reactions to one's ideas, enhanced access to important information, and increased cooperation and trust. In short, politically skilled people are perceived as possessing high levels of social capital, which enhances their reputation and ability to be influential.

Interpersonal influence. Part of the reason politically skilled individuals are expert networkers is their subtle and convincing personal style, which exerts a powerful influence on those around them. This is derived from the interpersonal influence facet of political skill, which captures the ability to adjust behavior to match the demands of a particular situation. That is, individuals high on the interpersonal influence dimension are capable of appropriately adapting and calibrating their behavior to each situation, often based on the understanding derived from their social astuteness, in order to elicit particular responses from others. Indeed, aspects of the interpersonal influence dimension capture what have been referred to as flexibility, which involves adapting one's behavior situationally to different targets of influence in different contextual conditions in order to achieve one's goals.

An important feature of flexibility that contributes to success at interpersonal influence involves focusing on goals and objectives and being able to remain calm and emotionally detached from the situation. Those high in interpersonal influence appear to others as being interpersonally skilled, and they use such behaviors to control their environments. Although these individuals are not always overtly political, they are seen as competent leaders who play the political game fairly and effortlessly. This facile political style is seen as a positive, rather than a negative, force within the organization. To identify these individuals in your organization, just think of those who seem to possess the ability to always know just what to say or do, no matter the situation. Further, when something doesn't seem to go quite as they expected, these individuals seem to be unflappable. Instead of retreating in fear or appearing upset, individuals high in interpersonal influence are able to quickly adjust, countering with another action or statement that makes them seem like they are ready for anything. In many ways, these individuals seem to perform social jujitsu on others at work—no matter what they are presented with, they seem capable of countering effectively such that they end up on top.

Apparent sincerity. Finally, in Dale Carnegie's best-selling book *How to Win Friends and Influence People,* his first rule of how to make people like you (which, he argued, was a precursor to effective influence) was to become genuinely interested in them.[8] Carnegie's advice has been much discussed and promoted over the years, and it can be summarized as never finding fault, never arguing, flattering people at every opportunity, and appearing sincere. Thus, a final aspect of political skill is an ability to appear genuine or sincere, which reflects the true execution component of political skill. That is, it is not just what behaviors politically skilled individuals exhibit, but more that they demonstrate influence attempts in ways that appear to be sincere and genuine, without ulterior motive, and that inspire trust and confidence. In fact, researchers who study influence processes have appealed for research examining the way influence attempts were executed, focusing on the interpersonal style component that he argued gave the appearance of sincerity.

Politically skilled individuals appear to others as possessing high levels of integrity, authenticity, sincerity, and genuineness. They are, or appear to be, honest, open, and forthright. This dimension of political skill strikes at the very heart of whether influence attempts will be successful, because it focuses on the perceived intentions of the behavior exhibited. Indeed, perceived intentions or motives are important and have been argued to alter the interpretation and labeling of behavior. For example, what appears to be helping behavior (e.g., offering to stay late at work to help your supervisor) is labeled as "citizenship" if the intentions are seen as positive, but "political" if the intentions are perceived as instrumental or self-serving, whereby you expect to get something out of it. Influence attempts will be successful only the extent to which the actor is perceived as possessing no ulterior motive.

Because their actions are not interpreted as manipulative or coercive, individuals high in apparent sincerity inspire trust and confidence in and from those around them. Their tactics often are seen as subtle, and their motives do not appear self-serving. They are capable of disguising ulterior motives when deemed necessary, yet others would not describe them as hypocritical. Instead, they appear to others as being "straight shooters," who can be characterized as "what you see is what you get." Whether these individuals are truly sincere and genuine is not the point—some people may be sincere and genuine in their behaviors but others simply do not perceive them to be. Political skill is required to inspire trust and confidence from others.

People High and Low in Political Skill

Now that you have a good idea about just what is political skill, here are some examples of people who are high in political skill and those we characterize as low in political skill. Interestingly, individuals we can "see through," and in whom we perceive ulterior motives, probably are not very good at influence attempts and continually "shoot themselves in the foot" even though they would love to be good organizational politicians. These people are low in political skill. However, individuals who come across as genuine, sincere, and authentic in their statements and behavior and who, in fact, do not appear to be trying to influence people at all, are indeed the ones who are high in political skill. In the high versus low examples of political skill, we can also see people who have very good and noble intentions but just do not inspire a comfort and trust level because they are not politically skilled.

Clinton versus Gore. In many ways, Bill Clinton is an embodiment of political skill. From his earliest days in politics, Clinton was said to have meticulously recorded information about those he interacted with and regularly called them just to check in and see how they were doing. Often, he'd learn of something they needed during these calls and would attempt to help, never asking for anything. However, when it came time to run for higher office, you can bet he made calls, drawing on years of untapped social capital. Further, after making it to the White House only to be later mired in scandal, Clinton survived an impeachment partially due to his political skill. Clinton may have been genuine, sincere, and authentic in his public statements and interactions, or he might have been simply playing a role to manage favorable images—we will never really know because he is so politically skilled that he "appears" to be genuine and convincing.

In contrast is Clinton's vice president, Al Gore. Although in his post–political office life Gore has become known as a passionate advocate for environmentalism, he was not viewed as a charismatic figure while in office. In fact, during his own presidential campaign, he often came across as "wooden" or fake. Beyond just appearing boring or uncharismatic, it was difficult for many to see Gore as someone they could believe. He might have been an honest, caring individual who really wanted to be influential and inspire people to trust and follow his ideas, but he just didn't come across that way. As a result, many Americans, seeking someone they could trust, didn't see Gore as authentic or believable, which likely cost him much-needed support during the election.

Broadcast News. One movie that seems to depict the success between those high in political skill and those low in political skill is the 1987 film *Broadcast News*. In this movie, Tom Grunick (played by William Hurt) is an attractive and politically skilled news anchor who can't write and lacks the intelligence to even understand the news he is reporting. The audience loves Tom as a news anchor—he is engaging, seemingly genuine, and authentic in his news delivery. In spite of his low IQ, he is successful because of his political skill.

Aaron Altman (played by Albert Brooks) is extremely bright, well read, and motivated. He has everything it takes to be a successful news anchor except the political skill. Aaron has no clue how to relate to others and, perhaps as important, does not understand why it is important to deal well with others. He simply wants to report the facts—and he is good at getting and assembling the facts. Unfortunately, because of his lack of political skill, not to mention his arrogance, Aaron is stranded in the newsroom, and is branded as boring, uncharismatic, and unappealing to the network's audience. This is another example of how political skill can lead to success and is independent of intelligence. Clearly, having both intelligence and political skill is a valuable combination. However, for many positions, having political skill is more likely to lead to success than having a high IQ.

Measuring Political Skill

Because of the importance placed on political skill for career success, you're likely wondering how politically skilled you are. Well, with the Political Skill Inventory (PSI),[9] which will allow you to assess your own level of political skill, you can find out. Additionally, scores can be computed for each of the four facets of political skill. By answering 18 questions and performing a handful of math operations, you can know how politically skilled you are, as well as whether you are higher or lower on social astuteness, interpersonal influence, networking ability, and apparent sincerity.

Assessing Your Political Skill

The PSI questions, presented here and at politicalskillatwork.com, are answered on a scale that ranges from 1 (Strongly Disagree) to 7 (Strongly Agree). An overall PSI score is computed by summing the responses on all questions and dividing by that number of questions (i.e., 18). You will have an overall political skill score between 1 and 7. Larger total scores indicate people who have higher political skill, and smaller scores identify individuals who have lower political skill.

Social astuteness has 5 questions. To determine your social astuteness score, simply add up your responses for questions that are labeled "(SA)" and divide that number by 5. This can be done for each dimension, with the caveat that you will need to divide the sum for networking ability (NA) by 6 (it has 6 questions), interpersonal influence (II) by 4 (it has 4 questions), and apparent sincerity (AS) by 3 (it has 3 questions). Like your overall political skill score, your score for each of the four facets should range from 1 to 7.

Take a few minutes to complete the PSI for yourself. Of course, many surveys are fairly transparent, such that you know how to come out high or low on this scale. (Especially because we just gave you the scoring system!) The important thing to remember is that you need to be honest with yourself when completing this survey in order to get an accurate self-assessment. On the pages that follow the PSI, we'll discuss what conclusions you might draw based on your scores for the overall construct, as well as for each of the facets.

Asking Others to Rate Your Political Skill

Self-report measurements of political skill can be useful and enlightening. However, even when prompted to be honest, we often tend to respond to questionnaires with some bias due to social desirability, which leads to a less than accurate reflection of our true scores. Given this, you might also consider asking someone close to you, such as your immediate supervisor, peers or coworkers, or perhaps even subordinates to rate your political skill. In so doing, if you and your other chosen rater(s) obtain similar levels of overall political skill and the four dimensions, you can have greater confidence that you understand how interpersonally effective you are, and why, as well as what areas you might want to work to develop.

POLITICAL SKILL INVENTORY

Instructions: Using the following 7-point scale, place the number before each question that best describes how much you agree with each statement about yourself.

1 = STRONGLY DISAGREE

2 = DISAGREE

3 = SLIGHTLY DISAGREE

4 = NEUTRAL

5 = SLIGHTLY AGREE

6 = AGREE

7 = STRONGLY AGREE

---

1 – I spend a lot of time and effort at work networking with others.   NA

---

2 – I am able to make most people feel comfortable and at ease around me.   II

---

3 – I am able to communicate easily and effectively with others.   II

---

4 – It is easy for me to develop good rapport with most people.   II

---

5 – I understand people very well.   SA

---

6 – I am good at building relationships with influential people at work.   NA

---

7 – I am particularly good at sensing the motivations and hidden agendas of others.   SA

8 – When communicating with others, I try to be genuine in what I say and do. — AS

9 – I have developed a large network of colleagues and associates at work who I can call on for support when I really need to get things done. — NA

10 – At work, I know a lot of important people and am well connected. — NA

11 – I spend a lot of time at work developing connections with others. — NA

12 – I am good at getting people to like me. — II

13 – It is important that people believe I am sincere in what I say and do. — AS

14 – I try to show a genuine interest in other people. — AS

15 – I am good at using my connections and network to make things happen at work. — NA

16 – I have good intuition or "savvy" about how to present myself to others. — SA

17 – I always seem to instinctively know the right things to say or do to influence others. — SA

18 – I pay close attention to people's facial expressions. — SA

KEY:

Social Astuteness = (SA) 5 questions (add items together and divide by 5)

Networking Ability = (NA) 6 questions (add items together and divide by 6)

Interpersonal Influence = (II) 4 questions (add items together and divide by 4)

Apparent Sincerity = (AS) 3 questions (add items together and divide by 3)

Understanding Your Political Skill Score

Overall political skill is the combination of social astuteness + interpersonal influence + networking ability + apparent sincerity. If you have calculated your overall political skill, you should have a number between 1 and 7, which would make a score of "4" the midpoint. Thus, if you have a total PSI of 4 we consider that to be a moderate level of political skill. In general, scoring a 1 or 2 is considered to be low; 3, 4, or 5 is considered average; and scoring a 6 or 7 is considered to be high. Successful employees, and especially managers, tend to score fairly high on the PSI. However, remember that there are four dimensions of political skill. Thus, it is important to consider these scores to understand exactly *why* you received the overall score you did. The following sections can help you understand more about your score for each dimension.

Social Astuteness

If you scored *low* (i.e., a 1 or 2) on the social astuteness dimension of the PSI, you likely have a low level of understanding or a low desire to understand the motivations or intentions of others' behaviors. A low score means you have little intuition or savvy about how to present yourself to others and you do not always know the right things to say or do in order to influence others.

An *average* score (i.e., a 3, 4, or 5) on this dimension means you have a satisfactory ability to understand people and a reasonable ability to read people's motivations and detect any hidden agendas they may have. Further, average scores represent a satisfactory level of intuition and savvy about how you come across to others. Finally, if you have an average score, you often know the right things to say and the right things to do in order to influence others.

A *high* score (i.e., 6 or 7) on the social astuteness dimension means you have an excellent ability to understand people, sense their motivation, and detect any hidden agendas. You have outstanding intuition and the savvy to know exactly how to present yourself. Also, when influencing others, you seem to instinctively know exactly the right things to say and do.

Networking Ability

If you score *low* on the networking ability dimension, you either have a low ability to develop relationships with others at work or you lack the motivation to spend time and effort developing these relationships. Low scores on this dimension also mean you probably lack a large support network that can be used to advance your work goals.

If you have an *average* score, you have a satisfactory ability and motivation to spend time and energy developing work relationships with others. Average scores in networking also mean you probably have a reasonable formal and informal network of people that can help you move work-related goals forward.

If you scored *high* on networking ability, you are an excellent networker. You have both the ability as well as the motivation to develop positive work relationships. You are especially good at developing good relationships with influential people. You probably have a very large number of support networks, both formal and informal, that you often use effectively to move your goals forward in the organization.

Interpersonal Influence

A *low* score on the interpersonal influence dimension means that you have a fairly low ability or motivation to make people feel comfortable and at ease with you. If you have a low score, you may not have a smooth communication style with others at work. Further, you likely have a limited ability to develop a good relationship and rapport with most people.

An *average* score means you have a satisfactory level of ability to make people comfortable and at ease around you. Further, you normally are able to communicate with others, but not everyone. You have a reasonable ability to establish a good rapport with most people.

If you have a *high* score on interpersonal influence, your ability to make people feel at ease around you is very strong. You likely have a very effective communication style with others and are able to establish a very good rapport with most everyone you meet. Most people are quickly drawn to you because you know how to make yourself likeable.

Apparent Sincerity

If you scored *low* on the sincerity dimension, this reflects a limited awareness of the importance of appearing genuine and sincere. If you have a low score, you likely show a relatively low level of genuine interest in other people and do not place a high value on being perceived as a genuine and sincere person.

If you have an *average* score on this dimension, you have a satisfactory level of awareness regarding the importance of appearing genuine and sincere. You likely show a genuine interest in some of the people with whom you work, but not everyone. You also place a reasonable value on being perceived as genuine and sincere.

If you scored *high* on the sincerity dimension, you have a very good appreciation for the importance of appearing genuine and sincere to everyone. You aspire to demonstrate a sincere interest in others at all times. Finally, it is very important for you to be perceived as being genuine and sincere.

Conclusion

As you now understand, politically skilled individuals more accurately understand the needs of organizations as well as the employees within organizations. Further, those who have political skill can use that knowledge to influence others within organizations. We examine the four dimensions of political skill—namely, social astuteness, interpersonal influence, networking ability, and apparent sincerity—and we provide the political skill scale for your self-assessment. As you read through this book, you will discover how political skill (in general, as well as the specific dimensions) can be used to affect others. You will also learn how best to increase your political skill by focusing on the specific dimension(s) upon which you need to improve.

Research Highlight

Lvina, E., et al. (2012). "Measure Invariance of the Political Skill Inventory (PSI) across Five Cultures." *International Journal of Cross-Cultural Management, 12*(2): 171–91.

The failure to consider cultural dynamics is a common criticism in organizational research, especially when it comes to concepts that deal with interpersonal interaction at work. Why? Well, different cultures often have different expectations about how people interact, particularly at work and *especially* when it involves supervisors and subordinates. As a result, research on political skill began to expand to other cultures, employing translations of the PSI. Given this, it became important to examine the psychometric properties (i.e., the scale validity) of the PSI across cultures.

In a series of studies published in 2012, Lvina and her colleagues undertook this work. Using more than 1,500 employees from the United States, Germany, Turkey, Russia, and China, they provided evidence that the PSI could be used to evaluate political skill as a stable construct across cultures. That is, the survey instrument performed consistently across the cultures surveyed, and any differences found in the scores were considered to be a result of cultural differences.

More specifically, the authors concluded that uncertainty avoidance and a low- versus high-context style of communication are two possible sources of differences in PSI scores. Regarding uncertainty avoidance, cultures at the high end of the spectrum (e.g., Germany) demonstrated a somewhat constrained endorsement of political skill. Additionally, high-context cultures (e.g., Turkey and China) that emphasize indirect communication style as well as the importance of relationships, were found to score especially high on the social astuteness and networking ability dimensions.

2

OPPORTUNITY RECOGNITION, EVALUATION, AND CAPITALIZATION

"**Y**ou need to look at this," the analyst said as he laid several photographs taken from a U-2 spy plane.

"A soccer field?" his supervisor seemed perplexed with the analyst's urgency.

"Yes, it's a soccer field," he said and then paused, waiting for a reaction. None came. "It's a soccer field in Cuba."

"So, there are soccer fields everywhere," the supervisor intoned and pushed the photographs back to his subordinate.

"No, you are missing the point. Cubans don't play soccer, they play baseball." The analyst pushed them right back toward his supervisor.

"And the point is?" the manager asked with frustration growing in his voice.

"The Soviets play soccer."

A moment later, the supervisor was on the phone. "Get me the Director."

Although the dialogue was added for dramatic effect, this is a true story about one very perceptive Central Intelligence Agency (CIA) analyst. After the Bay of Pigs disaster in 1961, President John F. Kennedy was hesitant to act on reports suggesting Soviet forces were moving missiles onto Cuban soil. In need of evidence confirming these clandestine movements, Kennedy ordered the CIA to obtain photographic evidence. The CIA then launched a U-2 spy plane to carry out his orders. Pouring over the images, one analyst noted the presence of a soccer field. This tugged at something in his brain. A cultural and geographical expert, the analyst was well aware that Cuba was a baseball-loving country. Cubans just didn't play soccer. However, he knew who did— Soviets. Ultimately, this photo became part of the initial evidence pointing to the possibility that the USSR likely had a foothold or base camp already established on the island.

And herein lies the heart of this chapter: patterns exist all around us, but they often are invisible to the untrained eye. In this instance, an analyst not familiar with Cuban culture may have viewed that photo as completely meaningless. Yet the content of the photo, the image itself, would have been exactly the same. That is, the relevant information contained within that photo was both visible and invisible all at the same time. The soccer field was present, but the meaning underlying its presence would have been lost. This is why the CIA is well known for hiring and training a diverse body of agents who become masters of their assigned country's politics, culture, geography, and a multitude of other factors. It is not just so they can better blend into their new surroundings, but so that they can identify patterns—or in this case—elements that don't fit established patterns.

This example shows why expertise is intrinsically linked to pattern recognition. Experts are more likely to have been exposed to patterns or their components, and, thus, they should be skilled at recognizing them. Fortunately, political skill is just that—a skill, and therefore achieving expertise is a possibility.

We believe that those with political skill are not just better at recognizing patterns in their environment but also at evaluating and capitalizing upon the opportunities that those patterns offer—a feat that can be just as difficult as recognizing patterns. Consider opportunity evaluation and capitalization as the method you use to leverage insider information in a way that moves you closer to achieving a goal. Why is it sometimes difficult to leverage a pattern that has been recognized? Again, that analyst and his supervisor had to find some way to convince a world leader that the USSR was moving missiles onto Cuban soil... based on the picture of a soccer field. Simply recognizing a pattern (or opportunity) is only one part of the equation; the successful and timely exploitation of that information is also just as difficult to facilitate.

In this chapter we discuss how and why pattern recognition, as viewed through the lenses of opportunity recognition, evaluation, and capitalization are the underpinnings of political skill. By the end, you will see why your ability to see patterns in your environment lead to improved outcomes at work and in innumerable other contexts.

Why Political Skill Is So Effective

Political skill is one of the most powerful predictors of success in the workplace. The relationship seems intuitive: those people able to better navigate their environments, network with colleagues, and effectively influence others should fare well in professional environments. Yet each of these critical behaviors doesn't *just happen*. For example, influencing others is not a simple skill; it is accomplished through successfully leveraging a network of interlocking competencies. In many ways, an explanation that relies solely on these behaviors falls short of truly defining and explaining what is actually happening when political skill is put into action. Without a more concrete explanation, it is difficult to understand how to improve political skill and exactly why it works so well.

Researchers' efforts to understand political skill have been underway for over three decades. In this time, great progress has been made toward understanding what political skill predicts (e.g., increased pay, promotions) and how those with it differ from those without (e.g., reduced stress). Recently, research on political skill has turned inward, and there is now a greater emphasis being placed on understanding the *how* and *why* behind this skill. One particularly meaningful contribution resulting from this new attention is the idea that political skill is underpinned by something called social pattern recognition. In essence, politically skilled individuals are capable of recognizing meaningful patterns in their environment. Just like the CIA analyst and the soccer field, the patterns recognized by the politically skilled illuminate something that is invisible to others. Whereas the intelligence analyst extracted critical evidence, employees use political skill to extract information that signals potential opportunities for advancement or goal attainment. Political skill makes people so effective because it allows them to recognize patterns in their environment and, ultimately, to capitalize upon the information contained in those patterns.

Pattern Recognition

Take a few moments to imagine the scene presented in the following paragraph. Don't skip ahead or peek at what comes after, just conjure up an image in your head based on the words that follow:

You knock on the door of a family member's house. No one answers, but you expected that on a day like today. You turn the handle and as you walk in, you see several children in the living room seated around a man wearing white gloves and a black top hat and vest. You look into the dining room and you see that on the table are several rectangular objects, each brightly adorned with colored wrapping. Where are you?

Did you find yourself at a child's birthday party? Do you recall the clues that led you to that conclusion? Perhaps it was that no one answered the door because the kids were being entertained or the parents were out of earshot. Maybe it was the children gathered around the feet of a traditionally dressed magician. Last, and perhaps the most concrete piece of evidence, were the presents on the table.

As you read through the description, you likely began to

synthesize those clues in such a way that connections formed between them. Any one of those things in isolation would only hint at the correct answer. The presents could point toward a birthday party, certainly, but they could have been for anyone (not just a child). Or, if you did not know the setting was a home, perhaps you would have assumed the magician meant you were at a library, fair, or other special event. Yet when these pieces of evidence are woven together: family home, presents, magician, kids—your presence at a children's party is unmistakable.

This is a pattern. It is a *social* pattern. Most of our conscious experiences with pattern recognition tend to revolve around visual or tangible patterns. Perhaps we see patterns on the latest fashionable dresses or on ornate rugs. Sometimes they come in the form of riddles or puzzles (e.g., what number comes next, how many triangles are in the picture). Yet reducing pattern recognition to a mere aesthetic element or amusement undercuts the important role patterns play in our lives.

Consider the importance of what psychologists call routines and scripts. A script is understood to be a person's general understanding of how a sequence of events is supposed to unfold. A script, like its namesake, stems from the idea that people essentially memorize their lines and stage movements to such an extent that they can play their "roles" (e.g., host, guest, waiter, diner) with *any* random partner and still make it seem as if the performance was well-rehearsed. One of the most classic examples of a script in action is how we go about eating at a restaurant. Consider our two protagonists: the diner and the waiter. The diner enters the restaurant and (generally) waits to be seated. After being seated, the waiter will come to ask what the diner would like to drink, to which the diner is fully prepared to answer because that is part of the script. While the waiter retrieves the drinks, and perhaps delays their delivery for a few minutes, the diner reads the menu so that when the waiter returns, food can be ordered. This intricate dance continues, and it wouldn't take Shakespeare to finish the script: the food arrives, the check is brought after a suitable amount of time, the diner pays and leaves a tip, and then the diner leaves the establishment. If the meal goes according to the script, we barely notice the elaborately choreographed dance that took place and we are likely only going to comment on the quality of the food and conversation.

However, when one of the parties involved in this act suddenly forgets their lines—when there is a violation of the script—we immediately notice the problem. It can feel as if we are at an eighth-grade production of *Romeo and Juliet* and the final line is started, "Never was there a tale of more woe, than that of..." and left unfinished. Everyone in the audience wants to shout "...Juliet and her Romeo" because we know how this story ends. This is how it feels when you give the waiter your credit card and it takes 20 minutes for him to return it. You know the waiter's line and you expect it to be delivered *on time* (just as they expect you to put your credit card on top of the receipt in a timely manner).

Sometimes, when the script is violated, confusion takes hold and we are forced to either ask for our *line* or begin to improvise. Consider the awkward feeling associated with walking into a restaurant and finding no host or sign stating "Please seat your-self." The whole script grinds to a halt and immediately we feel as if something is wrong; perhaps we will stand near the doorway waiting for further instructions ("Line, please!") or we will impro-vise and find a table on our own. Regardless of the choice, the routine itself is slowly thrown off track and we must wait until the next scene until we can again get back on script.

It should be obvious now that a script is essentially just a social pattern; as soon as we recognize the pattern (e.g., eating at a restaurant) we can easily identify the next action, behavior, or event that will occur. This is why pattern recognition is so import-ant, not just in our work lives but in every facet of our lives. Pat-terns make life more efficient and they tell people how to behave and interpret information. This could be something as innocuous as recognizing that the parking lot fills up early on Monday morn-ing to matters of life or death. For example, the military trains pilots to recognize a variety of anti-aircraft weapons by teaching each component of the weapon itself. This allows pilots who are only able to see the barrels and the mount to begin to piece together the composite whole.

And this is the most important aspect of pattern recognition: individuals must possess some form of a mental prototype upon which they can overlay those pieces of the pattern found in their environment. A prototype is a robust cognitive framework, that is, a mental model of what something—from a physical object to a social interaction – is supposed to look like or how it should occur.[1] Prototypes provide us with the framework necessary to see patterns, and they must be created and improved upon through education, training, or experience.

Consider the role of experience. Again, returning to the restaurant example, it is due to the lack of a firm prototype that, as soon as they are seated, children ask, "When are we going to eat?!" Without understanding the prototype, they simply cannot sequentially order the events (e.g., drink, food, check). However, if we provide them with this knowledge (e.g., build their prototype), they will begin to see the pattern and understand when the food is *supposed* to come (although they likely will still ask that question at least 10 times before the food comes).

Similarly, consider what a meteorologist sees when looking at a weather map. The various lines, arrows, and numbers are not independent of one another; they are a series of interlocking *patterns.* Meteorologists, having the appropriate education, training, and experience, possess the necessary prototypes to identify and interpret those weather patterns. What happens when a high-pressure system is approaching this ridgeline? A prototype built from the study of previous high-pressure systems near ridgelines allows them to predict the weather's behavior.

Each person possesses countless numbers of prototypes for various aspects of their life. These can be personal, professional, or anything in between. If a utility bill comes once a month, then its absence might be noticed on the thirtieth. Similarly, if at work, you might recognize that the boss is a little more edgy on the day he engages in a voluntary fast. Patterns are constantly forming around us, and they allow us to effectively identify and then quickly organize bits of data into meaningful information.

Thus, the question is where does political skill first intersect with pattern recognition? The answer: opportunity recognition.

Opportunity Recognition

Opportunity recognition is the process by which people recognize new and potentially successful ideas within their environment. The two factors contributing to opportunity recognition are individual characteristics and contextual/environmental factors.[2] The environment provides the patterns; as mentioned earlier, patterns exist almost everywhere and even though 20 people might live and work in the same space, only a few might be capable of recognizing patterns or opportunities. Those chosen few are the people who possess the appropriate individual characteristics necessary to observe and interpret those patterns for what they could be—opportunities.

Who are those chosen few? The politically skilled.

At its most fundamental level, political skill is what allows people to recognize opportunities in their environment. If you drill down into the very core of political skill, to its very center, you will find that it is a highly directed form of pattern recognition focused on social environments like the workplace.

Without a doubt, you are already engaging in opportunity recognition at work. Consider how you might be able to tell which projects and/or teams are the most visible and the most important to your supervisors or the company as a whole. Or perhaps you are able to recognize the value of certain accounts and how success with those clients in particular is directly tied to your success and upward mobility. These observations are a direct result of your ability to parse your environment for important information that can inform your future actions.

Some readers may consider these previous observations to be intuitive. It is true that, to many people, noting which accounts are the most important or recognizing that trying to get in a word with your boss after a rough day is generally a bad idea seems relatively... basic? Simple? Before assuming that *surely*, everyone must possess these abilities, consider your past coworkers, subordinates, and bosses. How many of them were good at their job— they could audit like no one else or seemed to speak to an oracle in regard to market movements—but simply missed the forest for the trees when it came to company matters. We all know those people who can get the job done but then fail to feel a change in the wind and find themselves upstream without a paddle. Basically, don't sell yourself short here; this is a skill.

Just like any other high-level skill, the effective use of political skill requires people to successfully execute several lower-order skills. As stated in the last chapter, these skills are expressed through the four dimensions of political skill: interpersonal influence, social astuteness, apparent sincerity, and networking ability. Specifically, the networking ability and social astuteness dimensions of political skill help people recognize opportunities by helping them embed themselves within their organizations.

Networking effectively, and efficiently, allows access to otherwise inaccessible knowledge and information. It is the isolated employee who is the last to know. Friendships, professional relationships, and/or just being present for the daily gossip can provide a flow of information that often rivals the official chain of command. Bereft of a diverse set of relationships, the basic knowledge of the organization's inner workings can seem opaque and confusing. This is one of the primary reasons mentors are so effective; a strong mentor who is senior and has served longer understands the nuances, players, and the history of an organization. Mentors can leverage their diverse network and provide mentees with information that explains past and future decisions.

This information is valuable and can be critical to success within an organization. Perhaps a certain project is going to become the new focal point for the organization—this might mean a strategic move from your current team is in order. Or, there might be rumors that your current team's product is going to be discontinued. That might indicate that a swift and tactical move to another team is in order.

All of this information likely will not come in a nice and easy-to-understand package. More than likely, you might hear rumblings of downsizing or that a supervisor is looking for a new team. Perhaps someone from sales heard that they need to liquidate all of the product your team supports. These are all just pieces of the pattern. Your network will allow you to acquire enough pieces of information, hopefully, to *see* the pattern before it sees you. If you are able to decipher the pattern, then it is likely that you recognized an opportunity—to exit a failing team or to join the team developing the new flagship product. However, even with an expansive network, the politically skilled individual must be constantly searching for signals in a sea of noise—they must be socially astute.

Social astuteness works hand in hand with networking ability because it allows people to identify relevant clues (i.e., pieces of patterns) within their social environment. The reality is that we are constantly searching our environment for information; sometimes we do it intentionally, and other times it occurs at a subconscious level. Intentional searches, what we term *active search*, is a deliberate process by which people intentionally seek out information that will help generate a usable pattern.

To better understand active search, imagine that you recently landed in a foreign country and have no knowledge or experience with their customs. Unfortunately, the company you came to do business with sent a delegation of four senior managers to meet you at the plane. You have no idea what is appropriate in terms of greeting. Fortunately, you are the fifth person to exit the plane, and as you walk down the stairs there should be no doubt that you will be carefully watching and listening to every person who comes before you in the hope that you can figure out the appropriate greeting. This is the process of active search.

A passive search is different in the sense that you are not actively looking for relevant pieces of information. In many ways, a passive search is more a measure of our overall *readiness* to identify patterns within our environment. To continue the above example, imagine that after a few days of meetings in this new country, you and your colleagues have a chance to explore the city. This is a moment to relax, completely free from your professional obligations. While standing in line at a local store and thinking about your family back home, you notice that every customer in front of you taps the counter twice and then fist bumps the clerk before paying. You were not intentionally looking for this and perhaps, if your *script* for how a normal transaction in your home country goes (e.g., clearly with three taps and a handshake, right?) was not so engrained in your mind, this could have gone unnoticed. We argue that our passive search ability is made more effective when we have stronger, more robust prototypes and/or more pieces of a pattern already at our disposal.

Both active and passive searches operate in tandem to help identify information that can result in opportunities. An active search could be as simple as walking from desk to desk asking your colleagues what sports the CEO plays. That might be a bit clumsy, but it is an active search for information nonetheless. A passive search is less intentional and likely operates off of previously digested information. Perhaps you are a former collegiate tennis player, and in a conversation with one of your senior coworkers she mentions that your mutual supervisor, Jan, is an avid tennis player. The savvy and socially astute among us will naturally pick up the clue and might consider what to do with that opportunity.

Determining what to do with a potential opportunity is the second step of this process. Simply recognizing the opportunity is only a small piece of the puzzle. As mentioned earlier in the chapter, opportunities are recognized all the time. The first question we must ask ourselves, before we even consider capitalizing upon that opportunity is, *Do I want to pursue this opportunity and, if so, how do I do it?*

Opportunity Evaluation

Consider how even the best opportunities often have some costs associated with them. It is all too easy to conjure up any number of stories about how the pursuit of an opportunity led to ruin (this is a common theme in film and television because it is so inherently relatable, and it resonates with audiences). Consider the woman who yearns for a promotion simply because she wants to add the word *Regional* to her current title of *Manager*. If she recognizes an opportunity to ascend to that lofty position, has she taken the time to evaluate the risks or challenges associated with pursuing that goal? Is this rapid ascent tied to her engaging in some pseudo-coup against the current regional manager? Will it mean sacrificing relationships? Will there be a social penalty for moving up the ladder *too* quickly? If her attempt to capitalize on this opportunity were to fail, would she be left vulnerable or even find herself on the way out the door? Does she even care about these potential ramifications?

This is why the opportunity evaluation phase is so important in the process of recognizing and capitalizing upon opportunities. There will be very few, if any, opportunities in life that carry no risks or downsides. Yes, a promotion generally is good, but what are the other, sometimes detrimental, effects it could have on your life? Or, what is needed to capitalize upon that opportunity? Evaluating each opportunity is a critical step in the process of deciding whether to capitalize on recognized opportunities. We argue in favor of three particular assessments that must be considered when evaluating an opportunity: goal, power, and risk assessments.

Goal Assessment

Once an opportunity is recognized, it becomes critical for people to begin determining whether or not pursuing that opportunity is in line with their personal and professional goals. In its most basic form, motivation stems from our desire to reduce any discrepancies between our current state and our desired end state. More plainly, we simply want to reach our goals, and the only way to do that is to reduce the distance between us and our goal. Our *motivation* then is nothing more than the term we use to explain the *want* we feel to close that gap. This is why when we are motivated to earn the next bonus-tier at work, we work harder to close every deal and to find the time to make every extra phone call we can. We are motivated to decrease the distance between our current sales numbers and those required to hit the larger bonus numbers.

In many cases, the opportunity you recognize will result in the ability to reduce the discrepancy between you and your goal. Perhaps you find out through an administrative assistant that one of your colleagues is leaving next month; this might be the perfect time to talk to your coworker and find out which clients you should be trying to snag before they are divvied up in an otherwise orderly but completely random manner. This is an opportunity that directly improves your chance to attain a desired goal—a larger bonus—and, thus, if you wish to achieve higher sales numbers, you should pursue this opportunity vigorously and attempt to capitalize upon this "insider" knowledge.

However, there are going to be instances when you recognize opportunities that are readily available to you but do not actually help you attain your goals. For example, Microsoft employees are not required to follow the typical corporate pathway of working their way into managerial positions in order to progress in rank and salary. Instead, Microsoft encourages and retains expert employees not interested in management positions by increasing their "level" (higher levels correspond to higher pay and better benefits) within the organization. If a senior Microsoft employee who is more interested in becoming a leading expert in their field than a manager discovers an upcoming opening in their group's leadership team that offers higher pay, they need to evaluate if that recognized opportunity is worth pursuing.

In sum, understanding whether an opportunity will help us achieve our goals is a major consideration when making a decision. It is all too easy to say yes to a promotion or new, higher paying job, but do those opportunities help us reach our goals? Maybe they do. However, if the answer is no, then it is worth reconsidering your initial enthusiasm. One reality of vigorously pursuing a goal is that it usually requires us to reduce the time and effort we spend in the pursuit of other goals and on other activities. This means that determining important goals is not as simple as "I want to be the boss," because being the boss might also mean sacrificing family time, personal hobbies, and/or professional relationships. Accurately assessing whether an opportunity aligns with your own goals is critical because no one should pursue opportunities for opportunities' sake; this would result in a generally haphazard approach that could see you using up all of your social capital and goodwill pursuing something that you don't really value. To be sure, that social and political capital will be needed in the future and that is why it is important to continue evaluating recognized opportunities by conducting a power assessment.

Power Assessment

Next, conducting a *power assessment* will help in evaluating the viability of a recognized opportunity. All employees are capable of possessing and/or developing their power within an organization. Broadly, power can be broken down into types: formal and informal. Formal power derives from the authority granted by the organization; this includes people in managerial and leadership positions or those placed in charge of valued resources. Informal power is instead derived from other factors that tend to be less visible; some sources of informal power include expertise in a relevant work area and being well liked or respected by coworkers.

The reality, however, is that power is not evenly distributed or even equally sought after by members of an organization. In other words, some people have it and other people do not. The deft use of political skill can help you acquire power within your organization and use it more effectively, but that can take time. Even if you possess power, you still must ask yourself if you possess *enough* to fully realize a recognized opportunity. Consider a situation where you recognize that there will be an upcoming opportunity to move to a new district in a city more to your liking. Due to your keen sense of social astuteness and well-developed network, you have access to this information before your peers. However, you are well aware that several of your colleagues—all of whom possess more power than you—likely would vie for this job if it were to become publicly available. You might assess the situation as being one where, despite your foreknowledge, you simply do not possess the power to take that position without a costly battle that could hurt your reputation and your future in the company.

Power is fickle and often very difficult to accurately measure. Yet it is a ubiquitous fixture of any workplace that should always be taken into account. It is not just about possessing power, either. As in the example above, often it is about assessing your colleagues' power. It can hurt to volunteer for a job or land a spot on a coveted team, only to find out a day later that you have been bumped off and replaced by someone with a stronger base of power to draw from.

Pursuing some recognized opportunities can be rather innocuous, just as some situations within the workplace can be considered relatively inert and not prone to causing trouble. Yet for those more dynamic and potentially incendiary opportunities, evaluating your power within an organization naturally coincides with the final consideration—risk assessments.

Risk Assessment

Even pursuing opportunities that appear safe and beneficial can carry some risk. This risk could range from minor (e.g., the feeling of defeat if you are unable to capitalize) to major (e.g., the loss of a job or position). In the situation described above, you may have decided that the risk of throwing your name into the hat to move to a new district was too high; it would be great to be in that district, but if your colleagues see you as someone trying to work deals behind their back it might negatively affect your career in the long term. This is why accurately assessing the risk associated with pursuing a recognized opportunity and judging your own risk tolerance is an important step in this process. Even if an opportunity is recognized, you might judge that attempting to capitalize upon it might not be worth the risk. Therefore, before deciding to pursue an opportunity, the risks must be assessed.

As another example, one of the authors has a relative who recently received a new manager for her team. To all appearances, this manager seemed to be a fine addition to their well-established sales team. In her initial remarks to her new team, the manager mentioned how happy she was to be part of a team that represented such a core component of the overall company's business. She even went a step further and stated that this team was one she had sought a spot on for quite some time. As expected, the team met her arrival with enthusiastic optimism and had high hopes for her leadership. However, less than one month later, the team found out that this same manager was already interviewing for a management position within a different group. Needless to say, the group was nonplussed by this development.

To be fair, this manager likely had various motivations for attempting this move that we simply are not privy to. It is possible that one of those reasons was an intent to move upward and onward within the company as fast as possible. The other team she had applied to join did have a more visible product, and her success there likely would gain more notice. We can assume that she recognized an opportunity to move to a new group, one with a higher potential for success, and then started assessing the various aspects associated with that move.

By the same token, it is just as possible that she failed to assess the risk of her team finding out about her attempt to leave their group so soon after joining and in direct contradiction to her opening speech. When this woman did *not* get the job, she found herself amidst a team that was less than pleased. They viewed her words as hollow and any enthusiasm for their performance as purely manufactured and fake. The team continued to work and meet expectations, but the manager was always held at arm's length. Within the year, she was gone from the group and the entire company.

The bottom-line of risk assessments is this: no influence attempt or political maneuver is without risk. If the level of risk were the only factor, then offering advice on what opportunities to pursue would be much simpler. However, some opportunities might be judged to be worth the risk, and even more importantly, everyone has their own personal risk tolerance. There can be no absolute answer; what works for one of your colleagues may not work for you. This is why it is imperative that you assess the risk involved when determining if you will vie for some recognized opportunity. The negative effects of failed influence attempts are real (e.g., no one wants to be caught ingratiating the boss), and before you stride boldly toward your goal, take a moment to look for any potential hazards you may encounter.

Opportunity Capitalization

Once you have recognized an opportunity and assessed whether it is worth pursuing, it is time to work toward capitalizing on that goal. The result of all the assessments (i.e., goal, power, risk) is, hopefully, that you have now selected the best course of action regarding how to pursue the opportunity you recognized. All that is left to do is to work toward your goal.

Like its sibling, opportunity capitalization means exactly what you think it does—taking advantage of a recognized opportunity and exploiting it to the fullest extent. Also, like opportunity recognition, the process of capitalizing on opportunities is aided by political skill; whereas recognizing opportunities focused on being socially astute and well connected in order to recognize opportunities, the capitalization process relies on your ability to influence others to help you move closer to your goal.

Political skill is many things, and, at its core, it is a skill that allows us to effectively influence others. It is actually in the space between deciding to act and achieving a goal where much of the *skill* component of political skill resides. Specifically, the ability to influence others and to appear sincere or genuine is of the utmost importance.

A brief example will be helpful in illuminating the importance of these two facets of political skill. Consider a situation in which Tom, our plucky protagonist with a desire to continue his upward ascent at PoliSkill Inc., has recognized an opportunity to get to know his manager better. This manager, Karen, is an avid tennis player reputed around the office to have an absolutely killer backhand. Fortunately for Tom, he played collegiate tennis and still has a passion for the sport despite moving a bit slower around the court nowadays. Tom recognizes an opportunity here; getting to know Karen in a friendly way outside of work by enjoying a shared passion could help him when it comes time for the next promotion. Even better, Tom assesses that this opportunity will help him achieve his goal of becoming a manager himself, is well within his power, and carries a pretty low risk because *everyone* knows Tom is a tennis player (the constant updates on the US Open three years in a row gave it away)—so it won't look like he has just picked up a new hobby in order to woo the boss.

One option for Tom is to stop by Karen's office on his way out from work. He gives a few jaunty knocks and she invites him into her office. After a few pleasantries, Tom mentions that he heard she likes to play tennis. Warmed up now, he rolls into a semi practiced monologue about how much he enjoys watching the US Open. Just before wrapping up, Tom drops the main part of the message: he likes to play tennis on the weekends, and it would be great if Karen could join him. The move may be considered somewhat forthright, but Tom presents his case in an easy, casual manner, and, as a result, all that really shines through to Karen is his love of the game.

In another scenario, Tom haphazardly decides to stop by Karen's office about two weeks before his annual performance appraisal is due. He raps twice on her door and gives her a wave with his left hand; his right is currently holding a tennis bag and he is wearing a sweat bracelet. After a few pleasantries in which, much to Tom's chagrin, tennis does not come up, he awkwardly says farewell and raises his tennis bag in a "good-bye" gesture. Karen, fully aware that Tom wants to be asked about the tennis racket in his hand, obliges. Tom smiles, the sweet taste of victory on his lips. "Oh, do you play tennis?" he asks Karen, full well knowing the answer. Unfortunately, Karen also knew full well that her hobby was not unknown throughout the office. "I guess you could say I used to play," Karen says while using the toes of her heels to slowly push her tennis bag farther under her desk. "But I just don't have as much time as I used to. Maybe we could play when things slow down at the office" (subtext: things never slow down at the office so this will never happen).

In both of these scenarios, let's assume that Tom has the same, rather innocuous, intentions: to better his chances of becoming a manager by getting to know Karen. True, he is treating her somewhat as a means and not an end, but let's give Tom the benefit of the doubt and say that he also would value finding another friend who plays tennis. Just for a moment, consider that Tom's intentions are exactly identical in both scenarios. That means the same opportunity was recognized (i.e., getting to know Karen) and the same evaluative process was completed leading to a decision to act (i.e., invite Karen to play).

Despite these similarities that led to Tom's motivation and decision to act, the actual execution (i.e., capitalizing on the recognized opportunity) varies greatly in these two scenarios. So much so that they probably will result in quite different outcomes. While the first scenario may be viewed by Karen as a friendly attempt by one of her team members to find a tennis buddy, the second may come across as some thinly veiled attempt to influence his upcoming performance ratings. Consider how arriving at the office with his tennis racket may seem disingenuous if there is no on-site gym; Tom could just as easily have left it in the car. In other words, his attempt may appear forced or fake.

Not only might this lead to Tom not achieving his desired outcome, but it may lead to a host of other negative repercussions that he had not even considered during his risk assessment. This is why opportunity recognition and capitalization must go hand in hand; simply recognizing an opportunity is not entirely special or useful if you are not able to capitalize upon it. Fortunately, this book is about political *skill*. And, as will be touched upon again and again—like any other skill—political skill can be developed.

Conclusion

Our world is full of patterns. Knowing this, it is inevitable that you will begin to take more note of them. Of course, you likely have been aware of them to some extent, but now you will be able to pick them out more consciously and appreciate them for what they are—important bits of information that can serve as clues to help us better understand the world around us. Through the three-fold process of opportunity recognition, evaluation, and capitalization, those patterns are converted into opportunities. In the end, this is exactly why political skill is such a powerful tool; it not only helps people see *more* opportunities than their colleagues, but it also helps them to capitalize upon them.

Research Highlight

Wihler, A., et al. (2017). "Personal Initiative and Job Performance Evaluations: Role of Political Skill in Opportunity Recognition and Capitalization." *Journal of Management*, 43(5), 1388–1420.

People often talk about organizations and managers wanting employees to show initiative. However, research has shown that organizations actually vary in the extent to which they value employee initiative. Given this, it is crucial for employees to be able to recognize opportunities that are ripe for such behavior and then to be able to capitalize on them. In their 2017 study, Wihler and colleagues examined the role of political skill in this opportunity recognition and capitalization process. Across three independent studies, they tested the argument that political skill would facilitate both the successful identification of climates for initiative and the effective execution of initiative.

They found that the social astuteness dimension of political skill facilitated opportunity recognition, as the relationship between an organization's climate for initiative and the employees' displayed personal initiative was stronger for those higher in social astuteness. Additionally, they found that employees' political skill facilitated opportunity capitalization, as the relationship between displayed personal initiative and job performance ratings from supervisors was stronger for employees higher in interpersonal influence ability.

As important as the above findings are, the authors also found that the job performance ratings of employees low in interpersonal influence actually were *lower* when they displayed more initiative. Based on this, it seems that when the politically skilled show initiative they are likely to be viewed as proactive, whereas those without political skill are just seen as pushy.

3

DEVELOPING YOUR
POLITICAL SKILL

Ivanka Trump, the impeccably polished professional running several of her own businesses while simultaneously serving as an advisor to her father, the president of the United States, might well be held up as evidence that political skill can be developed over time. Why? Well, there is good reason to believe that Ms. Trump is a master of political skill. In recent years, Ivanka has received only minimal criticism when compared to what has beset the rest of the Trump administration, as well as her husband, father, and brothers, from all sides. Ivanka's training began earlier than most, due to her family's fame and the elite social scene she was forced to enter at such an early age.

The daughter of wealthy parents who were fixtures in Manhattan's upper-crust charity events and nightclubs, Ivanka was thrust into public life early on. Some of the earliest photos of her are as a six-year-old attending exclusive galas with her famous father. As she grew older, those photos would change from her being just another person in the photo to her being the focal subject. Whether gracing the cover of *Seventeen* magazine in 1997[1] or just being caught on film walking down the street by paparazzi, Ivanka seemed to lean into New York's social forces.

In a controversial documentary released in 2013, *Born Rich,*[2]

Ivanka starred alongside several other now-adult heirs and heiresses born into families of immense wealth. Jamie Johnson, a child of the family who own Johnson & Johnson, helmed this documentary. Being a member of the same elite circles his subjects traveled provided him the opportunity of a lifetime; Jamie leveraged his personal friendships with the interviewees to put them at ease and, consequently, they shed their normally protected exterior and offered candid thoughts on their wealth and position in life. The result? *Born Rich* did not portray its subjects in a flattering light. Those interviewed tended to come off as snobbish and spoiled at best but cruel and detached as a rule. In one telling scene, Benjamin Luke Weil, another wealthy elite, tells a story about dealing with people who bother him: "I can just say, f**k you, I'm from New York. I can buy your family..." When the director asked Juliet Hartford, heiress to the A&P grocery-store fortune, about her plans for all of her money, she said, "Give it all to the homeless. Just kidding. I'd just have a few houses in like the Bahamas and London, and animals and a plane. A big art studio."

Ivanka, however, projected quite a different image than her costars. Where many of those appearing in the film *still* regret their appearance, Ivanka's performance was viewed as a triumph for her image. One film critic noted that "while snobbery is par for the course for many of [the] subjects, the poised daughter of Donald and Ivana Trump, 21-year-old Ivanka, stands out from the well-bred crowd as a young woman who appreciates her position and is making it work for her." Sam Dangremond, an editor for *Town & Country* wrote that Ivanka was especially "adept at using this moment to her advantage."

Ivanka has been especially astute to her social environment and has consistently demonstrated a propensity to recognize when and how to revise her image. The transformation of Ivanka's style has not gone unnoticed by body language and speech experts. One such expert, Patti Wood, noted that Ivanka has transitioned from a more sensual appearance to something much more polished, in a conscious effort to present herself as more educated, sophisticated, and formal. Similarly, Anett Grant, CEO at Executive Speaking, Inc., explains that today, her voice is much richer and the sound rounder, which she couples with added energy stemming from a newfound comfort in her voice.[3]

Ivanka Trump's transformation from wealthy socialite to polished professional emphasizes three important tenets of political skill development. First, political skill is partly inborn, but it can be trained and improved through dedicated practice. Without a doubt, Ivanka has a natural talent for understanding social situations, but the dramatic changes to her personal speaking style and body language suggest she deliberately practiced the behaviors necessary to achieve her specific goals. Second, just as Ivanka's rapid change hints at external coaching and mentoring, the development of political skill almost necessitates outside feedback and mentorship to help you realize gains. Third, the development of political skill should be focused on each dimension (i.e., social astuteness, interpersonal influence, networking ability, and apparent sincerity), but it is likely that training will naturally cut across and simultaneously improve several dimensions. The improvement in Ivanka's speech and body language likely was focused on improving her interpersonal influence, that is, her ability to influence others. However, it is not much of a stretch to imagine that her improved speech and ability to control her message also aided her apparent sincerity and networking ability.

The question of whether, and how, political skill can be developed has been discussed since research on political skill began. The term political skill suggests that, like any other skill, it can be improved through training. This is to say that political skill is not something akin to a personality trait in that it is unlikely to change much over time. Instead, political skill is amenable to training. Yes, some people possess a natural aptitude toward political skill, but without practice aimed at developing this skill it will not be realized. If you have any capacity for political skill—and that capacity is far more widespread than many people realize—we believe there is much you can acquire through careful shaping and development. Thus, the real question is *how* to train people to be more politically skillful.

It's Just Like Any Other Skill

This seems like it should be an easy question to answer. If we replaced "political skill" with any other activity, like basketball or basket weaving, the path to getting better would be clear: *learn, listen, and practice.* Do you want to improve your public speaking skills? Take classes on public speaking. Do you want to be a better spouse or parent? Ask your loved ones how you can be a better mother, father, husband, or wife. Do you want to become a better runner? Run more.

At first, political skill seems an awkward fit for these solutions. Currently, there are no classes that can teach you political skill (though we would argue this book is a good place to start!). Also, it may feel awkward to ask your bosses and coworkers for feedback on how you can improve politically within the workplace. Finally, unlike running, using political skill often is not as simple as lacing up a pair of shoes and walking out the front door.

The problem of understanding exactly *how* to develop political skill stems from the fact that it almost certainly cannot be trained all at once. Almost all of the skills mentioned above—public speaking, basketball, being a good partner, and running—all appear to be straightforward skills that can be taught and mastered. However, this is not exactly true. Public speaking is the umbrella term we use to capture a series of smaller skills such as breathing, body language, cadence, tone, pacing, and many others. Similarly, being good at basketball means having competence in a wide array of skills, including shooting, defending, passing, dribbling, and on and on. Most skills are comprised of several smaller subordinate skills or abilities that work together to allow us to be considered successful at a superordinate skill or task. This is no different for political skill.

Political skill is comprised of four dimensions and each of these dimensions contributes to your overall political skill. As in the other examples, being politically skilled means having the ability to influence others, network effectively, be astute to your social environment, and appear sincere or genuine. These are the four skills that need to be practiced in order to develop and improve your overall political skill. Note that these skills are not as easily fit into a specific practice drill as, say, passing or free-throw shooting. Fortunately, we believe these skills are amenable to the basic principles of cross-training.

Let us consider running for a moment. Yes, we know, most people dread this activity and believe it's nothing more than placing one foot in front of the other thousands (even tens of thousands) of times in a row. Running is a skill that is seemingly so easily mastered that even toddlers pick it up, though with the occasional bump in the road. However, the act of running is actually a multifaceted activity; it involves the muscular system, the cardiovascular system, neurological functions, and an awareness of several factors like pace and monitoring hydration levels. These individual systems work together to allow us to run, yet they also require training dedicated to each specific component. In this way, to improve as a runner, it might be possible to just *run*, but it is just as possible to work on each of these systems individually.

Of course, roadblocks in the form of injuries or bad weather are simply inevitable. If running is not an option, runners will turn toward similar activities that allow them to cross-train—engage in one activity that develops the skills or abilities used in a different activity. For example, swimming is different from running, yet swim training will result in improvements to your running ability because both activities rely upon the cardiovascular system. Likewise, lifting weights improves the muscular system; cycling can improve your brain's ability to send impulses to your legs (e.g., neurological); and even reading about how temperature affects pacing can improve your running ability without you ever even lacing up your shoes.

We believe that this type of cross-training is also possible for political skill. This is beneficial to all those looking to develop their political skill because although we use political skill on a daily basis, it is not the same as running in that when and how we practice is solely under our control. Instead, daily life is like being in an actual race. This is because we don't necessarily find ourselves in a controlled, nonthreatening environment within which we can practice political skill. Additionally, the execution of political behavior relies on at least two, if not all, of the political skill dimensions. Thus, being able to develop just one dimension at a time can be of particular benefit to those interested in becoming more politically skilled.

Not Just Practice, Deliberate Practice

Improving your political skill is a two-part process. First, you need to know what it is you are trying to improve. In chapter 2, you were asked to take the Political Skill Inventory, a measure of your current proficiency in each dimension of political skill. With that now complete, you should be able to determine where to focus your efforts for improving political skill.

All that remains now is to practice. However, practicing political skill is not the same as using political skill; perhaps this is why some people who have spent 30 years in the workplace—the consummate political arena—are still rather inept when it comes to political skill. Just as with sports, simply playing game after game is not enough to ensure improvement. If the film is not watched, the plays not analyzed, and the individual motions not studied and practiced, overall skill growth will be stunted. Those who want to improve their political skill put in the time and effort both inside and outside of the office to ensure that the next time the game is on the line, they make every second count.

In 2008, to the dismay of children everywhere, Malcolm Gladwell popularized the claim that mastering a skill requires 10,000 hours of practice.[4] On that fateful day, parents around the world likely began timing and tabulating all the hours their children spent at the piano or kicking a ball down the field (*"Only 9,264 hours of practice to go, Susie."*). However, that adage, like so many other catchy proverbs, is incomplete. For instance, take the well-known saying "Money is the root of all evil." This is a great maxim; it is concise and packs a moral punch. Yet it's wrong (at least in form). The quote, taken from Timothy 6:10, is actually, "The love of money is the root of all evil."[5] Note how the removal of just three words radically alters the meaning of this saying.

This same *omission* of important information occurred when the "10,000-hour rule" (as it is usually referred to) was introduced and its message distilled down to something simpler and more memorable: *all you need is 10,000 hours of practice.* However, this is not what the researchers said, and the omission of a single word truly muddled the heart of the idea. What people actually need to become an expert is 10,000 hours of *deliberate* practice.

Deliberate practice occurs when you attempt to learn new skills that are just beyond your current ability level. Essentially, you must deliberately build upon your current skill set as opposed to just repeating those tasks you have already mastered. Thus, learning how to play "Twinkle, Twinkle" on piano and then repeating it for 10,000 hours will not lead to mastery of the piano. Instead, those 10,000 hours have to be spent stretching the limits of your abilities: first moving on to songs like "Mary Had a Little Lamb" and then slowly building up to the complex works of Mozart, Beethoven, and Tchaikovsky. This type of practice is generally uncomfortable because we are always struggling with something new and more difficult; no matter how far your skills progress, you deliberately decide to push yourself into uncharted waters rather than fall back on skills you already mastered. Invariably, this is uncomfortable as it is relentlessly challenging.

Anders Ericsson, a professor at Florida State University and a leading researcher on expertise, suggests that deliberate practice is so difficult not just because of the discomfort experienced, but because of the planning and feedback necessary to be successful.

Harnessing the power of deliberate practice essentially requires that challenging, well-defined goals be set and a teacher/mentor be available to provide accurate feedback. Much of the heavy lifting of deliberate practice can be completed on your own. However, it can be difficult to track your progress without a coach or mentor. Although you may find yourself in a situation where you have to go it alone, this is yet another reason that you should constantly be searching for a mentor, teacher, or coach who can help you develop your skills.

One reason to develop a relationship with a mentor is that research suggests there are few skills where the presence of a teacher/mentor is more important than political skill. Despite all of the benefits attributed to deliberate practice, research demonstrates that activities and environments where results are less predictable generally don't benefit as much from deliberate practice. Why? Let's revisit running, a highly predictable activity. Each mile run can be quantified through objective data: pace, heart rate, calories burned. The link between the behavior (e.g., running) and the outcome (e.g., pace) is both predictable and observable. On the other hand, office politics are highly unpredictable. In fact, the success or failure of an influence attempt is often hard to determine; even if you are successful, it can be difficult to define *why* you were successful. Unlike running, when engaging in office politics we tend to receive minimal feedback from our efforts and that which we do receive is almost always subjective.

Hence, we need mentors. We need teachers. Let's say you want to develop your public speaking skills; presumably you already know how to speak and at your fingertips is an endless supply of TED Talks from which to draw inspiration. Yet despite the ubiquity of public speaking, it is likely that you are *not* an expert (why else would you be focusing on it?) and, as such, are less capable of judging your own performance. Want to improve quickly? Hire a teacher who can provide you with instant and accurate feedback. There is an entire industry online built around instructors offering free lessons; on YouTube, some of the best teachers in the world offer free lessons that are only a few clicks away. You might wonder why they are giving away their knowledge for free. Well, they're not. At least, not exactly. Tutorials and videos are helpful, but without the constant feedback of a teacher, your skills will stagnate. The instructors know this, and they recognize that without their guiding hand, the lessons they provide are simply not enough to spur real skill development. This is why so many online instructors also offer private lessons to their viewers – this time for a fee.

Have we convinced you about the need for deliberate practice and working with a teacher or mentor? We hope so, because now we are going to discuss how to actually improve your political skill.

Developing Your Political Skill

Touchy Feely. That is nickname students gave to the most popular elective at Stanford's Graduate School of Business. The course's primary goal is to instill in students the idea that building relationships is the key to effective management. One account of students' experiences likens it to group therapy because of the emphasis on sharing, perspective-taking, and feedback. *Poets & Quants* explains that various activities include

" 'Crossing the net,' meaning going over to another person's side and assuming their thoughts and intentions; 'showing appreciation,' so that for every one thing you criticize, you express appreciation for 10 others; and 'turning toward versus away from people,' which means being receptive to proffered information; turning away means ignoring or shunning."[6]

The crux of this course is learning to be aware of what you're doing. Learning how your actions affect others, understanding their reactions, and bridging divides are just a small sampling of the skills taught here.

Does that sound like a typical business course to you? Probably not, but the students have voted the course the most popular elective for 45 consecutive years, and it's[7] taken by over 90 percent of Stanford MBA students.[8] Most MBA programs today are enhancing the typical accounting, strategy, and finance offerings with new classes that emphasize learning the softer skills required by today's business leaders. As society begins to recognize the importance of human relationships, more universities are offering, and often requiring, their students to complete courses on how to effectively lead and manage in the workplace (known more formally as "organizational behavior").

From the authors' perspective, the most critical aspect of Touchy Feely is its emphasis on feedback. One student of the course, Maria Lambert,[9] writes that "sharing feedback is not easy; asking for feedback is usually harder." In her recounting of one exercise, The Influence Line, she explains how she was given the task to silently order her peers from most influential to least influential—and then place herself in the line. She points out that overtly ranking her peers, thereby forcing her feedback to be known to all participating, can be a stomach-churning and difficult task. In a particularly poignant moment of clarity, Maria wrote that this activity taught her that "in the absence of feedback we make up stories." Whether her peers ranked her near the top or the bottom, she immediately generated stories justifying their choices.

The problem is that there is no room for stories when training and developing your political skill. Without accurate feedback, the success or failure of every influence attempt will be supported by a story conjured up from the influencer's own subjective perceptions. The story *could* be correct, but it also could be wildly off base. Without proper feedback, it is almost impossible to develop political skill because the variables are too numerous and your available perspectives too few. Thus, your first step in developing political skill is to find a mentor.

Informed Learning through Mentorship

Dante had Virgil. Luke had Yoda. Daniel had Mr. Miyagi. Mentors factor heavily in the stories told in literature and film. The role of these fictional mentors is important; their presence allows the protagonist to attain all the skills necessary for them to win their final battle. More important, without mentors there could be no montages. And without montages, there would be no movies produced between 1976 and 1990.

Just like Rocky needed Mick, you need a mentor as well. This is perhaps the most important advice you will find in this book. It is also the most straightforward: *Find a mentor. Now.* However, it can be the most difficult advice to execute because finding a mentor is difficult. Not just the act of asking someone to be a mentor, which can be at best uncomfortable and at worst unnerving, but additionally the work required to search for and identify the *right* mentor. You don't want just any mentor; you want a mentor who can fulfill three key responsibilities: provide accurate and *honest* feedback on your personal performance; dedicate time to your professional development; is willing to protect information that you share in confidence.

Ideally, the mentor you choose also will be someone who can observe your professional interactions and/or have access to information or networks that you may not be privy to. This is of the utmost importance because, as mentioned earlier, dedicated practice is most effective in environments where outcomes are predictable.[10] Because the underlying reasons for successes and failures are not always obvious, having a mentor who can better parse the information and provide objective feedback can result in learning and improvement where it would otherwise be wasted effort.[11] Thus, the primary role of a mentor is to reduce ambiguity and help you better understand how or why your influence was or was not successful.

Next, a mentor can open doors to new opportunities that otherwise would be unavailable to their mentees. This can occur directly, with the mentor actively lobbying for their mentee, but it can occur indirectly as well. Simply having access to a mentor's network, perhaps through brief introductions, has been found to yield opportunities that would otherwise be inaccessible.[12] Imagine being introduced to senior leaders in your organization by your mentor. Perhaps a few weeks later they recognize the need for a more junior leader to step up and take charge of a project—you may be the first person who comes to mind. Without access to that network, you may never have been selected—not for lack of expertise or knowledge but instead for lack of positioning.

Especially skilled mentors will provide targeted feedback on your use of political skill in the workplace. They may accomplish this by modeling successful influence behaviors, helping you better understand your social environment, or simply discussing the how and why of the nuances of your organization's political landscape. Effective mentors will not just rely on one-way lectures but will make time for robust and in-depth discussions that facilitate learning and a wider breadth of understanding.

Organizational mentoring relationships focus primarily on building political skill in a protégé (you) and helping the mentee develop a richer and more informed understanding of the work environment. Such relationships do a great deal to promote personal learning, because good mentors increase learning that relates to both job skill and interpersonal competencies, including political skill. Essentially, mentors provide their protégés with the necessary road map depicting boundaries of the game. Successful mentoring involves the informal training and development of what, when, and with whom to do things in the work environment, along with building the interpersonal and social effectiveness competencies that round out political skill.

Executive Coaching

You may find yourself in a situation where mentors simply are not available. Perhaps you are already at the executive level and finding an internal mentor within your organization is impractical or simply not possible. Maybe you feel that your current level of political skill is severely lacking, or that you want to improve as fast as possible, and a mentor simply cannot commit that much time to your personal development. If these or similar situations arise, you may want to consider hiring an executive coach.

As one moves up the hierarchy, technical expertise becomes less of an issue, and political skill becomes increasingly important for successful managers as the scope of their jobs becomes broader. In fact, one of the highly acclaimed findings of the long-term "executive derailment" studies at the Center for Creative Leadership (CCL) was that lack of social effectiveness skills was a leading cause of derailment.[13] Success at this level is largely determined by possessing the political savvy to obtain scarce resources and muster support for a new concept.

Therefore, as one progresses up the chain of command in organizations, political skill becomes increasingly important while technical "know how" becomes less so. The CCL derailment studies outlined 10 fatal flaws that led to executive derailment, and more than half dealt with issues such as insensitivity to others, being perceived as arrogant, failing to delegate, being overly ambitious, inability to adapt to a boss, and overdependence on someone. Only one of the 10 flaws focused on failure to make the business work. Political savvy and interpersonal issues appear to be far more difficult for managers to master than technical issues, and when these managers find themselves in positions that require political skill, they often need professional development to assist them, increasingly calling on executive coaches for assistance.

The executive coaching process usually begins with an assessment by the coach. Using the assessment as a guide, the coach and the executive jointly determine what issues the executive is dealing with. At this point, a strategy can be formulated concerning types of changes that need to be made and skills that need developing. In line with CCL results, the change and development process generally focuses on the areas we label "political skill."

Executive coaching is an ongoing process that depends heavily on the relationship between the two parties. No one has found any quick fixes when developing the kind of behavior that coaching is designed to facilitate. We believe it is a good idea to set up a coaching contract that runs at least a year; anything less than six months may do more harm than good.

An executive coach helps the executive identify issues that will likely affect performance in the executive role. The coach also works with the executive to develop new behaviors and provides ongoing feedback to develop the subtle changes in behavior that can enhance the executive's effectiveness. After considering various alternatives and evaluating likely consequences, the executive can choose a way to approach this situation and perhaps act such strategies out through role-plays with videotape feedback. There is no guarantee that the executive will alter others' behavior, but the approach is likely to be better thought out since the behavior has been rehearsed and feedback has been provided by an independent observer before the "real" interaction occurs.

Executive coaching increases psychological and social awareness and understanding, increases tolerance for ambiguity and a range of emotional responses, and increases flexibility in and ability to develop and maintain effective interpersonal relationships, all of which are central to political skill. A skilled coach can help an executive become more conscious of politically charged environments and a more astute observer of political situations and people. Over time and with practice, executives can refine novice skills into a well-integrated skill inventory and smooth functioning style that will help them more effectively deal with a wide array of situations.

Deliberately Training Political Skill

Each of the four dimensions of political skill can be trained individually. Below, we provide various resources for developing your political skill. As noted above, reliable mentors will help you improve your skill across all four dimensions.

Developing Social Astuteness

Sherlock Holmes, the character created by Sir Arthur Conan Doyle, is known for his ability to quickly identify clues, often overlooked by others, and to piece them together in such a way as to ascertain facts about a crime that were previously unknown. He is lauded as a master of deduction, a true detective who can piece together any crime and discover the culprit. However, does Sherlock actually rely on deduction to solve crimes?

We take for granted the term *deduction* because it is much more common than its close sibling, *induction.* Deduction first involves the presence of a theory or hypothesis and only then does it take into account observations. Essentially, this is what is known as a top-down approach because the intent is to confirm a theory. Induction, however, relies first upon observations. This bottom-up approach allows the observations to be formed into a pattern and then into a theory. Take a moment to consider one of Sherlock Holmes's deductions:

> Now he was a fisherman, scarring pattern on his hand is very distinctive—fishhooks. They are quite old now, suggesting he has been unemployed for some time. Not much industry in this part of the world, so he's turned to his widowed mother for help. Widowed? Yes, obviously. She's got a man's wedding ring on a chain around her neck, clearly her late husband's and too large for her finger . . . (Sherlock Holmes in Hartswood Film's recreation of Sherlock, *The Hounds of Baskerville,* for the BBC.[14])

Notice that Sherlock's true skill does not lie in deduction but rather in induction. He observes his surroundings, taking in every small detail, and weaves them into a coherent pattern that eventually morphs into a theory about the crime he is solving. Even though Doyle's famous detective likely would have been lost to history were he to have relied upon deductive reasoning, there is no inherent benefit in the one form of logic over the other. However, certain environments, positions, and a host of other factors can make one form superior to the other in a specific situation. Thus, depending on how we choose to improve our political skill, we need to employ each effectively and at the appropriate time.

Be Actively Astute

Unless we are looking for the car keys or worried that the person laughing and pointing from across the office is making fun of us, we tend to be passively astute to our surroundings. Recall from the previous chapter that passive search is a constant, unintentional process that alerts us to important features of our environment. However, this passive search of our environment is likely to result in missed opportunities because it does not involve active attempts to try to discern the *why* behind others' actions and behaviors. This active search represents the inductive approach to understanding our environment.

Thus, we recommend that the development of social astuteness begins with directing effort toward being actively astute to your environment. This is perhaps the most cost- and time-effective training tool available for developing social astuteness. To be actively astute means that instead of just accepting the machinations and outcomes of your organizations' politics, you attempt to understand the *why* and the *how*.

Does Janet from accounting seem to have an outsized amount of power for her position? Ask yourself *why*. Every organization has both a formal and informal hierarchy; is it possible that Janet has substantial tenure with the organization and the respect of all her peers? Look beyond the job titles and job descriptions and begin to understand the players. Similarly, if you find yourself being given a coveted role on an upcoming project, don't just congratulate yourself. Ask yourself, *How did I get this promotion?* Was it just hard work? Did you network effectively with your boss, or your boss's boss?

Make every attempt not to be a passive consumer of the workplace. This is a difficult task to measure and we recommend that you consider taking notes. Annie Murphy Paul, author and journalist, argues that seeing is not the same as observing.[15] Taking "field notes" can help make your observations more scientific and may even make you a more acute observer of others. We don't recommend you start catching the eyes of those in your office, noticing something, and then furiously writing in a notebook. However, learning to observe the most salient aspects of your environment and discarding the unimportant will help calibrate and improve your social astuteness.

Critique and Feedback Sessions

In some cases, you simply will not be able to objectively evaluate yourself or your environment because of the ambiguity inherent in political environments. In this case, you want to be more deductive in your approach to improvement. Perhaps you think that you are being too aggressive in the workplace—this is your *theory* or *hypothesis*. One way to test this theory is to gather information by asking for feedback or candid criticism from those around you.

Critique or feedback sessions can range from 360-degree feedback from subordinates and coworkers to one-on-one sessions with your boss. If such interactions are positive, constructive, and developmental as opposed to negative and personal, they can be very effective in diagnosing where you need to improve your interpersonal effectiveness. These feedback sessions can be valuable to all participants because they provide an opportunity to better understand others' perceptions of similar events or environment. This can result in real-world learning that may aid in future efforts toward perspective-taking, as well as in understanding others' behaviors and emotions. In addition, participants who already possess political skill can use their abilities to model appropriate behaviors and skills to the other participants.

Filmed Role-Playing with Feedback

Another technique to better understand how to effectively interact with others is to record role-play sessions with your colleagues.

Ideally, your role-play partners will be members of your current organization who are familiar with its norms and expectations. As individuals role-play some of the challenging interpersonal dilemmas faced on the job (e.g., hiring or firing decisions, dealing with insubordinate employees) they gain a better understanding of the skills required to be effective. The intent of the role-play is to teach problem-solving and interpersonal skills to support the employees in developing viable resolutions to their problems. These skills are made even more prominent when the role-play is recorded and played back for immediate critique by the participants. The result is a video record that provides a unique view to those role-playing; now they can see themselves and all of their good and bad habits on full display. Pausing the video and offering feedback at critical junctures allows participants to evaluate other ways of delivering information or more effective use of taken-for-granted interpersonal skills (e.g., eye contact, gestures). An important by-product of such role-play sessions is that individuals become more aware of their own social skills (or where they are lacking) and how their behaviors can elicit a variety of responses from their partners.

Broaden Horizons

Michael Simmons's five-hour rule is a simple guideline to live by: [successful people] "set aside at least an hour a day (or five hours a week) over their entire career for activities that can be classified as deliberate practice or learning."[16] In today's busy society, where walls that once enclosed the workplace have now been replaced by borderless digital communications, it may seem impossible to carve out that much time for personal study. However, the benefits are vast and when that effort is focused appropriately, it should yield benefits to your social astuteness.

At its core, social astuteness is the ability to understand others' emotions, thoughts, and desires within a particular environment. Consider setting aside a few hours each week to read classic literature. The classics are just that for a reason—the authors found a way to tap into, extract, and (quite literally) spell out human nature. Jane Austen's Elizabeth Bennett, the protagonist of the immortal *Pride and Prejudice*, can provide a master class on the multitude of forces that shape our opinions and actions. Homer's "Odyssey" is an epic poem of leadership, loss, and tenacity. If you do not know where to start, we recommend reviewing *The Western Canon* by Harold Bloom or simply choosing something you were supposed to read in high school but somehow found a way around it.

Another option is to put yourself into uncomfortable situations, because getting to know yourself is just as important as understanding others. It is difficult to understand emotions in others if we cannot understand them in ourselves. You may not have felt fear lately. Consider taking a few days to go to an outdoor survival school with a group of people you have never met. Perhaps you have not suffered lately due to a winning streak in your life. This might be the perfect time to volunteer to help those less fortunate than you. When you go to volunteer, don't just engage in the volunteering—engage with those you are helping. Strike up conversations and listen. Your leaders, coworkers, and subordinates arrive at your organization from a wide range of backgrounds; get to know as many people as you can and learn to understand their motivations and desires.

As a note, many uncomfortable things we strive to accomplish are decidedly solo efforts. Running a marathon, writing a novel, and skydiving are activities that might put you out of your comfort zone, but they do tend to be done alone. All forms of personal improvement and experience will be beneficial, but it is important to engage in those activities that allow you to engage with others so you can learn more about them while also learning more about yourself.

Developing Interpersonal Influence

Perhaps more here than for the other three dimensions, developing skills to persuade and ultimately control the behaviors of others will require knowledge of multiple training methods in order for greater comprehension of each unique situation and behavioral flexibility to occur. Critique/feedback sessions and recorded role-play with feedback, which are used for training social astuteness, are effective for this component as well. Other particularly valuable techniques for increasing one's influence skills include leadership training, behavioral modeling, and developmental simulations.

Leadership Training

Leadership training programs and experiences are more widely available than ever before; they range in content from in-depth case analyses, problem-solving, and communication exercises to rigorous high adventure experiences designed to develop leadership skills and confidence. The increased breadth of skills being imparted to these leadership acolytes is a direct result of society's high expectations for our leaders. More than just being able to manage projects and deadlines, today's leaders need to be effective communicators, empathetic in their actions, virtuous in their behavior, and a host of other things that are constantly added to an ever-growing list of roles and responsibilities.

Rather than just fulfilling the roles of leader or manager, the new expectation is that they are also coaches, teachers, and mentors. These are not easy roles to play. If anything, industry has trended toward requiring leaders to possess finely tuned interpersonal skills that allow them to maximize follower performance. Consider finding a leadership training program focusing on the development of interpersonal skills. Again, the best way to improve is through deliberate practice and accurate feedback. A leadership training program, even a short intensive, will provide you with that opportunity to practice new skills and receive immediate feedback while doing so.

Behavioral Modeling

Based on Bandura's social learning theory and often incorporated as part of overall leadership training, behavioral modeling is perhaps the primary interpersonal skills training technique used in business today. Its efficacy for training effectiveness has been widely validated.[17] Experts typically use the role-play format to demonstrate the proper way to implement particular skills. Once the new skills are modeled, repeated practice by participants is needed for effective transfer of training, optimal skill acquisition, generalization, and maintenance to occur. Because behavioral repetition is an essential key to permanently increasing one's behavioral flexibility, the most effective behavioral modeling programs require participants to practice the newly learned skills. We suggest that the best way to practice influencing others is to use the new skills in any social setting in which an influence situation occurs. These settings may or may not be in a work capacity.

The following example is illustrative of ways in which these techniques can be combined to develop influence skills. Initially, trainers might explain the definition of political skill to the trainees, with particular emphasis on the four facets. Then the trainers (or actors) could act out a vignette concerning how a common problem is handled poorly (i.e., with little or no political skill) and then handled effectively (i.e., with high political skill). The trainees will see the two different approaches showing political skill in action in real-life situations. For example, there's a subordinate (played by a trainer) who is perceived to have excellent potential but has yet to live up to that potential by performance review time. A supervisor (played by a trainer) with low political skill might come on too strong by focusing solely on that poor performance and by asserting their authority with threats (e.g., insisting that such performance will not be tolerated for much longer). Discussion can follow this "negative" role-play.

Then, a role-play for the same situation is performed with a trainer playing a highly politically skilled "supervisor." In this more "positive" role-play, the supervisor can demonstrate expert use of two or more of the political skill facets. For example, an astute supervisor might first ask the subordinate's views on the subordinate's own performance. In many cases, the subordinate will already recognize that they are performing poorly and will express a desire to do better, perhaps even offering solutions for improved performance. After hearing the subordinate's views, the supervisor can then adapt his/her approach to each subordinate.

If the subordinates appear to be devastated by their own poor performance, for example, the trainer can model good political skill by offering feedback on subordinates' comments (i.e., to show that they were listening intently), and by telling subordinates to not be too hard on themselves. With this new information (i.e., that the subordinate is devastated already), supervisors can choose to use a more soft-handed influence approach (e.g., use of reason versus assertiveness) in advising subordinates on ways to improve performance.

In addition, supervisors might refer a potential mentor from their social network in order to help subordinates work on areas that need strengthening. Throughout the role-play, trainees are encouraged to take notes and ask questions. After the role-plays are finished with the actors (i.e., trainers), trainees can then be matched with other trainees and practice the newly learned skills with real issues facing them in their organizations.

Developing and Managing Networks and Social Capital

Bill Clinton, the 42nd president of the United States, has always been considered a master politician. Not just in regard to the traditional meaning of politician, but additionally in regard to the way he wielded a carefully honed, razor-sharp political skill. Regardless of political persuasion, at the time of his initial campaign for the presidency, it was hard not to be swayed by the charm of this saxophone-playing, smooth-talking man who seemed to pull everyone around him into his orbit.

Although he could be considered an example of how to excel in any of the four dimensions of political skill, we have chosen to highlight his ability to network and harvest social capital. Before even beginning his career in politics (though he knew that was his desired goal), he was an active networker who did not pull any punches about his ambitions and reasons for networking. The following is an account of Clinton meeting a graduate student named Jeffrey Stamps at Oxford in 1968.

"Clinton promptly pulled out a black address book. "What are you doing here at Oxford, Jeff?" he asked.

"I'm at Pembroke on a Fulbright," Jeff replied. Clinton penned "Pembroke" into his book, then asked about Stamps's undergraduate school and his major. "Bill, why are you writing this down?" asked Stamps.

"I'm going into politics and plan to run for governor of Arkansas, and I'm keeping track of everyone I meet," said Clinton. (from Never Eat Alone, by Keith Ferrazzi)[18]

Note that networking is not simply about building a network. A network, once constructed, must be maintained lest it fall into disrepair and you into anonymity. It is possible that building a network is even simpler than the maintenance portion. It is natural to meet new people in our daily lives, but less so to reach back into our contacts and cold call an acquaintance. However, this is often required in order to maintain a network, and Bill Clinton knew it.

By some counts, the index cards Bill Clinton made of his contacts totaled a staggering 10,000 by 1980. These cards did not lie dormant. Instead, they were carefully alphabetized in a box until the next election. As opposed to waiting until he *needed* to leverage this network, he dedicated time to maintaining it. Every night, Clinton would pull a few cards out of the Rolodex and write them letters or simply give them a call. After each interaction, he would take notes on what they spoke about or what he had learned and add it to the file; the next time they spoke he could refer to those notes (*Hey, has your daughter graduated from Duke yet?*) and it seemed as if he remembered *everything* from their past conversation. When it came time to leverage that network (to win the presidential election in 1992), he was in possession of a list of people who felt as if they were connected to him, not just someone who traded business cards. More succinctly, Clinton devoted time to *maintaining* his network in order to keep his connections strong.

Social networks are just as important for managers as they are for politicians. Building and maintaining a strong social network is a sign of effective political skill and an essential part of its exercise. Knowing the right people—the people who can help you meet your goals and objectives—can lend confidence in your ability to acquire resources, gain access to private circles, and otherwise exercise your influence. As the aforementioned story shows, successful networking requires more than knowing how to build connections, allegiances, and contacts; you also have to understand how to use social capital to develop coalitions when support needs mobilizing. More than simply exchanging favors, building a network also involves skills in inspiring people to support and follow you.

Building a network can be viewed as an individual effort, but we encourage you to consider ways to tap into others' networks. Mentors can serve as entryways into well-established networks that you might otherwise not have access to. Carefully networking on your own may lead to contacts that can then help you gain access to new, highly sought-after networks as well. If you find your networking ability is lacking, consider trying to improve this dimension by using the following techniques.

Getting Out There and Building Credit

Effective networking relies heavily upon the importance of being—and therefore being seen as—a valuable partner. People must remember that they become part of the network of anyone who enters their network. It's a mutual relationship. What we need to realize is that oftentimes, the nature and strength of that relationship gives one of the two parties a certain level of social capital to draw from in the future. Commonsense ideas for building social capital include volunteering to help your networking partner, being generous with favors, doing high-quality work, getting the job done on time, and getting others excited about working with you. Effective networkers form allegiances and coalitions with other effective people by demonstrating their understanding and ability to help with the job. They are scrupulous about honoring their commitments, promises, and allegiances.

Additionally, effective networkers never lose track of the point that networks can go on for a long time. Lack of any current need for a particular person's assistance does not mean that it may not be vital in the future. Never burn your bridges with anyone. Every contact you maintain will help develop a resource-rich network that will ultimately aid you in your various work and non-work endeavors.

Active Networking

Don't settle for going to networking events, conferences, or dinners and just offering a passing "Hi! I'm so and so" when meeting new people. Exchange business cards. Take notes about the people you meet and what you spoke about. As per the story at the beginning of this section, you need to *actively* network. Never has it been so easy to maintain and organize your contacts. Although Bill Clinton's index cards system worked well in the 1990s, you can do so much more with any number of online systems. Something as simple as Google Contacts can be used to store any number of important pieces of information about the members in your network.

Instead of putting the umpteenth business card in your desk drawer, start creating profiles for each member of your network. Most modern scanners will recognize business cards and create neat, perfectly sized images to upload to your contact list. Have trouble remembering faces? Go to your contact's LinkedIn page, connect with them, and download a recent photo for your own records. Write brief notes in the "Description" section of your contacts about how you met, who they are, and the last time you contacted them. This is the type of information that you *will* forget if you do not write it down. Don't be a passive networker! Be active and learn how to maintain, cultivate, and leverage your network.

Online Networking

Social media has taken a starring role in modern-day networking. Sites like LinkedIn and even Facebook allow us to connect with colleagues on a more personal basis. Although it is tempting to simply connect via LinkedIn and consider your network maintained, this is simply not the case. Social media sites embrace somewhat of a "set it and forget it" style. This is what makes these sites so easy to use. It provides the feeling that we have networked with hundreds of people, when really we have done nothing more than agree to be reminded of everyone's birthday once a year. By all means, leverage this tool to keep up with your connections. You can look to see if they have changed jobs, been promoted, had a child, or any number of life events. These milestones provide a great opportunity to call your connections to help maintain and strengthen your network. And, for the record, just commenting, "Congratulations on the new promotion," will *not* cut it. Call. Write. At a bare minimum, record it in your notes so that the next time you see them—you can mention it and congratulate them with a handshake instead of a few keystrokes.

Counseling

Individuals who experience social anxiety or are frightened to take risks to expand their social contacts might consider counseling. A professional who is skilled in helping clients improve social relations can be particularly useful. Counseling is not only valuable for the timid but for assertive individuals as well. For those who "come on too strong" in a manner where their extreme extroversion eventually wears out its welcome with others, counseling can probe for causes of such behavior and encourage individuals to consider being more parsimonious in their outbursts.

Developing Genuineness or Sincerity

On April 20, 2010, the largest marine oil spill and worst environmental disaster in the history of the United States began with the explosion of the Deepwater Horizon drilling site. The devastation it wrought on marine life was vast and the disruption to the lives of residents and workers in the Gulf states was extreme. Jobs were lost. Fish populations were devastated. Home values plummeted. Just a month later, Tony Hayward, the CEO of British Petroleum (BP), made an apology: "The first thing to say is I'm sorry. We're sorry for the massive disruption it's caused [residents'] lives. There's no one who wants this over more than I do. I would like my life back."

He starts off strong with a simple "I'm sorry." We teach this basic lesson to toddlers. Even when the act that required the apology was an accident, we simply say, "I'm sorry." As long as it is not said ironically or harshly, the words themselves have a somewhat magical effect in our society—those two words express remorse. However, just like a chemical can be inert in isolation, mixing "I'm sorry" with other words can make the message become unstable and dangerous. Hayward's addition of "There's no one who wants this over more than I do" manages to transform his initial message of remorse into one of annoyance and entitlement. This is even before he adds the true accelerant: "I would like my life back."

Deceivers and Believers

For purposes of simplicity, we propose that there are essentially two types of characters who reflect high political skill and use it to influence others. Furthermore, we suggest that the prognosis for the long-term effectiveness of their influence efforts is different for each character.

The two types of characters are "Deceivers" and "Believers," and they differ not so much in their observable short-term or immediate behavior, but rather in the believability or perceived sincerity of their interpersonal influence behavior over time. Deceivers are concerned with the immediate accomplishment of the influence objective. They concentrate on playing a role convincingly enough to elicit the desired response from the target or object of influence.

This would be synonymous with "surface acting" in the drama-turgical literature, and, therefore, even if Deceivers can be effective in the short term, it is unlikely they can continue to play the role convincingly with others day in and day out.

On the other hand, Believers fully embrace and internalize the persona they demonstrate when influencing others. They are not merely playing a role, even one that has been well scripted. They literally become the person they intend to represent in the inter-personal influence attempt. This would be synonymous with the term "deep acting," and it is likely that believers will be effective in successfully demonstrating influence behavior in a sincere way both immediately and over the long term because they are just being themselves.

In the moment, it was hard to know if Tony Hayward was a Believer or a Deceiver. Did he sincerely mean his apology to the people affected by the Deepwater Horizon tragedy and sim-ply bungle his presentation? It is difficult to know if an apology is meant sincerely; even a well-executed, seemingly heartfelt apology could come from a place of insincerity if the person is a Deceiver. Just as executing an apology well does not make you a Believer, a jumbled apology does not make you a Deceiver. Of course, we hope you truly are apologetic (a Believer) if you are apologizing for something. However, some people have problems *appearing* sincere or genuine even when their words are heartfelt and authentic.

This could be for any number of reasons. Perhaps this per-son is not good at expressing emotions. They may come across as wooden or stoic in their presentations. It is not just apolo-gies either. Consider being given an award for excellence by a rather impassive leader who does not appear at all enthusiastic about your accomplishments. Again, perhaps this leader is over-the-moon excited for you, but they simply do not know how to demonstrate it. For this reason, leaders need to ensure they can express the appropriate emotions at the correct times. Essentially, they need to be able to appear sincere and genuine.

The Theater

Just over three decades ago, the *New York Times* reported on a then new form of training for managers and executive that involved taking acting classes.[19] Now, with hundreds of companies employing this technique to instruct and train employees and managers, this drama-based alternative has become a successful industry. More than ever, today's training must be compelling, realistic, practical, relevant, and lasting. The training should also encourage risk-taking and facilitate improved awareness and behavioral flexibility. Drama-based training does that by providing an opportunity to step outside your real-world role and personality. Participants actually learn and attempt (rather than merely hear about) emotional regulation and control, recognition and response to nonverbal cues, management of tone of voice, and so forth.

We interviewed New York actor and acting coach Mara Hobel to gain greater insight into the art of acting. She contended that in order to appear authentic, an actor must not only understand the role but also "capture the essence of that character." Hobel explained that techniques such as tone of voice, voice inflection, and facial expression contribute to a genuine stage presence that is "absolutely essential for a believable performance." She indicated that actors must use all dimensions of their being to engage the audience. Hobel added, "It is most captivating when the actor suppresses emotion. The audience reads the body language on a subconscious level, like pantomime." Therefore, self-control is a major factor in making a true emotional connection.

In her role as an acting coach, Hobel communicates to her students that on stage and in life, actors "need to take responsibility for 'who' and 'how' they are influencing others." Hobel told us, "I tell my students my shortcomings. I'm honest. They need to know I'm human. When I speak to people, I'm not acting. I'm being myself." Thus, self-awareness, sensitivity, and being confidant in who you are contribute to an authentic presence off and on stage. As veteran stage actor Lewis Stedden aptly stated, "You can't be a phony on stage."

Proper shows of emotion and use of nonverbal cues translate to perceived sincerity and the appearance of being genuine. These are both cornerstones of political skill. Again, this is not intended to be a lesson in how to deceive others, but rather an appeal toward expressing your desired emotion in such a way that others can feel it too. Is it any wonder that Ronald Reagan, the 40th president of the United States, was considered a master at influencing others? Prior to his presidency, he was a Hollywood actor—his political skill enabled him to bring together Democrats and Republicans. When he left the presidential office, his approval rating was 68 percent—one of the highest ratings for departing presidents in the modern era.

Conclusion

Like any other skill, political skill can be improved over time. However, simply engaging in political skill at work will not result in improvement. Instead, you need to deliberately practice the various dimensions of political skill. In a perfect situation, your efforts will be accompanied by a mentor who can provide you immediate and accurate feedback.

For this reason, there is absolutely no excuse for being satisfied with possessing only a modicum of political skill. Make no mistake, this is a critical competency in the workplace, and it will yield benefits for you, your employees, and your organization. It will not be easy or comfortable to train each of the four dimensions, but it will be worth the effort.

Research Highlight

Brouer, R. L., et al. (2009). "The Moderating Effect of Political Skill on the Demographic Dissimilarity—Leader–Member Exchange Quality Relationship." *The Leadership Quarterly*, *20*(2), 61–69.

As we've noted, mentors are a great resource for developing political skill, and for many people, supervisors are a natural source of mentoring. Given this, it is important for employees to develop high-quality relationships with their supervisors. However, this can be easier said than done, as a number of factors can hinder relationship development. Unfortunately for employees, some of these factors are out of their control, as things like being demographically different from your supervisor can prevent the development of a high-quality relationship.

Brouer and her colleagues set out to see whether political skill could mitigate the negative effects of demographic dissimilarity on relationship quality between employees and supervisors. They hypothesized that the interpersonal savvy of politically skilled employees would enable them to develop higher-quality relationships despite the demographic differences. Results from their study showed that demographically different subordinates without political skill reported significantly worse relationships with supervisors than those who were demographically similar. Not only was this negative effect mitigated for politically skilled subordinates, they actually reported slightly better relationship quality than those who were similar. This suggests that the politically skilled might even be able to capitalize on differences with supervisors in a strategic manner.

4

POLITICAL WILL:
THE MOTIVATION TO
SUCCEED

The Challenge of Political Will

Barack Obama ascended to the presidency on a wave of national optimism. His campaign used carefully crafted messages, oratorically graceful speeches, and modern technology to create a coalition of voters that redefined the way in which we understand the electorate. Obama rose to power because of his intellect, his oration, and his projected hope that there were more values that united us than divided us. He won the presidency overcoming lingering racial tensions, his relative inexperience, and, as he joked, his funny name.

Sitting in the oval office in the beginning of his term, President Obama was faced with a dilemma on how to use the political will he had garnered from his election win. Knowing he could use it for big policy gains, he set his sights on two critical ideas: healthcare reform and fighting climate change. Either policy choice would result in the investment and loss of collective political will and personal social capital. He chose to address health care and within a year of taking office, the bill passed Congress on a nearly party-line vote. The political consequences for President Obama were predictable and devastating. His approval rating fell

18 points from what it had been on election day (67 percent) and his unpopularity increased 31 points to 44 percent,[1] due to what was now being labeled "Obamacare" and was widely seen as a main factor in the Democrats losing control of the House of Representatives in the 2010 midterm elections.

The Power of Political Will

It is without question that political skill is a powerful predictor of career success and played a paramount role in Barack Obama's road to the presidency. Indeed, anecdotal and empirical evidence indicate that those leaders and employees who possess higher levels of political skill will experience better work performance, stronger social networks, decreased job stress, and overall greater success in their careers and in their lives. However, political skill cannot be seen as a panacea in careers or organizations. Political skill alone cannot predict success or political behavior.

For example, we are all familiar with the caricature of the office "yes man." That "suck up" in the blue suit and red power tie who agrees with whatever the bosses say; even to the point of contradicting themselves, hurting their coworkers, and compromising their own values. Or the "blunt instrument" that keeps pushing for their agenda but lacks political acumen, which always dooms their cause. Each case depicts the complex nature of the relationship between political skill and its motivational counterpart, political will. In short, an abundance of motivation accomplishes nothing without a requisite amount of skill, and the most skilled political actor will accomplish nothing without the desire for personal or contextual change.

Understanding political will as a motivator for action for individual employees and leaders helps us to better appreciate political skill as a personal resource that can be used to garner power and influence of others. It also helps us to see political will as a finite yet renewable resource for both individuals and collectives. In this chapter, we introduce the concept of political will and explain how it impacts the implementation of political skill. Further, we explain the role of political will in leadership and destructive behavior.

Defining Political Will

Until recently, political will was a concept only addressed in the aggregate. That is, researchers and the popular press discussed political will as being held only by a collective and little, if any, discussion was had regarding the political motivation of individual actors. Despite widespread recognition of the concept in the popular lexicon, academic definitions and understandings of political will have varied greatly. Some definitions of political will do, however, demonstrate both individual and ecological level considerations. For example, Kpundeh (1998, p. 92) defined political will as "the demonstrated credible intent of political actors (e.g., elected or appointed leaders, civil society watchdogs, stakeholder groups, etc.) to attack perceived causes or effects of corruption at a systemic level."[2] Post, Raile, and Raile indicated that "political will is the extent of committed support among key decision makers for a particular policy solution to a particular problem."[3]

While these scholarly definitions are notable, they only acknowledged, rather than articulated, a view of political will as a personal characteristic. Considering that every change initiative in organizations or society begins with a single voice in the darkness, a more direct understanding of personal political will seemed appropriate. Thus, personal political will can be thought of as "the motivation to engage in strategic, goal-directed behavior that advances the personal agenda and objectives of the actor that inherently involves the risk of relational or reputational capital."[4]

From this perspective, we see that utilizing one's political skill requires a willingness to risk personal assets, real and perceived, that the actor has cultivated through previous actions. Thus, we recognize that political actors cannot invest themselves in all relationships, achievements, or causes. They must select which issues or initiatives are of the most importance to them and one's political will in a particular context serves to predict action.

Understanding Your Political Will

Political skill is a resource. When individuals possess this resource, they achieve an abundance of positive outcomes for themselves, their causes, and their organization. And, as we make the argument that politics per se is not a bad thing by pointing to leaders throughout history who have built movements from the ground up to change society by engaging in political behavior to build coalitions for change, it is important to understand how both instrumental and altruistic motivations can activate political skill and social capital. No one can deny that Martin Luther King Jr. had tremendous political skill in building his "coalition of conscience" to fight for equal rights. More important, however, he demonstrated exceptional levels of political will to knowingly risk not only his social capital but his life for the cause of justice. This type of positive outcome of an influencer who possesses both political skill and high levels of political will confirms that political behavior is not simply "many ticks" sucking the blood out of their competitors, but rather there are individuals who are driven to selflessly expend their political resources for the benefit of others.

However, what about Adolf Hitler's political will? He unmistakably possessed high levels of political skill. This is evident in his ability to motivate a nation toward rising from the ashes of World War I and galvanize energy and resources toward an abhorrent ideology that committed some of the most immoral acts against humanity in history. Like Martin Luther King Jr., Hitler was a talented and relentless communicator of his vision. Unlike Martin Luther King Jr., Hitler's anti-establishment views were directed toward exclusion rather than inclusion and a concern for his, and his followers', own self-interest at the cost of others' interests. It is these types of bad intentions that spurred researchers to investigate whether political will could be two sides of the same coin in that it might drive individuals to both pro- and anti-social behaviors.

Taking up this charge, academics have recently expanded on the political will construct in an effort to better understand if a political actor's motivation can determine whether they strive for only their self-interest or for the interest of others. An individual's political will could be driven by an interest in others or themselves and a concern for instrumental or relational outcomes. Further, even if individuals are highly motivated toward a particular cause, they still might not act if they perceive the risk to be too high. Those with greater levels of political skill should be expected to more accurately assess the risk involved with action and therefore be less likely to make foolish political plays that will result in disproportionate damage to their social capital.

Recently, a scale was developed that allowed researchers to assess an individual's political will.[5] The resultant scale supports the notion that political will had both self-serving and other-concerned components. Specifically, the Political Will Scale (which is at the end of this chapter) validation found that individuals have both a self-serving and benevolent orientation to engage their political resources. Accordingly, self-serving political will was shown to correlate with behaviors that most benefit the actor, whereas benevolent political will seems to relate to political activity that might benefit others.

Political Will and Career Outcomes

The nascent stage of political will research has yet to yield an abundance of empirical results. It is perhaps not surprising, however, that political will relates to a number of important career-related outcomes such as status in the workplace and career growth potential. This implies that political will helps the actor to effectively manage a positive reputation that assists them with later career opportunities. Interestingly, this relationship exists for both self-serving and benevolent political will, thus suggesting that each motivation is critical to have in order to advance one's career. This further points to the important self-regulatory nature of political will in assessing the context appropriateness and risk inherent in one's political behavior.

Political will is manifested in both the quality of enacted political behaviors and through the specific political behaviors that are selected. Thus, individuals' political will affects not only their willingness to *try* to influence others, but also the particular political behavior *chosen*. For example, individuals with self-serving political will are more likely to try to influence powerful people, even those above their direct supervisor, and less likely to engage in influence tactics that emphasize rational arguments for their position. Thus, we would characterize those with high levels of self-serving political will as engaging in more aggressive political tactics. In contrast, those with higher levels of benevolent political will are more likely to build coalitions and attempt to influence their targets by using rational arguments.

Among the riskiest behaviors within the workplace is when individuals decide to "speak their mind." That is, speaking up to powerful others in the organization to express concern or to ask for changes in their work. Whereas individuals with higher overall levels of political will are more likely to speak their mind, those with benevolent, rather than self-serving, political will are the most likely to do so. Of course, individuals can be low or high on both dimensions as well as low on one and high on the other.

Perhaps you are high in both self-interested and benevolent political will. Or, similarly, you are in a situation that activates your high level of either self-interested or benevolent political will. In these cases, you will be prone to invest yourself in multiple causes, thus depleting the political and social capital (which are your personal resources) you have accrued. Given that these are diminishing resources, individuals must be cautious not to overextend or outstrip their own social capital. Unchecked political will can lead to a martyrdom complex in which the actor "takes a bullet" for every cause in the organization. In the end, these overzealous actors will become decreasingly effective as each bullet wound leaks out their reputation, time, credibility, and influence.

Political Will and Leadership

At the aggregate level, political will can be seen as a measure of leadership effectiveness. A cursory Google search of any failed regulatory or social issue will see multiple references to the lack of political will as being the reason for its failure. In fact, some have argued that political will in the aggregate form is defined and known only in its absence.[6] Indeed, political science definitions imply that the degree of political will attached to a particular cause or initiative can be reflected in the number of policies or regulations that the collective efforts result in.

In contrast to this results-oriented view, we suggest that individuals are enacting their own political will every day, in ultimately significant, and not so significant, ways. Organizations are a shifting sea of coalitions with both congruent and divergent interests, and as such, the definition provided by political science is unfulfilling in understanding the process by which these changes occur. In fact, within these work constellations, members with high political will are more likely to be recognized by their colleagues as informal leaders.[7] However, high political will does not ensure that these informal leaders will be successful; it is only those with high political *skill* that are able to convert their advantageous social status into increased job performance.

As we begin to investigate the interaction of political will and political skill, we cannot help but be drawn to the concept of leader charisma. Much as we have pondered how political behavior can be used for socially appropriate and destructive means, charismatic leadership scholars have tried to rationalize the charisma of Gandhi with that of Hitler. Charismatic leaders can possess one of two dominant orientations. The first, socialized charismatic leadership, is based on norms of equity and focused on the collective. The second, personalized charismatic leadership, is aligned with personal interests, narcissistic behavior, and self-aggrandizement.[8]

Thus, leaders will be motivated to engage in socialized leadership when they possess high levels of political will and to enact personalized leadership when they have increased levels of self-interested political will. Based on past research we would expect that while a leader's political motivation directs them toward a particular target, they are likely to be identified as charismatic and effective when they possess high levels of political skill. Indeed, political skill is often associated with personal charisma. For leaders or aspiring leaders, the development and understanding of personal and collective political will should be a cornerstone of their development.

Political Will as an Outcome of Leadership Processes

In the end, we may be left with the same puzzling dilemma that has plagued political scholars for decades...how to know when political will has been effectively implemented. Indeed, political will is still most recognized by its absence, and with this in mind, it may be most helpful to view political will as an outcome of change; accepting that any personal, organizational, or societal change is the result of competing wills. In these contests, individuals will either overcome the status quo or be lost to the winds of history in failing to chart a new course for their initiative.

Individuals who have a benevolent type of political will help to explain why leaders throughout history have sacrificed their own comfort and risk their own lives to benefit the broader society. It helps explain why Martin Luther King Jr. risked his own life to engage in influence behaviors to improve justice in society. Perhaps more important, it also explains all of the unseen acts of defiance and civil disobedience along the road to civil rights performed by unnamed, but concerned, citizens. This collective political will cannot be measured solely by policy gains but must be viewed through the lens of collective activity.

Unlike previous generations, technology allows for us to understand the power of our message in ways never seen before. Your ability to generate collective action can be seen in retweets, likes, hashtags, online petitions, and followers well before more significant steps must be made toward achieving policy changes. While each of these technological actions has a relatively low entry barrier to "join a cause," they serve as a tangible gauge of the volume of awareness political actors have gained for their cause. This facet of collective political will represents a recognition of the "New Power" elements of modern social movements like the Me Too movement (movement against sexual harassment and sexual assault) and the ice bucket challenge (dumping a bucket of ice water over a person's head to promote awareness of amyotrophic lateral sclerosis [ALS]). These technology-driven, low-entry-barrier movements have resulted in significantly elevating the level of awareness around an issue. However, each of these initiatives has struggled to institutionalize its changes into the types of lasting structural changes that the political scientist's view of political will would see as being connected to societal paradigm shifts. So, whereas these viral social movements may have altered the conversation about their causes and technology presents an easy way to quantify their effectiveness in doing so, we are still left with the challenge of converting these conversations into lasting change.

Political Will and Destructive Behavior

The self-serving dimension of the Political Will Scale shows why, perhaps, political behavior has gotten such a bad rap in society in that it details the types of self-serving motivations most of us find appalling at their most extreme. We have all seen these motivations in the individual who will offer to help a colleague because the boss is in the office that day. It explains why some people operate in a finite pie scenario where they can only make their slice of the pie larger if they reduce your slice. While certainly all organizations have temporally finite resources, the view of the collective as expanding together rather than fighting one another affects the manner in which we approach problems and others.

Though research has not yet established the link between political will and destructive leadership behaviors, some scholars have argued, and it's a modest logical leap to suggest, that individuals who possess high levels of self-serving political will are likely to engage in a more destructive pattern in relationships in general and leadership in particular. One such personal characteristic, Machiavellianism, correlates positively, and strongly, with self-serving political will. Machiavellianism reflects one's disposition to prioritize their own self-interest at the expense of others. Those possessing high levels of this personality trait have a view of morality that deviates from societal norms and drives them toward unethical acts, including behaviors that may seem directly related to political activity such as deception and manipulation.[9] Thus, we might expect that as leaders with self-serving orientations gain status in organizations, they will be prone to engage in ever increasing abuse toward their subordinates.

How Do Political Skill and Political Will Interact?

So how do we predict the effectiveness of a political actor when we incorporate one's motivation with their skill? The matrix below describes four types of political actors as predicted by their relative political skill and their political will toward a particular event, cause, or context.

Figure 1: Political Will–Political Skill Integration

	Low Political Skill	High Political Skill
High Political Will	Yes Men	Influencers
Low Political Will	Sheep	Bystanders

Yes Man: A yes man possesses high levels of political will but lower levels of political skill. In this scenario, it is likely that the actor's initial blunders and/or overt overtures to gain influence will be seen as harmless. However, over time, these ongoing socially inappropriate or awkward behaviors will move the target and/or observer toward annoyance. As these yes men are motivationally driven to gain the approval of those in power, over time they are likely to contradict themselves and appear to others as disingenuous or simply as blatant liars. These contradictory images will lead others to dislike and distrust these individuals and ultimately lead to their demise.

As political actors, these individuals are useful to gain momentum for your effort. These yes men's intentions are obvious and their ability to detect your influence behavior toward them is low, and thus you are able to utilize your political skill to move them and/or their resources into your coalition, keeping in mind that their resources may be minimal and their reputation either underdeveloped or tarnished. Because of the risk associated with including these individuals, use caution before enlisting them as a meaningful component of your coalition.

Sheep: Individuals who possess little political will and political skill will struggle to survive in any organization regardless of formality, education, industry, or culture. In fact, it can be hard to imagine someone whose traits classify them in this quadrant throughout their lifetime. It is probably more accurate to suggest that there are low-skill participants in organizations, but while individuals may have generally lower levels of motivation, they can be motivated on specific issues to engage their resources toward a goal. Thus, the low-motivation "slacker" may be readily willing to speak out against environmental abuses in her/his local community but is not concerned with the impact of human trafficking in their city. We would thus expect these individuals to be low-impact and low-performing in their careers.

When interacting with sheep, it is important to understand their potential. They will never become critical thinkers on an issue because it requires too great an investment of resources to obtain and perhaps too much social understanding that they do not possess. However, when their shallow pool of interests does overlap with yours, you may be able to count on them to engage in simple, low-investment tasks. This effect is similar to low-information, single-issue voters. When attempting to influence these individuals, simple messaging and low-investment calls to action will be most effective.

Bystander: The low political will, high political skill individual is likely to be seen as the most shrewd or cunning by others because they are seen as leaders by others while remaining unwilling to stick their neck out for others. These individuals are likely highly self-focused in their motivations and will likely only risk their social capital in a context that stands to promote their status. This implies that very few change agents can be classified as bystanders, and it is further likely that these individuals will be disliked by their colleagues due to their selfishness despite being respected for individual accomplishments.

Bystanders can be both valuable and dangerous to your coalition. They are valuable because when engaged, their political skill will bring elevated resources and stature to a project or initiative. Their danger lies in the degree to which the same issues they bring to bear on the situation can overwhelm the project and cause it to lose traction because of power struggles caused by the bystander's participation, or it could lose focus because of the weight of visibility the bystander brings to the project. In these cases, value alignment and partner selection are key considerations for the actor. To the degree that you can ensure that the reputation of the bystander enhances, rather than detracts, from your goals and you can be sure that the individual is not looking to subsume you and your cause within their own agenda, then the bystander may be helpful in building a stronger coalition.

Influencers: When elevated levels of political skill are met with commensurate levels of political will, change and growth are nearly guaranteed. We have already discussed the many benefits of possessing political skill, but when that level of ability is combined with a level of motivation that ensures that not only action will be taken, but that action will be successful in achieving the influencers objectives.

Conclusion

On January 20, 2017, Barack Obama spent his last day in office as president of the United States. After going "all in" with his political will to win an important victory for healthcare reform, some thought not only might his popularity not recover, but he would likely not win a second term. However, President Obama left office as one of the most popular presidents in modern history (59 percent approval rating). Among his administration's accomplishments were leading the country out of the Great Recession and into the longest period of economic expansion in modern history, increasing the reputation of the United States around the world, passing the Lily Ledbetter Fair Pay Act, ending the Iraq War, ending "Don't ask, don't tell," and passing sweeping Wall Street reform. The Obamacare battle in which he invested his political will had led to the smallest number of the population being uninsured of any time in the modern history of the United States and had begun to bend the healthcare cost curve downward. His story shows how politically skilled leaders who understand the nature of political will as renewable can adeptly invest their capital and weather the storm of shortsighted criticism to ultimately gain heightened levels of respect, accomplishment, and social capital for future endeavors.

WHAT IS YOUR POLITICAL WILL?

For each of the following items, rate yourself on a scale from 1 to 7 where 1 is "very strongly disagree," 4 is "neutral," and 7 is "very strongly agree."

1 — Doing good for others sometimes means acting politically.

2 — I would engage in politics to serve the common good.

3 — When I am right, I am willing to act politically.

4 — I would use political tactics to improve my working conditions.

5 — Engaging in politics is an attractive means to achieve my personal objectives.

6 — I would employ political tactics to be in my boss's inner circle.

7 — Prevailing in the political arena at work would prove my competence.

8 — I would engage in politics to preserve my self-esteem.

- Add up your scores on questions 1, 3, 5, and 7 and divide that total by 4. That is your self-serving political will score. For reference, studies have found that 2.99 is an "average" score for this dimension.

- Add up your scores on questions 2, 4, 6, and 8 and divide that total by 4. That is your benevolent political will score. For reference, studies have found that 3.98 is an "average" score for this dimension.

- Add up all 8 items and divide by 8. This is your total political will score. For reference, studies have found that 3.49 is an "average" score.

Research Highlight

Shaughnessy, B. A., et al. (2017). "An Integrative Social Network—Political Conceptualization of Informal Leadership: Performance Consequences of Need for Power, Informal Leadership, and Political Skill in a Mediated Moderation Model." *Journal of Leadership and Organizational Studies*, 24(1): 83–94.

In any group, a leader will always emerge. Right? Well, if your experience tells you that is the case, the question for researchers is why. Why is it that certain people emerge as leaders and the other group members recede to follower roles, perhaps despite their talent?

Shaughnessy and her colleagues postulated that it was because the motivations of some individuals made them more inclined to invest themselves politically in a group and thus more likely to be seen by others as leaders. In their study, they asked members of a small social services organization in the United States to anonymously identify same-level coworkers who were leaders in the workplace. They also asked each of these employees to rate their own internal political orientations. Their results showed that when employees had more political will, their coworkers were more likely to see them as an informal leader. Political skill, however, did not contribute to emerging as a leader, but it did affect the likelihood that these informal leaders were able to obtain higher job performance scores. This means political will can help make you a leader, but your success is dependent on political skill.

PART II

POLITICAL SKILL AND CAREER SUCCESS

5

GETTING THE JOB

Political skill is not the only quality you need to land a job, but having it can make a big difference during the selection process. After all, most openings draw a number of applicants with the requisite intelligence, education, and experience; therefore when hiring managers are weighing the qualifications of their top candidates, a politically skillful candidate can stand out and rise to the top.

People high in political skill tend to receive higher ratings of suitability for jobs and more actual job offers from interviewers—a point supported by research[1]. This is most likely because politically skilled people are viewed as fitting the job context better than less politically skilled individuals, and hiring for *fit* (roughly defined as appropriateness for the mix of personalities, the culture, and the values of the job, the organization, or the work unit or group) has become an increasingly prevalent basis for selection decisions.

In this chapter, we examine the hiring process in organizations today and how the notion of fit is increasingly being used to decide who gets jobs and who does not. We also describe the role of political skill in assessments of fit and final hiring decisions and provide examples that illustrate the importance of political skill in getting jobs.

The Hiring Process

Most people make their living by working for others, and those others are almost always part of an organization. Would-be employees generally have to clear many hurdles to get hired. Although the official hiring process is sometimes bypassed out of favoritism or personal friendship, most selection systems call for information gathered over a sequence of steps with a final decision being made only after all information is gathered and compared on all job candidates.

Hiring was not always a systematic process. The rise of the factory system during the Industrial Revolution of the late eighteenth and early nineteenth centuries moved the manufacture of goods from individual craftsmen, operating out of their homes and shops, to large numbers of people brought together to work in ways that capitalized on economies of scale and mass production, which increased profitability for business owners. In those days, people typically were hired for jobs that required no prior experience and no special skills. Therefore, hiring was usually first-come, first-served—those who arrived first at the application office went to work.

Psychology in Hiring

In the very early years of the twentieth century, German psychologist Hugo Münsterberg relocated to the United States and settled in Boston. The discipline of psychology was still very new. Münsterberg had received his training in one of the first formal psychology programs in the late 1800s in Leipzig, Germany. Trained in experimental psychology, he believed that the basic principles of psychology could be applied to understanding people's behavior in the workplace. (He later became known as the "Father of Applied Psychology.")[2]

It just so happened that Boston was experiencing some problems with its transportation system. At that time, the conventional way to get around large cities like New York, Chicago, and Boston was on trolley cars operated by railway motormen. The requirements for holding the job of railway motorman were essentially nonexistent, so people were hired on a near-random, first-come basis. As a result of this hiring process (or lack thereof), Boston was experiencing a costly problem: poor performance, high turnover, and other on-the-job troubles.

Münsterberg approached the city and told them he could help fix the transit system by applying a more systematic and scientific approach to hiring the railway motormen. He first observed and analyzed the job to see what tasks, duties, and behaviors were required, and then he translated that information into the knowledge, skills, and abilities (KSAs) needed to perform these duties effectively. Then he identified the best ways to measure or assess these critical KSAs in job applicants, arguing that the applicants who scored highest on the key KSAs would show the best potential for the job.

Boston implemented Münsterberg's plan, and it worked! Railway motormen hired using this new system consistently performed better, stayed on the job longer, and generally saved the city a lot of money. What Münsterberg came up with was the first formal personnel selection system, which became the standard model for selection and hiring for the next century. Further, even this early, Münsterberg understood the critical nature of the human element; he noted that of the three great factors (in the terms of his day, material, machine, and man), man is not the least but the most important. Interestingly, within the past decade or so, more and more companies have been going about the hiring process with that insight in mind, and this approach seems to be driven by the concept of fit.

Selection Based on Fit

As university professors, we interact frequently with corporate recruiters who travel to college campuses a couple of times a year to interview students who are completing their undergraduate or graduate degrees. When chatting with the recruiters, we typically ask them what they are looking for in our students—usually for jobs in human resources management—and the exchange that follows has become quite predictable. The recruiters all quickly reply, "I'm looking for someone who fits." We ask just what that means, and the invariable response is, "You know, someone who fits." We explain that although we are confident that *fit* means something specific to them, we don't know what that is, and we ask if they could try to explain it. After some struggle, they inevitably say, "I can't describe it, but I'll know it when I see it."

The Nature of Fit

Herein lies the interesting and sometimes frustratingly elusive issue of fit as a criterion. Some efforts have been made to study the notion of fit and to try to develop a more specific sense of what it means, but the outcome has rarely been of much general help. It's possible to be a bit more precise about the concept of fit if you can answer: Fit for what? In this case, it becomes clear that fit assessments can measure job applicants against different reference points in the organization, including the job, the team or work group they might be joining, the organization's culture, or perhaps even a set of values the organization embraces. The extent to which job applicants are viewed as fitting well with (or being similar to) one or more of the relevant criteria or reference points usually results in their receiving higher ratings of suitability for the job and improving their chances of obtaining job offers.

The Employment Interview and Fit

The employment interview has been—and will doubtless continue to be—the prevalent personnel selection device, the tool employers use to determine how well job applicants fit with the job and organization. Like the whole selection process, the employment interview puts people in a situation where they see it as in their best interest to manage the impressions of the other party—even though they each hope to gain an unmanaged, independent impression for themselves.

That is, recruiters will promote their organization's status, reputation, and other advantageous features in the effort to ensure as large a pool as possible of qualified job candidates. Applicants want as many alternatives for jobs as possible, so they will present attractive impressions of themselves in various ways in an effort to impress interviewers and lead them to assessments of effective fit. At the same time, both recruiters and applicants are anxious to see through these attractive screens to what is really behind them—a devoted and enthusiastic worker or a slacker, an upbeat and rewarding workplace or a sweatshop. Or, in less invidious terms, a potential employee who will fit in and succeed in that particular workplace, and a workplace where the applicant will fit in and succeed. On each side, political skill promotes success.

These intentional efforts to manage the image of fit can lead decision makers to make wrong decisions. True fit is never completely knowable at this stage of the selection process, when little information is available to either side. Some might characterize such a decision context as "It's not what you are, it's what you appear to be."

Political Skill and Fit

Fit, as we've seen, is not well defined, difficult to precisely describe, and more of an intuitive hunch than a definitive thing. Decision makers really do struggle with their ability to clearly define what they mean by fit, but they usually can tell you when they run across either very good or very poor fit. It's that hard-to-explain quality, that *je ne sais quoi*, that is similar to the feeling they get when they encounter someone high in political skill. Indeed, we suggest that politically skilled individuals are apt to be perceived as fitting well with job and organization contexts. Those high in political skill possess the social astuteness and adaptability to assess the situation and formulate the proper influence strategy (the one that incorporates the proper methods of influence), and to execute it in an influential way that is perceived as genuine, sincere, and authentic.

The successful use of influence by politically skilled people is a result of two things:

- First, you need to accurately and astutely read the situation and select the proper influence tactic or strategy for that particular situation.

- Second, you need to execute the tactic or strategy in a convincing way that will lead to its success.

Efforts at interpersonal influence in the employment interview commonly take the form of ingratiation or self-promotion. Ingratiation is a tactic used to increase how much the interviewer likes you, and self-promotion is used to manage the interviewer's impressions of your competence. Job applicants often use either or both of these tactics to promote greater perceptions that they fit.

However, less skilled applicants tend to employ ingratiation when self-promotion is more appropriate. In fact, research on impression management in the employment interview has shown that applicants exhibiting ingratiation in the interview tend to be evaluated lower by interviewers than those who demonstrate self-promotion.[3] The conclusion here—and one worth noting—is that discussing your strengths in an interview, if done with political skill, should enhance your chance of being hired over applicants who spend interview time complimenting the interviewer.

The informal rules of the game, and the implicit expectations in employment interviews, are that applicants are going to try to appear as talented, skilled, and qualified for the job as they possibly can. Interviewers usually expect people in these situations to be self-promoters. If an applicant goes against these expectations and does not self-promote but instead only tries to ingratiate, the effort might be interpreted as a character weakness in the applicant; that is, being too timid and perhaps even weak, resulting in lower evaluations from the interviewer.

Applicants should to size up the interview situation (determine the nature of the job they are applying for, the required skills and competencies, and what it will take to appear to fit this situation) and select the proper methods of influence. Politically skilled people usually know the proper tactics to employ in each situation. However, even when the proper tactics of influence are chosen, they won't be effective unless their execution is skillful. People low in political skill may select influence tactics that are appropriate for a given situation, but they are likely to encounter difficulties when trying to execute influence effectively. For example, self-promotion can be tricky to manage. For each interviewer, there's an optimal level that is not so much that the applicant appears arrogant or conceited (as a society, we tend to despise arrogance and conceit) but also is not so little that the applicant seems weak or incompetent.

It's essential to strive to demonstrate a level of self-promotion that identifies and presents your positive qualities in a confident rather than an obnoxious way. No one wants to hire a jerk! Individuals high in political skill will be able to fine-tune the execution of delivery in a way that achieves just the proper degree of social calibration—one that carefully strikes the proper balance and communicates just the right image: the image that fits.

Getting Hired by Getting Wired

The political skill of networking can also make a big difference in the hiring process. As noted in chapter 1, networking ability involves the professional connections, alliances, coalitions, and friendships built up over time, which constitute the social capital you will draw on when needed to exert influence. The adage "It is not what you know but who you know" contains a great deal of truth. Although this expression may be used cynically or realistically, and it comes across as a gross oversimplification, the fact of the matter is that some of both is needed—that is, what you know and who you know.

As you expand your professional network and are associated with influential people in important and meaningful ways, you will convey a strong and positive message about yourself and your abilities that can work to your advantage. Your networking ability and the resulting store of social capital can make it possible to call in favors, delicately mention influential names, and thus move to the front of the pack for job openings. Once again, politically skilled people will know precisely how to use such network information in an effective way, employing a subtle style that conveys an impressive image in an understated—never an offensive or overbearing—way. The impact of political skill on the development, maintenance, and leveraging of social networks will be discussed in depth in chapter 9.

Research on Political Skill in the Employment Interview

Lest you think we're simply relying on intuitive hunches about the importance of political skill and how it should equip job applicants for the hiring process, here are reports of some research that has been conducted on the topic. Not surprisingly, political skill appears to be closely tied to success in the employment interview setting.

Corporate Recruiters

One study was conducted involving corporate recruiters from a number of different firms who were recruiting soon-to-be-graduates from a large Midwestern university.[4] Students who registered with the placement office for on-campus interviews participated in the study, and they completed questionnaires measuring, among other things, their political skill. The recruiters who participated in the study completed questionnaires after their interviews with students, and they reported on how well they thought the student fit the job and the organization and whether they would recommend that the student be hired and how positively they evaluated the student.

The results of the data analyses showed that job applicant political skill was significantly and positively related to recruiter assessments of both person-job fit and person-organization fit. Furthermore, political skill of job applicants was also significantly and positively related to hiring recommendations made by recruiters and to their overall positive evaluations of the job applicants.

Public Utility Interviewers

The other research investigation we found examining job applicant political skill and recruiter evaluations was set up a little differently.[5] Interviewers employed by a large public utility located in the southeastern United States participated in this research investigation as an exercise, part of a training and development program conducted on-site by one of the authors of the study. In this hiring exercise, interviewers were given the job description for a customer service representative position, along with a résumé that presented the woman applying for the job as either very qualified or very unqualified.

All interviewers watched one of two videotaped employment interview segments featuring the applicant whose résumé they had assessed. Half of the interviewers saw an applicant who had been trained to display political skill: she made frequent eye contact, smiled frequently, showed feeling in answering questions from the off-camera interviewer, and demonstrated other behaviors in politically skilled ways. The other half of the interviewers saw an applicant who answered the questions without any feeling or emotion and who did not smile or demonstrate behaviors in any ways identifiable as politically skilled. Interviewers were then asked to evaluate their likelihood of hiring the candidate, how well she performed in the videotaped interview, and how well qualified she was for the job.

It turned out that the objective qualifications of the job applicant (which had been manipulated to appear either very strong or very weak for the job) had absolutely no effect on the evaluations. The only thing that made a difference was the applicant's political skill (or lack of), and it affected their likelihood of hiring her, the qualifications they perceived she had for the job, and how well they thought she performed in the interview.

Political Skill and Fit for Specific Hiring Targets

Political skill operates across the whole spectrum of employment. Here are two further examples, showing how it operates to establish fit in the hiring process for CEOs and college professors.

Hiring Corporate CEOs

Corporate chief executive officers set the vision and strategic plan for their organization. As a result, hiring the right CEO is perhaps the most critical decision an organization makes. The right CEO must be not only knowledgeable regarding the specific industry but also able to inspire trust, hope, and motivation in employees. Lee Iacocca's performance at Chrysler provides a vivid example of what this can mean. Iacocca has been called a "new kind of American icon—the celebrity CEO."[6]

John Marchica, a CEO himself, is very critical of some charismatic CEOs, asserting that they are responsible for talking up company stock to their employees but then dumping it themselves; he also points to disgraced top executives trying to avoid responsibility and to the massive bankruptcies they manage to ride out. At the same time, Marchica also acknowledges CEOs who have been able to turn companies around, such as Lou Gerstner at IBM and Steve Jobs at Apple, both of whom had the political skill needed to be successful but also the industry knowledge and personal fortitude to see the job through.

Political skill does not necessarily mean that leaders will be effective—they can be self-interested, even unethical. However, it is difficult to be effective without political skill. Thus, when hiring CEOs (or any top managers), it is important to consider their record for ethical behavior, their success, and their industry knowledge. Political skill should also be a primary factor in the hiring decision, just not the only factor. It can make the candidate's integrity, motivation, and industry knowledge likely to work well for the new employer.

Hiring University Professors

The personnel selection process for university professors usually involves a two-phase process of assessing fit:

First phase. The hiring university evaluates technical fit by considering the quality of the universities where the candidates received their PhD degree, the research publication records they have established, evidence of their teaching effectiveness, and the prominence and reputation of their various doctoral advisors (who provide recommendations). This technical aspect of fit might best be characterized as person-job fit, because it assesses the extent to which candidates possess qualifications for doing the job of professor. The outcome of the person-job-fit stage is the formation of a short list, say, three or four applicants, who are invited for campus visits.

Second phase. In this phase, political skill tends to be what differentiates the short-listed candidates from one another. All the candidates invited for campus visits have passed the person-job-fit stage, and they all possess the skills to do the job. Therefore, the key consideration will be how well the candidates fit with the group of faculty members in the department doing the hiring. Job candidates usually visit a campus for two days, during which time they participate in one-to-one meetings with individual faculty in the department; meetings with the PhD students, usually as a group; a formal presentation of their research; and perhaps a meeting with the dean of the college and sometimes other administrators as well.

Besides these formal meetings, there are breakfasts, lunches, dinners, and possibly a reception where interviewing and assessments of fit continue. These interactions might involve efforts to further assess the candidates' competencies, but the focus of the hiring department tends to center on these questions:

- Would the candidates be congenial colleagues?

- Does the faculty like them?

- Would the candidates be good organizational citizens? (That is, would they be willing to assume their fair share of departmental and college committee work, and so forth?)

Certainly, how the candidates conduct themselves, how they present themselves to faculty and students, and how astute and adaptable they are all go into the perceptions of fit the faculty forms of them. Therefore, politically skilled applicants stand out from less politically skilled but equally qualified candidates. Because competence was largely addressed in the first phase of fit, the second phase of fit focuses more on things such as liking and similarity to the group. Politically skilled job applicants are astute enough to read situations, gauge their audience, and calibrate their responses and behaviors socially in ways that facilitate the perception of high person-group fit—and thus solidify a job offer.

Diversity in the Interviewing Context

The importance of fit is seen using a classic occupational choice framework. Indeed, students with higher levels of political skill were found more likely to prefer social or enterprising careers.[7] But being different from someone else often signals misfit and has traditionally been a disadvantage in the interviewing context. Recent research indicates that having political skill can help demographically dissimilar job candidates overcome negative biases of interviewers.

Let's say you are a Hispanic American job candidate interviewing with a Caucasian hiring manager. Without political skill, the hiring manager is likely to rate you less attractive as a candidate for the position. However, politically skilled applicants are able to manipulate perceptions of their fit with the organization. More specifically, researchers have found that when applicants had higher levels of political skill they were rated as having higher levels of fit with the political climate and then rated more favorably in terms of hiring decisions.[8]

This effect is challenged if the dissimilarity is related to potential speech deficiencies. In experimental research, hiring decisions and venture start-up investment decisions were negatively impacted when the interviewee or entrepreneur was not a native language speaker. Specifically, non-native speakers were more likely rated as having lower levels of political skill and, in turn, less likely to have positive hiring/investment decisions than were native speakers.[9]

The idea of fit can lead us beyond the boundaries of an organization and into the normative behaviors of a society as a whole. It is from this perspective that we can see how gender-normed behaviors may or may not perpetuate the glass ceiling in organizations. If companies reward leaders who are seen as assertive and aggressive (male-stereotyped behaviors), it is likely that women receive mixed signals about the types of behaviors needed to get ahead in the workplace. The problem is that a woman who acts assertively and aggressively is typically disliked and thus not rated well as a job candidate.

With this in mind, Shaughnessy and her colleagues proposed that females with higher levels of political skill would be able to be less damaged by their use of assertive political behavior than their less skilled female colleagues. Unfortunately, the research showed that while politically skilled women who engage in softer political behaviors (i.e., ingratiation) were more often liked by their supervisors and thus given higher ratings of promotability, their political skill could not buffer them from the "backlash" associated with them using assertive behaviors. This shows that what society perceives to be indicative of leadership behavior is often dictated by gendered social norms.[10]

These cumulative results point to the notion that political skill is vital to the success of minority job candidates. This is because politically skilled applicants are better able to interpret the appropriate influence style for the interview situation and then project that style to the interviewer.

Conclusion

Getting hired in organizations today increasingly is determined by how well you fit the job, work group, or organization, but this notion of fit tends to be poorly defined by the companies and organizations. Indeed, fit is usually some intuitive judgment or feeling by the person doing the hiring. Political skill arms you with the savvy to know just how to approach the hiring process, strategically select tactics of influence, execute them successfully, and win out in the competition for who fits the job best and gets hired. Once you're hired, you will be concerned about performing your job effectively and managing a successful career. Political skill plays a central role here as well, and that is the focus of the next chapter.

Research Highlight

Treadway, D. C., et al. (2014). "The Roles of Recruiter Political Skill and Performance Resource Leveraging in NCAA Football Recruitment Effectiveness." *Journal of Management*, 40(6), 1607–1626.

Much of this chapter has been devoted to political skill's role in helping candidates get jobs. However, research indicates that political skill can be helpful for those on the hiring side as well. In one of the more unique political skill studies, researchers tried to understand if CEO reputation or recruiter political skill had a greater impact on the quality of the employees the organization was able to obtain during the recruitment process. To test this concept, they collected data on the political skill of a sample of Division 1 college football recruiters whose job is to convince high school athletes to commit to playing for the recruiter's school. The study used head coach winning percentage as a proxy for CEO reputation and through the recruiting service Rivals.com the researchers were able to assess the quality of the athletes that each recruiter was able to sign to a letter of intent.[11]

The results of this study yielded some interesting insights for both well- and little- known organizations. Having a coach with a good performance reputation improved the quality of recruits when the recruiter was politically skilled. However, recruiters without political skill did nothing to improve the quality of the recruits beyond the reputation of the head coach. These results suggest that if companies hire politically skilled recruiters, they can enhance the quality of the workforce due to the recruiter's ability to connect with the applicant and create a compelling vision of working at the company.

6

MAXIMIZING YOUR JOB PERFORMANCE AND CAREER SUCCESS

In 1974, a young and aspiring writer was living with his wife and their two children in a small trailer in Hermon, Maine. By day, the relatively unsuccessful author worked as a teacher—a significant step up from his earlier jobs working in a local laundromat and dying fabrics at a mill. By night, the author toiled at his wife's typewriter. Aside from some middling success with relatively unsavory men's magazines, the writer's work was not getting much traction. Who could blame him then when, after a night of writing, he looked at his work, felt dejected, and threw away his freshly inked manuscript pages?

As the author tells the story, he returned from classes the next day to find his wife had rescued the pages from the trash. She'd noticed them while emptying his wastebasket and instead of discarding them, she pulled them out and read them. When he got home that day, she asked him to keep working on it because she wanted to know the rest of the story.

The story that this wife rescued from the dustbin of history was *Carrie*, which became Stephen King's first published novel and the work that launched a career that now counts 61 full-length novels published across four decades.

Of course, for every Stephen King there are thousands of

aspiring authors who will never write a novel like *Carrie*, let alone be fortunate enough to have a spouse like Tabitha King who saves said novel from being scrapped. The story of Stephen King, just like those he writes, sticks with us because it is one of remarkable success. We love to focus on these grand successes—those who find a Monet at a garage sale, win the lottery, or help found Facebook. These are the stories that we feel compelled to tell over and over again.

But a focus on these types of successes is problematic because it distracts us from the smaller successes, and failures, that led to the big break. We remember the big promotion, but managing the small project that helped us hone our leadership skills was a stepping-stone to this success. If a career is analogous to chess, tell of the last moves, just before we capture the king and triumphantly roar, "Checkmate!" And in doing so, we overlook the instances where we somewhat routinely took another pawn off the board. Even more likely, we discount the instances where we silently sacrificed one of our own pawns in hopes of moving one step closer to our ultimate goal.

So, while it's fun to tell tales of grand and improbable success, it is really the little victories and strategic sacrifices that eventually result in success for the vast majority of society. The question that needs to be asked is not how you can get lucky enough to have your wife rescue your best seller from the garbage, but rather, how can you learn to build momentum through smaller successes and determine when to make small sacrifices that turn into what one day appears to be grand success?

Performance at Work

It almost goes without saying that organizations hire people to do specific jobs, and these days they spend a lot of time and money trying to predict which job candidates will perform best. The forward-looking among them also look for people with the potential to move on to greater things within the organization. If you get a job, clearly someone thought you could do well at it and probably do well by it, too.

Some of these jobs call for advanced skills in various realms of knowledge and technology that nothing short of years of toil will produce. But even for these jobs, technical abilities are necessary but not sufficient conditions for career success. This is because for most of the jobs in our society, we are required to work with and through other people. And where interactions with others are required, political skill can facilitate success. The evidence is clear and compelling. Decades of research has demonstrated that political skill is an excellent predictor of performance at work.

Building a record of consistently high job performance is important for securing rewards such as raises and promotions. Job performance is not the sole basis of the immediate or long-term rewards that make up overall career success, though. Your career is the collection of related positions, jobs, and experiences that defines your work identity over an extended period of time. How you move or progress through those opportunities and jobs, how you get identified and labeled early on and thus become well positioned to take advantage of opportunities—or create them—is a function of your political skill. It is what puts you in a position to take advantage of opportunities presented to you, as well as to create opportunities of your own. Salary, promotions, and even subjective assessments of career success are all facilitated by political skill.

What Do We Mean by Job Performance?

The nature of job performance has fascinated managers and researchers alike for decades. Typically, definitions of performance refer to only the formal tasks and duties assigned to each position. However, scholars studying performance at work have begun to recognize that job performance also has interpersonal aspects. In this expanded perspective, performance is not only about the work you do but also how your actions affect the work of others.

Facets of Job Performance

More specifically, job performance can be divided into facets: task performance and contextual performance. Task performance reflects the traditional understanding of job performance, capturing the duties central to a particular role and which typically distinguish one position from another. Contextual performance, though, refers to behaviors inherent in all jobs that help maintain the social fabric of the organization. These include cooperating with others, helping out when not asked, being a good sport when others get promoted, etc. Interestingly, even though these different types of performance rely on different sets of behaviors, research has shown that measures of political skill can often support predictions of which employees will fare well on either. Not surprisingly, though, the interpersonal savvy with which politically skilled individuals operate makes them even more proficient at contextual performance.

Objective versus Subjective Job Performance

It is also important to note that job performance can be measured in different ways. For jobs like sales, you can measure performance pretty objectively by capturing the revenue generated by a salesperson. Even in a job with an objective performance metric, like sales, performing well likely entails effectively interacting with others or obtaining access to resources through others, which is why research has shown a link to objective performance metrics. However, there are many jobs that don't lend as well to such neat, objective outcomes. Instead, organizations usually measure job performance by asking an immediate supervisor to rate the employee's performance. There is much debate regarding the level of effort supervisors put into this task, but even when supervisors are dedicated to the task, performance ratings are inherently subjective.

Why does this distinction matter? Because supervisors tend

to capture lots of things besides how well an employee performed on the job: the quality of relationship between supervisor and employee, whether the supervisor likes the employee or not, what the supervisor thinks of the employee's potential for the future, and so forth. This is compounded by the fact that performance ratings are often only captured once per year, which means that the supervisor can be more dependent upon their impressions of the employee than on the employee's actual accomplishments. In fact, some research has shown that performance ratings might actually tell us more about the supervisor than the employee!

Political Skill and Performance Appraisal

Of course, when it comes to subjective assessments of performance—whether from a supervisor, peer, customer, or even a subordinate—examining how political skill affects job performance means we are often actually considering how political skill helps shape others' *perceptions* of job performance. This inevitably allows for some nonperformance factors to enter into the evaluation process, such that employees can influence how they are rated by managing the rater's impressions. This only increases as we consider performance at higher levels within the organizational hierarchy. Yes, there are profit and loss statements or other objective metrics for some managerial jobs, but for many of these positions it is difficult to define performance with any sort of precision. As a result, politically skilled employees typically get rated higher than their less politically skilled counterparts because they are adept at altering others' perceptions so they are perceived in a more favorable light.

Effort and Goal Setting

One way in which this management of impressions occurs is through creating a perception of great effort exhibited toward the job. As the saying goes, "Motion creates emotion." However, because managers don't observe employees 100 percent of the time, they often must rely on proxies for effort, including things like the performance-related goals employees set. Goals take effort to accomplish, and the general assumption is that the harder the goal, the more effort required to achieve it. As a result, employees can use goals to manage their supervisor's impressions. Indeed, research on performance appraisal has shown that regardless of how well employees subsequently performed, the ones who set the highest goals received the highest performance ratings from their immediate supervisors.[1] Thus, politically skilled employees can set goals in ways that make their supervisors view them as ambitious, energetic, hardworking, and committed. When it comes time for a performance evaluation, this impression will be the lens through which the employee is evaluated and how well the employee actually performs their tasks becomes much less relevant.

Perceived Similarity

Similarity breeds attraction, in everyday life and at work. The fact is that human beings generally feel most comfortable with those who seem like themselves. This similarity can be based on demographic characteristics like sex, race, and age, as well as on attitudes, beliefs, values, and positions taken on different issues. Supervisors are no more immune to this dynamic than anyone else, and it can easily creep into performance ratings. You probably can't do much to achieve physical resemblance to your boss—but with political skill, you can present yourself as similar to them in terms of attitudes, beliefs, and values, which can positively influence your performance evaluation.

Take values. Values have received much attention and consideration in corporate America in recent years. The most desirable employees share and live the core values proclaimed by their organizations. In many cases, the most important characteristic managers seek in their employees is appearing to think like the manager, make similar decisions, and support the manager on matters of importance. Reflecting such similarity can lead to higher performance ratings and in-group status.

However, managing perceptions of similarity in attitudes and beliefs is a delicate process that needs to be carefully considered and thoughtfully executed to be effective. An attempt to present yourself as holding similar views to the boss could come off as insincere, especially if you tried to match up on *all* issues. Instead, this botched attempt at influence would likely be seen for what it is—an effort to suck up to the boss. Political skill can mitigate these concerns. Because of social astuteness, you will be able to read the boss and the context, determine which issues and beliefs they value most, and convey an impression of agreement on enough of those to come across as like-minded. Similarly, politically skilled employees will realize that disagreeing with the boss on occasion can be helpful, so as not to be seen as a yes man, and social astuteness can enable employees to make sure such disagreements are on matters that are relatively unimportant to the boss.

Ingratiation and Self-Promotion

We mentioned above that employees who try too hard to seem similar to their supervisor might come across as trying to kiss up. This also can be the case in other interactions, where employees use ingratiation or flattery to make the boss like them more by telling them how great they (the boss) are. Alternatively, employees might try to make their supervisors like them more by using self-promotion—sharing how great they (the employee) are. Some research on performance appraisals found that the use of ingratiation and self-promotion by employees led to quite different performance ratings from their supervisors, because each tactic affected how much supervisors liked the employees.

Essentially, supervisors tended to like employees who used ingratiation, and, in turn, assigned those employees higher performance ratings. The use of self-promotion toward supervisors not only did not help employees, it actually hurt them. Supervisors tended to dislike employees who used self-promotion, and that dislike led them to give the employees lower performance ratings.[2] Interestingly, this tendency existed even when there were no real differences in the actual performance of the employees. As we learned in chapter 5, self-promotion seems to be beneficial in job interviews (interviewers' rate those who self-promote higher). However, self-promotion does not seem to be an effective strategy after one has the job.

However, this doesn't mean that ingratiation is always successful. Indeed, we argue that the ability to use ingratiation effectively is dependent upon the employee's political skill. That is, those with more political skill—specifically, apparent sincerity—are better able to engage in ingratiation (as well as other tactics) in a manner that makes the flattering remark seem more genuine. In fact, in one study, politically skilled subordinates who engaged in ingratiation toward supervisors were less likely to be labeled by their supervisors as attempting such flattery.[3] Additionally, this led to an increased likelihood that the supervisors would rate the subordinates as being more helpful to colleagues.

Employing the Right Strategy at the Right Time

Beyond knowing how to deliver an influence tactic effectively, success also depends on knowing when to execute specific tactics. It doesn't matter how well you execute an influence tactic if it's the wrong thing to do at that time. Every context has an expected pattern of behavior, and politically skilled individuals, because of their social astuteness, can read situations to determine when a tactic is appropriate. Additionally, their interpersonal influence ability gives them the behavioral flexibility to conform their actions to the demands of the situation.

For example, although ingratiation has been shown to have a positive effect and self-promotion a negative effect on performance appraisals, this is not the case for job interviews. In fact, the opposite tends to be true. In the job interview, skillful self-promotion improves applicants' prospects, whereas ingratiation actually hurts them. Why? The situations are different and call for distinct influence strategies.

The implicit rules of engagement in the employment interview, where interviewers typically have never met the job applicants and know little about them, say that self-promotion is appropriate and approved, in part so the interviewer can learn more about the candidate's qualifications. However, in this context, ingratiation by applicants is seen as timidity and weakness of character. The performance appraisal process appears to have different implicit rules. The participants share a history and interact on an ongoing basis in a work relationship, and the supervisor has much more information about the employee. Thus, job applicants are expected to toot their own horns; employees are not—supervisors will read it as arrogance or conceit. Politically skilled employees realize this. They not only identify the most appropriate pattern of behavior to demonstrate but execute it in ways that appear genuine and sincere, which typically yields positive outcomes.

Political Skill and Career Success

Career success is usually indicated by the promotions that individuals receive and the salary levels they achieve over the course of a career. Because pay is typically linked to job level, the pay most people receive depends on their promotion, transfer, or reassignment to jobs higher up the company ladder. Of course, the nature of promotion is changing as companies downsize, restructure, and generally become flatter, with fewer layers in the corporate hierarchy. Flatter organizations provide fewer openings for traditional promotion. Promotions will continue to be made, but other types of recognition will grow in importance: perhaps reassignment to interesting, challenging, and prestigious roles or team projects. Although these may not constitute actual promotions, they can still be viewed as rewards.

In the internal contests for promotions, as well as for prestigious roles and positions, employees will come out much better if they have political skill. This is because politically skilled individuals will be able to make themselves seem more attractive than others, allowing them to take advantage of these opportunities. Much as good rebounders in basketball seem to know just where to go to capitalize on the angle the ball takes off the rim or backboard, politically skilled individuals can make sure they are positioned to capitalize on opportunities as they appear.

Politically skilled individuals accomplish this in several ways. In some instances, the network-building facet of political skill also contributes by enabling employees to become well-positioned in social networks, which can facilitate career success. For example, the results of one study found that network connections and social capital accumulation operated to enhance career success and found that the alliances, coalitions, and contacts people build up as parts of their network lead to greater access to information, resources, and sponsorship (or mentoring).[4] Additionally, because politically skilled individuals can effectively read the organizational context, they will at times be able to see when the time is right to create opportunities for themselves (e.g., proposing a new position that they could and should fill) when they previously have not existed.

Factors Determining Career Success

Political skill plays a role in all the main indicators of career success. Whether we consider promotions, pay, or job survival, the politically skillful come out ahead. Why? Because politics almost always are a factor in these decisions.

Promotions

To be promoted, you need a record of effective performance in the organization, but such a record is not sufficient. In addition, you need political skill. The two together make an unbeatable combination, but separately each can lead to an early career ceiling. You can perform well and fail if you are not politically skilled. You can have excellent political skill and fail if you make sufficiently disastrous or frequent technical errors. However, even if your performance is average, you can be considered an insider with potential to advance if you are seen as politically skilled.

Why? Because promotions are among the most political decisions made in organizations. Part of the difficulty with promotion systems is that the requirements or criteria for promotion may not be clearly specified. Managers generally wind up looking for people who fit best or show the most potential, or both; but fit and potential probably mean something different to each manager making promotion decisions. Most of the time, the definitions actually in use involve remarkable similarity to the characteristics and qualities of the manager in question. This process certainly seems to have been the dominant promotion model in organizations for quite some time.

It has been long recognized that one of the real keys to being promoted is to make sure you get noticed. Economics provides the useful concept of *market signaling theory*,[5] which describes the use of individual activities or attributes to convey information and alter the beliefs of others in a given market. Although the original theory tended to focus on characteristics such as education and experience, it could be expanded to focus on things such as ability (real or perceived), reputation (see chapter 7), and fit. Political skill is what allows you to transmit such information in subtle ways (but, as discussed earlier, not by trumpeting your achievements) to make sure that you are noticed and that your talents attract the attention of important top managers and decision makers.

Tournament theory is another useful way of considering promotions. A tournament is a way of identifying the most qualified candidate for a position by pitting individuals against one another in increasingly selective competitions. At each stage along the way, decisions are made regarding winners and losers. Winners are seen as stars, and they progress to the next stage, whereas losers are stigmatized and diverted to a losers' bracket. Winners gain higher positions, more attention from managers, additional training and development, access to privileged information, and—perhaps most important—an expectation that they will continue to be winners. Meanwhile, losers suffer lower status and reduced rewards and an expectation of being less likely to do well in the future.

Tournament theory seems to imply that winners of competitions are declared on some sort of objective basis, as if there were clearly specified criteria for winning. In fact, this does not appear to be the case. Promotion criteria are not clearly stated (or not stated at all), and decisions are highly subjective and thus quite susceptible to influence and manipulation. Furthermore, although sports tournaments devote much attention to the bracketing process and the levels and stages of play, work organizations have only one really critical round: the first one. This is when impressions of candidates are formed that carry into the future and influence subsequent opportunities. The attention and resources allocated to initial winners can actually result in their becoming the best candidates further up the hierarchy.

The general and ill-defined characteristics of fit and potential that so often drive promotion decisions can easily work to the advantage of politically skilled employees. However, even when a firm lays out more specific criteria or desired characteristics for promotion, the system still appears to work to the advantage of individuals with political skill. A survey of some Fortune 500 firms regarding the characteristics desired in those considered for advancement included the following: interpersonal skills, self-awareness, trustworthiness, character, empathy, street smarts, personal credibility, charisma, flexibility, influencing others, and integrity. Many of these are inherent to political skill, and the others are things that politically skilled employees are typically able to display effectively.

As with performance ratings, promotion decisions tend to turn on perceived similarity with characteristics of the decision makers. Likewise, the skillful use of ingratiation tends to help career success. For example, one study of life at General Motors pointed out that managers' chance of promotion was determined by how skillfully they flattered their boss.[6] It takes effective political skill to employ these tactics appropriately, but this is even more the case with the use of assertiveness—particularly in the context of promotion decisions, where influence is being directed upward. Any misstep here will likely be perceived as inappropriately controlling for someone in a subordinate position, which can lead to lower evaluations of promotability.

Again, although most people like to believe that ability drives the promotion process, in practice it seems to be crowded out by factors favoring those high in political skill. This is especially true when candidates are perceived to have adequate ability. Instead, things like getting along well with others and being perceived as a team player become more important. Politically skilled employees thrive in these situations because they can pick up signals from their bosses and other influential players in the work environment that indicate the right things to do and say at the right time to show themselves to best advantage.

This is even more true as you move to higher levels in the corporate hierarchy where variability on intelligence, past work experience, and performance narrows considerably. Because everyone looks about the same on these qualities, they are not going to be the basis for promotion decisions. Style differentiates winners from losers at the upper levels, and style is what we refer to as political skill. Furthermore, it is how you manage the impressions that your style is similar to, and fits with, the style of the managers making the promotion decisions that will lead to success.

Overall, we believe political skill positions people to be competitive and successful in the promotion process. Political skill can give you visibility, distinguish you favorably from others, and get you promoted. Because of massive organizational change, restructuring, and design, promotion systems are going to be ever more constrained, and political skill correspondingly ever more essential as you make your way to the top.

Pay

Decisions about employee compensation also tend to be mired in politics, and reasons other than merit and performance often influence their outcomes. Much like the research on promotion outcomes, studies have shown that effective use of ingratiation helps salary progression.[7] Also, similar to other contentions we have made here, behavioral flexibility with influence tactics is beneficial, as what researchers called a "tactician" approach to influence (the strategic selection of only the most appropriate influence tactics) has been found to result in higher salaries than those obtained by employees who used the contrasting "shotgun" approach (an indiscriminate use of many influence tactics).[8] Thus, because of its facilitation of the effective selection and execution of influence tactics, political skill is also beneficial for salary outcomes.

Also, political connections, part of the networking facet of political skill, are associated with higher pay raises, but only when employees emphasized the dependency of their manager or superior on them.[9] This dependency effect is an interesting one, and is a strategy that politically skilled people often employ to maximize both salary and promotion possibilities. Politically skilled people work hard at positioning themselves in a number of ways, but one way is to become indispensable to the boss, so the boss's effectiveness depends on their continuing service. If a boss who is talented and obviously going places learns to depend on you, you will go along for the ride as the boss rises in the organization, receiving attractive promotions and salary increases along the way.

A final issue concerning political skill and pay concerns the often-controversial topic of CEO compensation. Boards of directors are accountable for conducting performance evaluations of CEOs and for negotiating increases in compensation (which may include components such as base salary, bonus, stock, and perks). In theory, boards are independent entities that represent the shareholders, charged with viewing CEO behavior objectively and rendering unbiased evaluations of performance and determinations of compensation. But that has not been the case in many organizations over the years. Instead, a close and complex relationship often develops between the CEO and board members, a relationship that is strategically managed by politically skilled CEOs. Despite formal procedures for selecting new members to serve on boards and for other board procedures, the CEO often proposes new members and orchestrates support from existing board members.

Remember that board members are paid stipends to serve, receive expenses and meeting fees, and in some companies also receive generous perks. In light of this special treatment, compliments of the CEO, it is quite difficult for board members to be truly objective in the performance evaluations and salary determinations of their benefactor. It is a power and patronage relationship, carefully and thoughtfully orchestrated by skilled CEOs, and it leads to higher pay. The power involved is hardly ever blatant, direct, and overbearing; boards have their limits. Instead, CEOs successful at this process employ great political skill, applying their social capital, reputation, and the positioning that these assets produce to ensure a favorable outcome for themselves.

Job Survival

We have seen a number of top executives and politicians ruin their careers over bad decisions. But few have managed to survive as well as Bill Clinton did in the wake of the Monica Lewinsky scandal that almost dislodged him from the Oval Office.

Clinton, with his seemingly sincere plea for forgiveness, his heartfelt apology to his family, friends, staff, cabinet, and the Lewinsky family, as well as his willingness to take responsibility (albeit a long time after the fact) were all done in a very politically skilled way. Apologizing and asking forgiveness works only if you do it right, and Clinton knows how to do it right. Regardless of whether he actually felt these emotions—and who is to say he did not feel them?—he was convincing to many. Again, it is not only what you do but how you do it that leads to success and survival!

Further, Clinton knows how to network (a dimension of political skill) and with whom. As the press began to ask questions about impeachment and resignation, Clinton went out and got support from high-profile religious and work leaders, such as the Reverend Bernice King (Martin Luther King Jr.'s daughter) and Nelson Mandela. King and Mandela praised his work and asked Congress and the American people for tolerance and forgiveness.

In *My Life* (2004), Clinton wrote:

> As good as Mandela was, the Reverend Bernice King stole the show. She said that even great leaders sometimes commit grievous sins; that King David had done something far worse than I had in arranging the death in battle of Bathsheba's husband, who was David's loyal soldier, so that David could marry her; and that David had to atone for his sin and was punished for it. No one could tell where Bernice was going until she got to the closing: "Yes, David committed a terrible sin and God punished him. But David remained king."

Clearly, Clinton's networking and the political skill of his supporters were crucial to his continued presidency. These same principles, social astuteness, interpersonal influence, networking ability, and apparent sincerity, come into play for people trying to survive in any organization.

Sometimes organizations reach a point where they believe they must terminate employees for a variety of reasons, which typically include poor job performance, deteriorating financial performance of the firm that dictates downsizing, or simply what are known as irreconcilable differences with the boss. Some employees encounter these situations and lose their jobs, others keep them. We believe that political skill often makes the difference—survivors are those who persuade their employer that performance deficiencies can be made up, that others are less valuable and thus better to let go in a general downsizing, or that the irreconcilable can be reconciled after all.

Despite universities' efforts to prepare graduates for the work world, it looks as though they could be doing a better job of instilling the political realities of work environments. The incidence of job failure for managers and executives taking new positions is much higher than you might expect—about 40 percent fail and are terminated within the first 18 months. The most cited reasons for such job failure include "being unclear about what bosses want, inability to make tough decisions, being unable to build partnerships with subordinates and peers, and lack of political savvy."[10] Additionally, the Chicago outplacement firm of Challenger, Gray & Christmas found that "getting along with the boss is more important than job performance in surviving a corporate cutback."[11]

This all seems to highlight the realization that job survival may depend more on your political skill than just about anything else. In downsizing, companies sometimes apply a decision rule to dictate that a certain department or unit will be cut or dropped entirely. However, in many cases there is no decision rule, and then it can be hard to tell what determines who stays and who goes—but the decisions probably involve politics and judgments of fit. In unclear situations, top management may try to downsize in a way that preserves some sense of harmony, perhaps looking for a particular fit in those who will remain.

Politically skilled employees can manage that fitting-in process by demonstrating the extensiveness of their connections and networks with influential others and units, emphasizing key competencies that make them indispensable to the boss and organization, and drawing on the effective and friendly working relationship they have carefully cultivated with the boss.

Conclusion

Performance ratings and career success for most jobs in organizations today are determined increasingly by working smarter, not just harder, and demonstrating the ability to meet your goals working with and through others. For most jobs, no one is counting widgets to measure performance; instead, your boss is rating your performance based on your capacity to be influential and effective at what you do. This makes political skill one of the most important competencies you can possess if you wish to maximize not just your day-to-day job performance but also your long-term career success. Very much involved in the process of building a record of effective job performance and establishing a successful career is the concept of reputation, or what you are and become known for in the eyes of others. Chapter 7 develops the point that political skill is also a key ingredient in the formation and maintenance of your reputation at work.

Research Highlight

Harris, K. J., et al. (2007). "The Impact of Political Skill on Impression Management Effectiveness." *Journal of Applied Psychology*, 92(1), 278.

As much as we might want to believe that doing good work alone will translate to career success, we know that how we are perceived by others, especially our bosses, is often what matters most. After all, they typically rate our job performance, which determines our raises, bonuses, and promotions. Given this, managing the boss's impression of us is critical to career success, and, as we've argued above, political skill enables effective impression management.

Harris and colleagues conducted a study designed to investigate these effects. They asked employees to rate how frequently they used five different impression management tactics—self-promotion (highlighting one's accomplishments), ingratiation (flattery), intimidation (acting forcefully), supplication (highlighting short-comings to avoid certain tasks), and exemplification (presenting oneself as a role model). Then, they asked their supervisors to rate the employees' job performance across several categories.

As expected, the results indicated that employees' political skill influenced the effectiveness of employees' use of impression management tactics. The relationships between job performance ratings and ingratiation, intimidation, supplication, and exempli-fication were positive for those high in political skill. Perhaps more importantly, the relationships between job performance ratings and self-promotion, ingratiation, supplication, and exemplifica-tion were *negative* for those low in political skill.

Clearly, being politically skilled can help you effectively man-age your boss's impression of you, generating beneficial career outcomes. You can certainly attempt impression management without political skill, but you risk actually receiving worse per-formance ratings.

7

ENHANCING YOUR REPUTATION

Jean Valjean
#24601
Monsieur le maire

Each of these monikers refers to the same character from the famous musical *Les Misérables*, based on the book of the same name by Victor Hugo. Jean Valjean was imprisoned for stealing a loaf of bread, and his sentence was subsequently extended to 19 years after he attempted to escape. In prison, his name was replaced with his inmate number: 24601. Valjean's antagonist throughout the play, an officer of the law named Javert, mostly refuses to use Valjean's name, instead referring to him by his number. After his release, his name sullied by his time in prison, Valjean sheds his former self and creates a new identity where he becomes a successful businessman and even the *Monsieur le maire* (mayor) of a small town.

When Javert, searching for his former inmate who skipped parole, arrives in Valjean's town, he does not recognize his quarry. What is interesting is that there appears to have been no cosmetic subterfuge on the part of Valjean. Yet even in conversation, Javert does not recognize him. Javert is deferential to Valjean, as he is the town's mayor, and he even apologizes to Valjean after making an error in judgment. Yet when Valjean's mask is finally removed and his true identity revealed, Javert immediately reverts to his initial impressions of Valjean as a thief and outlaw.

The story provides a valuable lesson about the power of reputation. Valjean recognized that being a paroled convict would greatly inhibit his chances of a fruitful future because of his sullied reputation. However, he also recognized he could find his way into wealth and power if his reputation were different. Further, his position as a successful business owner and the mayor of a town created a reputation of being an upstanding citizen and pillar of the community that overpowered Javert's ability to recognize Valjean as Prisoner 24601. The man was the same, but he was viewed quite differently because of the nature of his reputation. The goal of this chapter is to understand how to better develop, maintain, and defend your reputation.

What Is Reputation?

Don't let the *Les Mis* example make you think reputation is simply about appearance. Yes, the manner in which we physically present ourselves to others can play a role in the formation of reputation, but it is a much more complex concept. It is an identity that people ascribe to you based on a combination of perceived characteristics, accomplishments, demonstrated behaviors, and images presented to others over a period of time.

Interestingly, the word itself can be both favorable and unfavorable in nature, as it is just as possible to develop a bad reputation as it is a good one. The dictionary defines reputation in three ways: 1. overall quality or character as seen or judged by people in general; 2. recognition by other people of some characteristic or ability; 3. a place in public esteem or regard.[1] Two of these three definitions are neutral in nature. Generally, reputation itself is a neutral term and it is only the *for* that determines whether a reputation is positive or negative. For example, very few people want to be described as "having a reputation." Yet most of us would be quite satisfied with "having a reputation *for*" something positive like always meeting deadlines or being a helpful colleague. Thus, reputation is a flexible term; it can take on multiple meanings.

Despite its flexibility, there are some core aspects that make up reputation. These individual qualities and known accomplishments combine to form reputation, merging in complex ways and weighted according to the context where the reputation applies. Further complicating things is the reality that contexts are variable and dynamic. So no one can imitate a reputation by duplicating the characteristics and actions of another person. Still, this doesn't stop people from trying to mimic the reputations of others to capture similar benefits.

Take Elizabeth Holmes, the now-disgraced founder of Theranos, as an example. Like Apple founder Steve Jobs, Holmes left college without graduating and started a technology company in the Bay Area. Then, as she and her firm began gaining fame, she made a wardrobe change, switching to Jobs's famous black turtleneck and jeans uniform on a daily basis. Although many leaders have begun to adopt a similar low-maintenance signature look, Holmes's selection was intentional. According to Ana Arriola, the former chief design architect at Theranos, Holmes was obsessed with copying Jobs's style, in part to signal that she had no time to think about clothing selections. In essence, she was trying to copy Jobs to cultivate a reputation as a tech icon with a devotion to Theranos that matched the intensity with which Jobs led Apple.

Holmes has since been exposed as a fraud. She has also ditched her turtlenecks and was recently spotted with a substantially changed hairstyle, perhaps in an effort (like Valjean), to distance herself from her crimes. However, we repeat that the aspects of individuals that make up their reputation are much more than just appearance. These additional aspects can be classified as forms of capital, both human and social. In many respects, it is these elements that form the foundation of one's personal reputation.

Human Capital

Human capital refers to individual attributes like personality, knowledge, and skills, as well as habits and other characteristics that contribute to one's ability (or perceived ability) to add value to an organization. As such, the knowledge, skills, and credentials gained by way of education and experience contribute to our human capital. For example, earning a college degree, obtaining specialized credentials (e.g., Six Sigma, CPA), and climbing the ladder in an organization all contribute to perceptions regarding our ability to add value. Further, *where* we obtained our degree and *who* we worked for provide additional credibility and status that alter the way people view us. Think about when you see someone's résumé. Sure, a master's degree and experience as a project manager might make a candidate look good, but how much better is that candidate perceived if the degree is from an Ivy League school and the projects that they managed were for a top consulting firm? Absent any actual information about performance, these aspects serve as proxies for ability, and they shape reputations in the workplace.

Similarly, individual aspects ranging from how we handle ourselves under pressure to our professional bearing and manners can make an individual more marketable and mobile. Interestingly, personality, sex/gender, and race/ethnicity also have strong implications for reputation, as these characteristics are often used as proxies for ability. This is why outgoing and confident individuals like extroverts and narcissists often end up in management roles. Their characteristics fit prototypes we have about leaders, so we assume they have the ability to lead well. However, this is often not the case and without anything more of substance these leaders will derail. Unfortunately, the use of race and sex as proxies often is born from bias and stereotypes, which can lead to discrimination. Still, these characteristics are very salient, and it is important to acknowledge how they interact with other aspects to affect our reputation.

Social Capital

Within organizations, the value of a reputation is strongly influenced by relationships and the influence wielded through those relationships. These alliances, coalitions, and even friendship networks make up our social capital. If social influence is the process by which you directly or indirectly influence others, then social capital represents a latent form of social influence based on the availability of social contact and network resources. And social capital, through network development, access to information, resources, and mentoring, has been positively related to career success.[2]

Social capital enhances reputation by conveying information concerning credibility to others. Let's say you are a high-performer. Sure, your boss will probably notice, and you might even enjoy a few good raises and bonuses. However, with a well-developed network, word will start to spread, enhancing your reputation throughout the organization, perhaps even the industry. Even better, when you want or need something, your network can deliver. Valuable resources are scarce, but they are easier to obtain when you have social capital to leverage.

The above is an example of leveraging your reputation *within* an organization. But a well-developed reputation throughout a social network can also give you significant leverage *with* an organization. This is due to the effect social capital has on voluntary turnover. When a member of an organization with strong and numerous ties to others leaves, others tend to follow. This outflow of talent is damaging to the organization. So, by positioning yourself as a central player in the social network, you become even more valuable to the organization than just your talent. You will be recognized as someone the organization needs to keep so that they can avoid suffering a great drain of human capital. As a result, your reputation within the organization can enhance your reputation with the organization.

The Importance of Reputation

As we've hinted at in the section above, reputations are important and valuable commodities because they give you access to greater resources and provide you with leverage. Perhaps more important, it appears that the combination of elements can be greater than the simple sum of the individual parts, particularly with positive reputations. Indeed, we would argue further that a well-developed reputation can be very difficult (if not impossible) to imitate or copy. As a result, reputation is an intangible source of immense value. Research consistently notes that strong, positive reputations help people get things done and perform well, as well as increase others' perceptions of their character or integrity. Those individuals who are able to build and then leverage that reputation will enjoy a sustained competitive advantage.

Even better, though, is the fact that reputations seem to have a flywheel effect. That is, because your reputation gets you access to more resources and information, it will undoubtedly yield further successes, which will only serve to enhance your reputation. Further, the more you are viewed as being well-connected, the more you will become regarded as having greater power and influence, which further enhances your reputation. It can keep feeding itself and building and building and building.

Finally, quickly building a reputation is especially valuable. Careers have been likened to tournaments, where those who experience early advancement are likely to find greater success over subsequent years. In this vein, reputation serves as a signal to decision makers, whereby fast-track employees are identified and subsequently promoted based on the reputations they built early on. Similar to the flywheel effect described earlier, once you have a reputation as a high-performer, much of your career will be perceived through that lens.

The importance of perceptions to reputation makes it essential to be aware of and carefully orchestrate work behavior and actions so they transmit the kind of image you want. Reputation is not simply about impression management, of course. You still have to come through and perform effectively. However, individuals with good reputations enjoy greater success over the long haul, as being known as influential and for getting things done allows for building social capital, which makes continued effective performance much easier to accomplish in the future. The question then, is how to effectively manage your reputation.

Managing Your Reputation

Reputation is not a monolith. Yes, it is often described as a collective perception, but it can exist in separate and distinct forms in the minds of others, as directly observed or as reported from secondary sources. Thus, reputation is subjective and can be considered as defined in the eye of the beholder as they interpret and ascribe meaning to observed behaviors and accomplishments, as well as the uncontrollable aspects we've discussed above (i.e., sex, race and ethnicity, age, etc.) that serve as signals or proxies for reputation. Although this subjective aspect of reputation might seem frustrating, it also makes it possible for individuals to actively manage the way they are perceived by others. That is, you can target individuals and groups and, like Valjean, tailor what they see in an effort to present yourself in a more desirable light.

Accepting that a reputation is probably best built upon actual behavior and real accomplishments, one of the best tools available for actively managing your reputation is political skill. Consider that political skill facilitates the adjustment of behavior and effective self-presentation in social situations. This is exactly the skill set needed to develop, maintain, and, when necessary, defend your reputation.

It's likely that you have amassed enough human capital that it is impossible to convey it all to others, or at least in an efficient manner. Consider how we often only discuss the most recent degree we obtained; very rarely do we find ourselves waxing poetic about our high school diplomas. Similarly, there are so many small components of our human capital (e.g., Red Cross CPR certification, half-marathon finisher) that there simply is not enough time or space to express them. In many cases, these aspects of human capital might be irrelevant, such as during career changes. For example, you may have been an incredible software coder at your previous tech job, but as you try to move into a managerial role, those skills likely won't be the best foundation on which to build the reputation you'll need to succeed in your new job.

Given this, it is incumbent upon you to determine what aspects of your human capital need to be highlighted and shared with others, and in which situations. Further, it is up to you to tailor the presentation of these aspects. Often, you will need to make sense of your human capital for others if you are to build the reputation you desire. For example, being known as a person actively involved in community service, a philanthropist, and a caring parent is likely to get you labeled as a good person, and that's not a "bad" reputation to have. On the contrary, many of us would want to be known for these things. However, these aspects of your human capital are of limited value to your career if you don't know how or when to highlight them at work. In isolation, these things seem irrelevant and if presented the wrong way might even get you labeled as a braggart. However, with some care in crafting, these aspects of your human capital can convey that you are an empathetic and caring individual, just the type of person that people want to work for, which makes you well suited to take on a leadership role.

This idea of properly contextualizing things isn't particularly novel. However, in the daily grind of a career, it can be easy to fall into traps that limit our success. Certainly, "just doing good work" is limiting given the political nature of organizations. This can lead people to think they "just need to know the right people" in order to get ahead. However, this too can fall short of being an effective strategy. Knowing the right people doesn't amount to much if they don't know the right things about you. You need to craft a reputation that conveys who you are and what your value is, especially as it relates to the specific context.

Political skill can make this a lot easier. As discussed in chapter 2, political skill allows you to recognize patterns in your environment. This means you can decipher social settings and identify what is valued. Once you know what is valued, you know what aspects of your human capital to highlight and what behaviors to spend time on. For example, research has shown that the social astuteness dimension of political skill enables employees to recognize key elements of the organizational climate.[3] Armed with information like this, you can then tailor your behavior to match the situation, enhancing your reputation as someone who fits the organization. Similarly, being able to understand the social intricacies at work can enable you to know what aspects of your human capital should be highlighted to give you the leg up over your competition.

In essence, political skill allows you to determine what the environment dictates for success so that you can select the human capital that supports a reputation best suited for that context. For example, let's say you are a military veteran who has entered the civilian workforce and you want to make the jump to the leadership ranks in your organization. First, it would be helpful to understand that guiding others under pressure and in unpredictable environments is valued. Because, if this is the case, you will want to highlight things that signal to others you have a reputation for displaying that skill. In this case, you will want to reconsider hanging your project management certificate on the wall, favoring instead a commendation from your time in the service. Or better yet, a picture of you from an overseas military deployment, perhaps one of you with your troops just after returning from an engagement with the enemy.

Sharing Your Reputation

The above is an example of building your reputation, but you also need to share it. As sociologist Erving Goffman (1959) pointed out more than half a century ago, everyday life can be regarded as a series of individual theatrical performances whereby people seek to control others through a projected image.[4] It is especially useful to think of life in organizations as made up of such performances, with members all presenting themselves in ways designed to guide and control perceptions that others form of them. Once you have selected the most salient parts of your human capital to emphasize, it is then time to begin communicating your reputation to others (and, eventually, having others communicate it for you).

However, simply telling people about your achievements is not quite the most effective method of sharing your reputation with others. This approach could come off as brazen or even bragging, something that might develop into a reputation you rather would not want attributed to you! Instead, it is best to *signal* your reputation to others. Signaling theory, as outlined by A. Michael Spence (1974), expands on the notion of theatrical performance and provides a useful perspective from which to consider reputations. More specifically, signaling theory suggests that individuals coexist in markets of exchange, and, within these markets, individuals signal others in the market in an attempt to convey information or alter their beliefs.[5] Spence classed any characteristic of an individual that could be observed by others and altered by the individual as a potential signal. In his view, a potential signal became an actual signal if it did exercise an influence on others. From this perspective, reputation can be regarded as an actual signal because it does influence others.

This is why political skill is so critical to the development of a positive reputation. Successful signaling generally is not accomplished through brute force but rather through social and situational savvy. The politically skilled communicate their reputation in the most effective way to influence others. Beyond facilitating knowledge of what to present, political skill enables you to present it in an effective manner. Take the example above about the veteran now in the civilian workforce. Shared at the wrong time or in the wrong way, tales of success in military combat might come off as just another war story designed to display machismo. Political skill enables these to be presented in a way that positively adds to the reputation you are trying to build.

Political skill does similar things for displayed behaviors. Consider this. In the first of a series of studies, researchers found that the social astuteness dimension of political skill enabled employees to recognize when an organization valued personal initiative. Not surprisingly, this led to increased displays of personal initiative by these employees. However, in a second study, these researchers found that instances of personal initiative didn't always lead to higher job performance ratings. Instead, these ratings were contingent on levels of the interpersonal influence dimension. With higher levels of interpersonal influence, employees' increased displays of personal initiative were related to higher job performance ratings from supervisors. Conversely, with lower levels of interpersonal influence, employees' increased displays of personal initiative were related to *lower* job performance ratings.[6]

This critical point bears repeating. It is important to be able to recognize what is valued so you can send the desired signals. However, it is even more important to know how to display these signals in a manner that actually results in the reputation you want. In the studies described above, employees were displaying very similar behaviors. However, those with political skill developed reputations as high-performing, proactive "go-getters," where those lacking in political skill likely developed reputations as pushy and problem-generating employees. Thus, signals are amenable to alteration and should be considered as intentional efforts to shape and influence others.

Putting It All Together

In sum, to build a reputation, you need to do more than just amass human capital in the form of credentials and experience. You need political skill to be able to recognize what your prevailing context, be it the organization or the industry, values so you can thoughtfully select the pieces of human capital on which you will build your reputation. Then you need to use your political skill to signal your reputation in a convincing and appropriate manner. This will make it more likely that people's perceptions of you and your actions are consistent with the reputation you want to create.

Reputation Maintenance

Creating a desired and beneficial relationship is great, but it is not enough to ensure long-term success. Reputations are dynamic, not static, and thus require consistent maintenance. This means that what others see you do must remain consistent with what they expect given your reputation. Any inconsistency, positive or negative, will result in adjustments to your reputation, which in turn redefine their perceptions of you. Unlike developing a reputation, however, maintaining a reputation mainly involves simply being aware of the reputation and acting in accordance with the behaviors prescribed in it.

We don't mean to imply that all maintenance behaviors are merely behaviors that conform to your reputation. Indeed, contexts are constantly changing, thus requiring a continuous calibration of the reputation you project. Additionally, reputations are typically nested within a particular context, and though they can transfer to a new environment, more aggressive maintenance may be needed to reaffirm the reputation. In fact, further development might be required to establish the best reputation in the new context. For example, if you were promoted from a lower level in the organization based on your reputation within that level, people would take you on faith for a while. If you failed to perceive the new context accurately and live up to the new expectations, however, you would probably soon see your reputation decline. Again, political skill can enable you to recognize the subtle shifts in the social landscape, providing you with valuable information about how to tailor your human capital and behaviors and leverage your social capital to facilitate success in your new context.

Reputation Defense

Reputation, no matter how arduously constructed and painstakingly maintained, is fragile. It can take a lifetime to build and a moment to destroy—consider the rapid fall from the national spotlight suffered by people like Bernie Madoff, Elizabeth Holmes, and Adam Neumann. Although these are extreme examples, sending mixed or detrimental signals can be devastating to your reputation, diminishing your credibility. As a result, people could lose confidence in your subsequent signals, and it can be difficult to rebuild the reputation you need for success. Thus, it often is necessary and worthwhile to defend your reputation.

We need look no further than our legal system to see defense of reputations in action. As David Logan (2001) points out, from 1980 to 2000, courts awarded more than $620 million to plaintiffs suing the media for damage to personal reputations.[7] However, Logan also notes that this figure is misleading and does not account for individuals unwilling to endure proceedings that put their reputation under close scrutiny. This implies that although some people will defend their reputations vigorously, others concede that the defense is more costly than developing a new reputation.

It has also been suggested that the best defense of a reputation is an active offense, using aggressive maintenance behaviors and keeping a close eye on changes in context to help prevent a crisis.[8] Again, being politically skilled helps in this regard, as social astuteness enables you to make sense of what you see unfolding around you. Perhaps you can thwart an attack before it manifests or avoid a misstep altogether by recognizing the implications of the shifting context and changing course before it is too late.

Still, sometimes hits are unavoidable. In these instances, as helpful as networks are in building a reputation, they can be brutally as effective tearing one down. In fact, networks serve as enforcers in this regard. Behave badly toward an influential member of a network and you can be assured their sentiment toward you will be reported to the rest, which puts a premium on maintaining the expected level of benevolent support. Here again, political skill is valuable. You need the skill to develop a broad and influential network that will give you the benefit of the doubt. In this way, a network can protect your reputation by minimizing the effects of the negative hits, should you make a misstep, by rallying to your defense.

Of course, you can't simply have others carry your water for you. Active and personal defense of your reputation is often necessary following an unfortunate event or even a deliberate attempt by someone else to damage your reputation, because no matter how often people decry the behavior, damaging a competitor's reputation by way of criticism, misinformation, distorting, or rumor *works*. Some subscribe to the maxim "When something goes wrong, the first thing you fix is the blame." Such individuals try to defend their reputations by structuring and manipulating perceptions formed by others concerning the causes of their good and poor performance. The idea is to engage in active efforts to influence the meaning attributed to the incident—and to reduce their perceived responsibility for whatever went wrong. As you can imagine, pulling off this strategy requires political skill so that the message can be delivered without backfiring.

Finally, sometimes the best option for limiting damage to your reputation is to step up and apologize for what happened, rectify any harm you have caused, and promise to change your ways. But even this is not as simple as it sounds. Apologies can do more harm than good if not well executed. How many times have we had someone say, "I'm sorry you feel that way," or something equally insincere? Similarly, public figures at the center of a crisis often step forward with an apology written by someone else. In these instances, it is often obvious that their words do not come from a place of genuine contrition. In both of these examples, the apology could have been more effective if delivered with political skill, as apparent sincerity enables individuals to present themselves in a genuine manner, such that their words and actions have the desired impact.

Regardless of the incident, it is important to work to limit its negative impact to your reputation. Clearly, there are many different avenues by which to pursue this end, including excuses, apologies, justifications, or attempts to reshape perceptions of the incident. Political skill can help you know just which tactics to employ, as well as how to execute them in convincing ways that protect your hard-fought reputation.

Conclusion

Your reputation represents the beliefs and opinions that others hold about you. In general, your reputation can determine your social standing in the organization and, hence, can affect the extent to which you are able to influence others. If you have a 'good' reputation, and you are held in high esteem, this can get you access to more resources, information, and connections with others. Political skill can make managing your reputation easier. Thus, developing political skill can enhance your reputation, which is critical for career success.

Research Highlight

Laird, M. D., et al. (2012). "Partial Mediation of the Political Skill–Reputation Relationship." *Career Development International,* 17 *(6)*: 557–582.

Although research had established a link between political skill and personal reputation at work, until recently little was understood about the mechanisms that explained this relationship. Laird and her colleagues argued that political skill leads to enhanced reputation for two reasons: politically skilled employees build better relationships with their supervisors and exhibit helpful behaviors toward colleagues. Together, these aspects work to establish a positive collective perception of politically skilled employees, so they develop a reputation for both character and results.

The results indicated that political skill was related to both higher-quality relationships with supervisors and increased displays of helping behaviors, as expected. However, there were interesting results regarding what led to specific aspects of reputation. Higher-quality relationships with supervisors led to increased reputation for character but not for performance. Conversely, higher instances of helpful behavior led to increased reputation for performance but not for character. This suggests that different aspects of reputation are driven by different aspects of interpersonal interactions. Not surprisingly, politically skilled individuals tend to excel at both, leading to better overall reputations.

8

MANAGING JOB STRESS

*F*ortnite. To the uninitiated, it might mean nothing more than an olden way to measure two weeks of time; to everyone else, it is known as a worldwide video game phenomenon that has been played by nearly 250 million people[1] and earns hundreds of millions of dollars each month.[2] *Fortnite* is one of the few games that broke into the public-at-large's consciousness: the most popular streamer, Tyler "Ninja" Blevins, amassed millions of followers and became a household name (at least for those with children) playing *Fortnite;* a veritable trove of news articles suggesting that *Fortnite* was responsible for everything from gaming addiction to failed marriages were published; and it was even banned in several countries for being too addictive.

Yet *Fortnite* almost didn't exist. In 2017, a relatively new type of video game genre, known as either battle royal or last man standing, began to gain huge market traction. The spark that led to this genre's ultimate success was a game known as *PlayerUnknown's Battlegrounds* (PUBG). This game sold 5 million copies in a three-month period and has gone on to sell 50 million copies since its release, making it one of the top five best-selling games of all time. To say it was a juggernaut within the industry is an understatement. Although there were battle royal games before

PUBG, the success of this game spawned innumerable variations that hoped to share in the success.

One of those games was *Fortnite*. In a weird twist of history, both games were released in March 2017. However, *Fortnite* originally did not include the *Fortnite: Battle Royale* mode. Thus, when the developer of *Fortnite*, Epic, realized that they could capitalize on the success of PUBG, they pushed out an entirely new game mode in two months. To put this in perspective, the development of *Fortnite* took several years. The only way to accomplish such a herculean task is to work hard and long. Epic did just that, and in doing so they created a culture that was known for pushing employees to the limits due to a never-ending *crunch*.

The crunch is a nearly ubiquitous term in the programming industry that covers the window of time right before a product's release into the world. This is the time when everyone is working nonstop to make deadlines; stories of employees working 24-hour days, sleeping in their offices, and sometimes receiving calls from their families asking, "Where are you?" abound. However, one thing about a crunch is that it ends. The product eventually launches, and the employees can take a well-deserved break, often at home with their families and friends.

Epic set a precedent with their decision to launch this new battle royal version of *Fortnite* in a mere two months. The problem with *Fortnite* is that the crunch never ended. The game launched to near immediate success and Epic decided it needed constant updates to its content and play. The result was employees reported working between 70- and 100-hour weeks, which led to a toxic work environment. At the heart of the matter was the contrast between management's position that the extra work was *voluntary* and the employees' perception that the work was *mandatory*.[3]

The ensuing work stress was extreme and led to emotional breakdowns, angry exits, negative repercussions at home, and countless other untold effects on Epic's employees. Unfortunately, there is no magic elixir for work stress. It simply is not possible for one to exist; work stress is a product of not just your own perceptions and feelings but also of your environment, coworkers, and the situation that is created when all those factors are mixed together. However, there is mounting evidence that political skill can help alleviate feelings of work stress. Those who are politically skilled tend to feel like masters of the environment and, thus, feel more in control of the factors that others perceive as doing things unto them. As a result, political skill can be viewed as a stress-reducing tool that will help you survive toxic workplaces and thrive where others may flag.

Causes of Job Stress

"We were told that we had to work 50-hour workweeks and complete 200 tickets a day. It's very, very exhausting, because we had to work really fast. When they announced that, I cried because I was just so tired and exhausted and it just felt like they didn't give a crap."—Epic Employee

Many of the factors that lead to employees experiencing job stress are very personal and so specific that they only apply to a single person. It could be maddening that Karen, the woman one cubicle over, constantly pops her gum throughout the day. Likewise, it could be that Jon, your colleague in accounting, always spoils the endings to popular television shows the day after they are released. Perhaps you keep adding pictures of your cat to your office door and everyone around you simply hates cats. The possibilities are seemingly endless.

We consider identifying all possible sources of job stress a nearly impossible task. There are too many unique individual and situational factors that can contribute to someone feeling stressed out in the workplace. What one person considers stressful may go unnoticed by their colleague. In the case of bubble-popping Karen, the employee to her left may pull his hair out all day, while the employee to her right copes by wearing noise-canceling headphones. As such, it is important to note that individuals within the same organization and position may experience and/ or perceive situations differently. Nonetheless, it is worthwhile to explain what we do know about stress to help highlight factors that tend, more often than not, to result in workers experiencing stress.

Job stress generally refers to the physiological and psychological reactions of individuals to demands encountered at work. It is important to note that this definition suggests that stress can be the cause of both your neck as well as your emotional pain. Many people consider stress to be associated solely with emotional or psychological stress. This is not so, physiological reactions at work can stem from minor pains to heart attacks. In fact, the link between work stress and physiological reactions is so well accepted that various police departments have adopted policies stating that if an officer, either on or off duty, suffers a heart attack, it is considered to be work related.[4] Yet we tend to focus on the host of psychological reactions to workplace demands like depression, anxiety, and anger.

Although the causes of these physiological and psychological strains are varied, extensive research has identified some stressors that tend to be problematic for most individuals. Organizational stressors experienced in the workplace include long hours, high workloads, conflicting or ambiguous demands, a fast pace, strict deadlines, job insecurity, interpersonal conflict, shift work, organizational politics, and harsh or controlling bosses. Certainly, some people will thrive in a fast-paced environment with strict deadlines, but in general these factors tends to be considered stressors for most employees. Thus, in general, workers in jobs in which a greater number of these stressors are present report higher levels of work stress.

No workplace is perfect; regardless of how strongly an organization or leader cares about their workers, stressors will never be eradicated from the workplace. Some stressors are isolated incidents that appear randomly, like your boss getting a speeding ticket on the way to work and then taking his frustration out on you and our colleagues. Others are more permanent fixtures of the workplace, such as a boss who constantly harasses employees on a daily basis. The primary difference between these two stressors is found in their duration. The sheer uncertainty of life requires that we deal with temporary stressors from day to day. This is not to say that they cannot be extremely stressful: giving a speech at graduation, interviewing for the next step up the company ladder, enduring the ire of an angry boss, and being let go can all be stress inducing. Yet they tend to be temporary stressors. Speeches wrap up. Interviews conclude. Bosses calm down. And new jobs are found. The real concern begins when the boss does not calm down or when a new job cannot be found. This is when these demands become chronic stressors.

Chronic stressors are those stressors that are persistent and show no sign of ending. These are the factors in our lives that we just can't seem to escape; they become a fixture of our time at work. That boss who is constantly abusive? We feel the stress while driving to work, sitting behind our desk, and when we lie in bed at night. And we feel that stress day in and day out. Chronic stressors can be debilitating. Some people may notice acute effects of this strain in the form of emotional burnout. Other effects are less visible and more insidious; research suggests that chronic stressors can weaken immune functions and lead to illness. In fact, the consequences of job stress can range from minor annoyances to quite severe.

Consequences of Job Stress

"It's killing people. Something has to change. I can't see how we can go on like this for another year."—Epic Employee

Job stress can do a lot of harm. In the past several decades, many studies have examined the relationship between job stress and a host of physical and mental ailments. Stress-related concerns include mood and sleep disturbances, upset stomach and head-aches, and conflict with family and friends. These symptoms of stress are relatively easy to see, but exposure to chronic stressors can also lead to illnesses that take a long time to develop, such as cardiovascular disease, musculoskeletal disorders, and psychological disorders.

These health risks should not be taken lightly; although they may take time to manifest, these ailments are serious, and the consequences can be deadly. Recent findings suggest that maladies resulting from job stress result in roughly 120,000 deaths per year. As reported by the *Atlantic,* this makes "work-related stressors and the maladies they cause, more deadly than diabetes, Alzheimer's, or influenza.[5]" The article continues to explain that the monetary cost is staggering as well, with job stress resulting in healthcare expenses of about $180 billion per year.

Current and future workplaces offer little hope for those unable to cope with workplace stressors. As competition in the workplace intensifies and the labor market continues to fluctuate—stress will increase. As current and yet-unforeseen digital revolutions eliminate jobs and change the very nature of our work—stress will increase. As employers continue to gain access to an ever-growing talent pool on the global market—stress will increase.

So how do employees cope with these increased demands and their associated increase in work stress? Certainly, the thousands of books, blogs, and seminars touting the benefits of individual approaches such as exercise, relaxation techniques, vacations, and so on will help for a while... but these tend to be predicated on the idea of putting stress "on hold." This is why research finds that even after a lengthy vacation, the stress at work almost immediately returns to pre-vacation levels. However, in stark contrast to this idea of putting stress "on hold," political skill serves as an antidote to the potentially devastating consequences of work stress. It serves as a protective mechanism that allows people to not simply withstand but even flourish in an intensely stressful environment.

Political Skill and Coping

People perceive, react to, and cope with job stressors in different ways. Some respond to stress better than others; some try to avoid it (either by fleeing the situation or by tamping down their response in an effort to stop feeling the stress), while others try to either adjust their behavior to suit the situation or adapt the situation to their preferences. Avoidance is most likely when people see no way to ease the strain through adjustment. Unfortunately, short of leaving the job entirely—which also involves stresses—avoidance rarely does much to improve the situation in the long run.

It stands to reason then that some people simply are able to handle stressors better than others. Recent research has shown that those with more optimistic outlooks are more robust than pessimists. Further, worrywarts seem to take a bigger hit to their immunity system than non-worriers.[6] Certainly, other factors exist that can help reduce the experience of workplace stress. One such factor is political skill; research suggests that people with political skill are more resistant to job stressors. Specifically, research has determined that political skill helped to buffer individuals from harm (including physiological concerns) due to chronic organizational stressors. Thus, being politically skilled is not just about succeeding at work and earning the next promotion, it is a matter of your health and well-being.

The idea that managers and employees need political skill is nothing new, of course, but what is new is our observation that the effective use of political skill can be a way to reduce job stress and thereby improve overall health and well-being. For one thing, simply having political skill can directly reduce the effects of organizational stressors. Research has found that concerns about self-presentation and managing impressions can lead to social anxiety with potential health risks. Employees high in political skill are free of such concerns; confident of their ability to control images, impressions, and interactions at work, they are less likely to perceive their situation as stressful. But why does political skill provide these benefits?

Adaptation and Flexibility

The world speeds along at a faster pace, more so now than ever before. Business deals are closed from behind a keyboard and documents are signed by various parties on as many continents. Likewise, leading companies are beginning to prioritize human concerns such as parental leave and diversity within their ranks. The results of these and the many other changes brought about by this new world is a radically redefined workplace that continues to be molded and reshaped to meet new demands and accommodate new strategies.

To be successful in their industry, organizations need to be both flexible and adaptable—not merely accepting change but embracing it. This is not a new idea. In 1987, Tom Peters's *Thriving in Chaos: Handbook for Management Revolution* argued that winning companies will be those who constantly change and adapt and who view chaos and ambiguity as market opportunities. Continuing this rallying cry are countless authors, journalists, and executives extolling the virtues of adaptability. An article in the *Harvard Business Review*,[7] "Adaptability: The New Competitive Advantage," provides the cold hard facts: "the percentage of companies falling out of the top three rankings in their industry increased from 2% in 1960 to 14% in 2008." When companies fail to adapt, they also tend to fail as companies.

Despite the idea of valuing organizational adaptability and flexibility being known for so long, only recently have we begun to value that same set of skills in our workforce.

Organizations need to adapt—we need to adapt, too. Although continuing professional education has always been a cornerstone of certain professions like accounting or medicine, this idea is beginning to creep into other fields as well because their tools and materials are changing at a rapid pace. It is easy for employees to become swept up in the change and, in doing so, lose their sense of balance. This feeling, like teeter-tottering on a balance beam, leads to uncertainty and, ultimately, stress.

Political skill helps people retain or regain their balance. When organizations undertake massive changes with the explicit purpose of increasing their chances for survival and success in turbulent environments—through restructuring and redesign, business process reengineering, technology adoption, and mergers and acquisitions—it is the soft skills like political skill that help the *employee* survive the changes and find success in their new operating environment.

It Comes Down to Control

> *"It got to the point where I was waiting for the message that maybe we weren't crunching that night, or that weekend. You're waiting for someone to say, 'Hey, we can actually not have you come in tomorrow.'"*—Epic Employee

People with political skill believe and feel like they are in control. This sense of control they feel contributes to the calm confidence that goes along with the high predictability of success. Why do the politically skilled among us feel in control? It is likely because they feel confident operating in ambiguous environments; politically skilled individuals know that they can quickly size up a situation, understand its inner workings, and find a way to achieve their goals.

This sounds simple, but it certainly is not. In fact, if this sounds like a simple task then some congratulations are in order because you can count yourself among the politically skilled. Most people do not do well operating in the gray, in that area that exists between fact and supposition. It can be an utterly maddening place to be because, oftentimes, existing in that space means not knowing truth from fiction, success from failure, or where you fit in the grand scheme of things.

Often, this frustration stems from a lack of control or a lack of *perceived* control. Researchers have been studying control and perceived control for decades. This body of research constitutes some of the most interesting and controversial research in the field of psychology. For example, in 1965, Martin Seligman investigated how a lack of control could lead to learned helplessness through a method that involved delivering electric shocks to dogs. What he found was that when the dogs could escape the shock (e.g., by pressing a lever or jumping away from the shock), they would learn to do so fairly quickly. However, if a dog was led to believe it could not stop the shock (even if it could), the dog would just lie down and accept its fate. This is learned helplessness.[8]

Job stress can often be like those shocks. We have all had coworkers, or we have been that coworker, who felt like there was nothing we could do to escape stress at work. At some point, this may have led them, or us, to simply give up the fight. To become overcome with stress. As above, operating in a gray area between the black and the white often hastens this breakdown, because if we can't make sense of our environment, we feel like we have no control. Suddenly, we stop trying to exert control. In other words, we lie down and accept our fate.

However, the politically skilled actor does not just lie down. Instead, they try to understand their environment and determine which levers need to be pulled. Without a doubt, even the politically skilled will receive a few "shocks" now and then, which is inevitable because life will always throw wrenches into the plan. Yet the main difference is that the politically skilled take up a position where they perceive some amount of control over their environment. They look around at all the actors to see who has the power and means to fix a problem, or they analyze a process to find its faults and then rally others to help fix it. They always try to maintain that sense of perceived control; constantly working to be a master of their environment, even when things start going poorly, allows them to do *unto* their environment as opposed to their environment doing *unto* them.

Organizational Politics

"Ruffling feathers is not conducive to getting where you want to get in the industry."—Epic Employee

Organizational politics are a fact of life and they are unavoidable. In fact, if you find yourself in an environment where you can see no evidence of organizational politics at work...be ready for trouble. It is much more likely that you are not *aware* of the politics happening around you rather than politics simply not existing!

The term itself, *politics*, is blamed for quite a few things in organizations and is almost always cast in a negative light. However, we define this as something more neutral in nature; it can be used for good just as well as it can be used for evil, yet it can also just be another means of getting things done. Is requesting maternity leave at your company a bureaucratic nightmare? What if you, as a manager, know that one of your subordinates recently became pregnant and will be requesting maternity leave in the next few months. Is it worth getting to know the CEO's assistant and maybe dropping some chocolate off on April 24 (i.e., Administrative Professionals' Day) so that you can slide the approval memo right to the decision maker? It might. If so, you have just played *the game,* and everyone is the better for it.

More succinctly, organizational politics refers to engaging in behaviors that are not formally sanctioned by the organization. As above, that could mean stepping outside the more formal lines of approval on memos or learning how to golf so that you can spend a bit of time with the CEO on the greens. Although the list of behaviors that can be considered "playing politics" is endless, we know that dealing with organizational politics has been identified as a key and even vital characteristic of effective managers.

It is clear that managers work in highly political contexts as they address competing interests, deal with scarce resources, and try to satisfy multiple stakeholders in efforts to enhance the organization's reputation and success. The efforts range from taking care of employees by distributing those scarce resources to speaking effectively with clients and partners when projects take a turn for the worse. Managers who can play politics effectively tend to feel more in control of their situation. Unfortunately, not all managers are equally adept and skilled at politics and thus may find the business environment threatening and stressful because of the demand for abilities they lack.

The recent Theranos scandal brought to light the management practices of its president, Ramesh "Sunny" Balwani. In stark contrast to the relatively savvy CEO, Elizabeth Holmes, Sunny was not a politically skilled manager and tended to favor using a hammer as opposed to influence when trying to motivate employees. As related by John Carreyrou in *Bad Blood: Secrets and Lies in a Silicon Valley Startup*, a work of investigative journalism, Sunny was a "force of nature, and not in a good way . . . [who] was haughty and demeaning toward employees, barking orders and dressing people down." His actions led to a "culture of fear" within Theranos and because he was so fond of firing people and then *immediately* removing them from the premises, the employees imbued "disappear" with new meaning: Sunny disappeared people. In several of his firings, the employees were forced to leave the premises *without* being able to collect their personal belongings.

Sunny's leadership resulted in Theranos experiencing an incredibly high turnover rate. A politically skilled leader would have realized he was dealing with intelligent, educated, and capable employees who wanted to make a difference in the world (an ostentatiously espoused virtue of Theranos from the very start). Yet he chose to check video logs of people entering and exiting the facility, openly questioning people about their commitment to the company and treating them without dignity. One of the disappeared employees wrote an email to both Sunny and the CEO stating that, "I was also told that anytime someone deals with you it's never a good outcome for that person." Sunny's sheer lack of political skill made him incapable of understanding his employees and the situation. Clearly, there were other, very serious problems underlying Theranos's woes, but Sunny did himself, the company, and even the overall deception, no favors.

Interpersonal Coping

We would be remiss if we did not mention one of the primary causes of job stress—our coworkers. Oftentimes we hear about how an organization is doing this or doing that, both of which are somehow ruining our lives. Yet it is the people around us who can somehow make a great organization awful and an equally awful organization wonderful.

Thus, it is not surprising that studies of job stress generally identify interpersonal relations as key contributing factors; disruptive and stressful relationships with coworkers are related to ill health, job dissatisfaction, absenteeism, and turnover. Even top management positions are far from immune to this sort of stress. Much of the work of management involves interactions with others, and that makes the ability to deal effectively with people with a wide variety of backgrounds, styles, and personalities indispensable for managers—and it makes any weakness in this area a key source of stress. If managers have political skill, they are less likely to experience stress from the interactions required in their jobs.

Work-Family Conflict

"I hardly sleep. I'm grumpy at home. I have no energy to go out. Getting a weekend away from work is a major achievement. If I take a Saturday off, I feel guilty. I'm not being forced to work this way, but if I don't, then the job won't get done."—Epic Employee

The push and pull between work and family has only grown in the past decade. As the working world continues to move toward equality and the economic realities of today often require that both members of a household work, the inevitable conflict that arises when separating work and family has become a reality for many working families. It is important to note that this is not a one-way road; family obligations can encroach on work just as much as work obligations can impinge upon family time. Whether it be a late meeting that was *just* scheduled during the time of your child's school play where they are in the starring role of J. Pierrepont Finch or because you cannot make it to the morning meeting because you are taking your aging mother to a doctor's appointment—work and family obligations tend to conflict.

The amount of research demonstrating the deleterious effects of work-family conflict is staggering and only continues to grow as the phenomenon becomes more widespread. Of course, this affects everyone in the workplace. However, women are particularly susceptible to the effects of work-family conflict because of the still-accepted/expected gender norms embraced by both society and the business world. Many people still expect women to devote more hours to dealing with family demands than their male counterparts. However, this expectation is a double-edged sword that cuts women both ways.

For one, women who work often find that they still need to accomplish many of the household and caregiving tasks. This is why a working mom may show up to her first meeting with green icing on her blouses—*before* going to bed, she baked cupcakes, then the next morning she woke the kids up, got them ready for school, dropped them off, and drove to the office while putting on makeup and driving with her knees. So, in this way, women are forced to manage 50 different expectations and *roles* (e.g., professional, mother, wife, baker). Failure to fulfill any of these roles likely will result in some sort of shaming or reprimand. If our fictional mother forgets cupcakes or her children's clothes are wrinkled—she will get the side-eye from the other mothers for not "doing her job." Similarly, if she doesn't notice the green icing on her blouse before the meeting, she might be deemed unprofessional.

Yet the situation gets no better when women request time off from work to care for family members. Historically, men's family involvement could vary depending on the demands at work, while the family demands on women tended to be constant and independent of the influence of work. There is no warm glow that surrounds a woman who takes time off to care for her children or her parents because it is an expectation. When a man asks for time off to spend time with his children or parents, he is considered a saint. Oftentimes, there will be a canonization ceremony right there on the spot—*before* he has even spent a moment with his family. And thus, the strange dichotomy that affects women's job stress in the workplace is complete.

The evidence of this strange disparity exists at all levels, from the bottom all the way to the top. A great way to discover this evidence was mentioned by Julia Greenberg in *Wired*: "Search for Yahoo CEO Marissa Mayer or YouTube CEO Susan Wojcicki's names with 'maternity leave' and you'll see dozens of stories about the choices they've made about new parents...," but do the same with any "top male tech exec and 'paternity leave' and see what you get." The problem is that these CEOs are held up as the templates for how professionals should act. If female CEOs at the highest echelons are receiving criticism for taking maternity leave, how will the rank and file women feel about taking leave? Similarly, if male CEOs do not take paternity leave, what message does that send to both men and women about expectations in the workplace?

Thankfully, the leaders of our business world are starting to realize that their personal decisions can have a great impact on their employees' well-being. In 2015, Mark Zuckerberg, CEO of Facebook, took two months of paternity leave, a move that received widespread plaudits for helping normalize professionals taking leave to care for children. As society begins to expect and/or realize that men will, or want to, share in the burden of caregiving we can expect things to change. This means that men's stress levels likely will increase as family obligations begin to impinge more upon their work than before. It is possible that women will begin to experience a bit less stress now that the burden of caregiving is starting to shift to a bit more equal position, but there is still quite a long way to go for that to become an accepted societal norm.

And this is why political skill matters. It is indeed possible to cope with work and family demands. Political skill seems to be an effective buffer between the two, if only because you realize *when* it is acceptable to say no, as well as *how* to say no. There are some early efforts to research the use of political skill in non-work contexts, and it is possible that this work will demonstrate that partners' political skill will help them better work together to manage work and family demands. Imagine if two politically skilled partners could recognize *when* and *how* to push back against work demands while managing all of their family obligations. For example, when the children's clothes are wrinkled, perhaps a father can take the kids to school because all the other moms will give him a pass for being a good dad who takes the time to drive his kids to school.

Implications and Benefits of Political Skill

What does this all mean? Based on approximately 50 research studies on political skill and stress, we know that political skill is the closest thing we have to an antidote to stress on the job. First, those high in political skill have good reason to believe—based on repeated experience—that they can control processes and outcomes of interactions with others. Thus, political skill creates feelings of success, accomplishment, and confidence, and such feelings tend to enhance physical as well as mental health. Second, employees with strong political skill will view interpersonal interactions as opportunities rather than as threats, so the same environment that seems stressful to the unskilled is merely invigorating to the skillful.

Political skill benefits employees in every single situation outlined in this chapter, as well as the hundreds of others we did not discuss—it truly is the multitool of stress management. Whether it be organizational politics and the ensuing ambiguity, unclear

roles, work-family conflict, or turbulent interpersonal conflicts—
political skill makes them all seem more manageable. Rather than
feel intimidated by the need to manage multiple and divergent
constituencies and interpersonal relationships, the politically
skilled employee will feel emboldened and ready. This is because
they know that they can inspire trust and confidence in others
and carefully manage any distress by channeling it away from the
current situation. Stressful situations that require political skill
are often seen as opportunities to those who have political skill.

The implications for political skill regarding organizational
politics and interpersonal relationships as stressors are straightforward. The ability to work comfortably in a political environment and define its dimensions as interpersonal suggests a natural
fit between the politically skilled person and executive-level work.
Rather than regarding the political and interpersonal aspects
of the job as threatening, hard to understand, and uncontrollable,
the skilled employee is apt to recognize that they are essential to
the job and they provide a chance to shine.

That is, situations that call for political skill are seen as
opportunities by those who are adept at using that skill. Those not
so adept experience frustrations and try other methods, such as
the intimidation tactics used by Sunny Balwani, or just ignore the
situation. This causes personal stress and creates stress among
employees and throughout the organization. The proper use of
political skill has the opposite effect: it reduces stress not only for
the users themselves but also for those around them, thus creating a healthier organization.

Organizational Benefits

The organization as a whole stands to reap great rewards if its
employees are better able to communicate, engage in interpersonal interactions, cope with accountabilities, operate in a turbulent
environment, and be flexible. As a result, formal efforts to improve
political skill have implications beyond feel-good employee

benefits. The organization enjoys better success, encounters fewer causes of anxiety, and enjoys better relationships with customers, suppliers, and potential allies in the market. Its whole operation becomes more effective, because every detail, from external negotiations to the shared work of teams and offices, runs more smoothly on a base of political skill.

Conclusion

The bottom line is that political skill can help reduce the strain that employees feel from the various stressors they encounter in the workplace. Just as a pair of headphones can silence Karen's continual popping of her gum and relieve you of that frustration, so too can political skill reduce much of the stress-inducing factors you experience—and in much the same way. Just as the headphones do not eliminate the cause of the stress, political skill will not eliminate stressful situations. Instead, political skill is a multifaceted solution: it helps you find solutions, understand situations, and overcome ambiguity. In doing so, you gain a sense of control over your workplace and you become a master of your environment.

Research Highlight

Perrewé, P. L., Zellars, K. L., Ferris, G. R., Rossi, A. M., Kacmar, C. J., & Ralston, D. A. (2004). "Neutralizing Job Stressors: Political Skill as an Antidote to the Dysfunctional Consequences of Role Conflict." *Academy of Management Journal*, 47(1), 141–152.

Stressors at work, when sustained, can lead to physical and mental strain. One such stressor is role conflict, which occurs when employees have competing demands for their roles (e.g., a phone-based customer service representative has pressure to satisfy callers but also complete calls as quickly as possible). Because this conflict is embedded within the role, the stressor is chronic and, unmitigated, likely to lead to strain, possibly even burnout.

Perrewé and her colleagues sought to understand whether political skill could serve as a buffer to the relationship between role conflict and strain. They argued that because political skill provides a heightened sense of control, which has been found to result in perception of fewer stressors and an increased ability to handle stressors that are perceived, employees with higher levels of political skill would show fewer signs of strain.

Indeed, the more politically skilled employees in their study, which took place over the course of more than a year, reported lower anxiety and somatic complaints, despite the presence of perceived role conflict. Even more impressive, these politically skilled respondents also had lower blood pressure, as collected in a biofeedback clinic associated with the study. Clearly, political skill is advantageous to employees as they navigate the complexities of organizational life.

PART III

POLITICAL SKILL IN SPECIFIC CONTEXTS

9

BUILDING SOCIAL NETWORKS

This millennium has been defined by a growing awareness that we are all embedded in a series of social networks. Obviously, our awareness has been catapulted in the non-academic realm through the monetization of social networks on platforms such as Facebook, Instagram, and LinkedIn. In this chapter, we identify social networks as a strategic source of social capital which, when effectively understood and leveraged, provides the capital holder with a series of unique career, reputational, and personal benefits. We also discuss how your political skill can help you get the most out of your social networking activity.

Social Networks in the Workplace

The term *Social networks* is ubiquitous in the modern workplace. Platforms like Facebook and LinkedIn have created global connections at a level never before seen. While some would suggest that this obviously indicates the world is more connected than ever, others might suggest that these casual, self-focused, "one-click" connections have decreased the importance of strong social network ties. These common understandings of social networks have not gone unnoticed by academics, and an abundance of research has been conducted to provide insights into the mechanisms and structures that aid in network development, maintenance, and implementation.

From an academic perspective, social networks are built upon a series of ties between nodes. In the real world, we call these ties *relationships* or *connections*, and we call the nodes *people* or *friends*. As you think about your various social networks, we are sure you realize that you interact with these connections more or less frequently, in different contexts, and/or for different types of assistance. It is also not frame-breaking to note that some of us have a larger number of connections than others, but it is often overlooked that the sheer number of connections alone does not ensure that we have the "right" connections to wield influence in our organization.

Each of our connections can be seen as either being a strong connection/tie or a weak connection/tie. If you evaluated your social network, you would probably agree that there are people who are in your inner circle and another group you are acquaintances with. Strong ties would be those that are in your inner circle and probably provide you consistent social and perhaps even financial support. These are the folks that always "have your back." Your acquaintances represent your weak ties and give you access to a diverse set of connections and resources. As you have success, these weak ties will draw closer; when things go wrong, they will distance themselves from you. Ultimately, we have to recognize that not all ties can be strong ones, and that there is a limit to the number of ties we can effectively maintain.

It is common to evaluate one's network on the number of contacts or followers accumulated on a social media platform. Until social networking or social media accounts existed, there was no easy way to quickly assess the breadth of a person's network. How big is your network? How many followers do you have on Instagram? Friends on Facebook? Connections on LinkedIn? Interestingly, research suggests that the maximum social network size in humans is approximately 153 contacts, with an average number of 124 people in a network. The authors suggested that this result is roughly congruent with what would be expected given the size of humans' neocortex, the part of the brain associated with higher-order functioning.[1]

Another way in which we can understand our social networks is through what researchers call centrality. Network centrality is understood as being a component of informal power in the workplace and represents the degree to which a particular actor has more connections within a particular network. This concept is at the core of social networks research across domains.

How might you know if you are central in a social network? Imagine if we asked all of the people in your workplace who was in their social network. Your centrality in the social network is simply a representation of the number of people who include you in their answer to that question. It is important to note that a person can be central in almost an infinite number or type of network. For example, among the abundance of networks one can be central in are those that reflect friendship, advice, dislike, or leadership. Whereas each of these different types of networks has different effects on your work performance, your centrality in any of these networks is a reflection of the amount of social capital you have at work.

We see that the currency of social capital is embedded not within your personality or characteristics but within the relationships you are able to cultivate and maintain. While certainly your personal characteristics contribute to your success, they only do so to the degree that they facilitate access to influential networks. We see these personal characteristics at play in everyday phenomena like the glass ceiling effect and the concept of white privilege.

The development of social capital comes from our networking behavior, and even Facebooking can lead to a greater sense of social capital development in the actor. Users of Facebook have been shown to perceive they are able to better integrate themselves into the communities in which they participate and be more connected with the world at large. Increased use of Facebook also elevates the user's perceptions of their ability to maintain social capital with their network connections.

Social Networks and Personal Success

Although perhaps intuitively we understand that social networks can be of benefit in the workplace, it is important to note that extensive research confirms these notions. From a performance perspective, our understanding of how social networks benefit us has most consistently been shown as a proxy for social capital and a predictor of various aspects of job performance.

Social Capital. As suggested above, our networks represent an important source of social capital. Whereas academics have disagreed on the exact nature of social capital, it is broadly accepted that it represents the *value* of the connections in one's social network. This touches on the idea that having a large number of connections is not, in and of itself, predictive of one's power in an organization.

Whereas having a large and diverse network increases employees' mobility within their organization, it is critical to have connections with powerful others. Of importance to you then is whether you can successfully understand the pattern of social networks in organizations, seamlessly insert yourself into those networks, and then advantageously leverage the social capital gained to benefit your career or your organization. Research suggests political skill can be a driver of your success in these endeavors.

We discussed earlier that there was an abundance of ways in which we can look at your social network—advice, friendship, etc. When you are central in work-related networks you tend to be more satisfied with your pay and upward mobility in your organization. And, while being a tie between two non-linked social networks might provide you with more power in your organization, this positioning may also lead to decreased satisfaction with your job.[2]

Social capital has been shown to have positive effects on organizations as well. In an interesting study of public-school achievement, it was found that internal social capital (stronger relationships among teachers), as well as external social capital (relationships among principals and stakeholder groups) positively predicted student performance on standardized tests in math and reading.[3] This type of research not only shows the importance of building social capital within and beyond organizational boundaries, but also it challenges us to think about the nature of our responsibilities in our roles as leaders. To what degree should we be consciously building organizational structures, cultures, and job descriptions to encourage the development of social capital?

Performance. Why invest your time and energy in improving your own social networks and/or your social networking ability? Not surprisingly, social networks have been found to be important in helping improve individual job performance. An analysis of 138 different studies found that being central in a network is positively related to both job performance and career success.[4] In contrast, being isolated from others leads to lower job performance.[5]

One of the obvious outcomes of popular social networking sites is their focus on increasing a person's popularity. Whether it is noted in "likes" or "followers," the success of today's internet "influencers" is solely an evaluation of their relative popularity. Social networks at work are, similarly, motivated by or reflective of an employee's popularity, and political skill can increase visibility and access in ways that enhance reputation and employee popularity.

Yet being popular at work and having a broad and strong social network is not without its challenges. When employees occupy a central position in a communication network, they are not only more likely to be seen as popular by others but also more likely to be subject to performance hindering behaviors from their coworkers (Scott and Judge, 2009). This type of behavior is to be expected. When a person's identity is threatened by participating in social networking, they are likely to experience hostile negative emotions, like envy. Thus, seeing oneself as not central or inferior might lead to increased hostility toward the central node in the network.

In fact, when Facebook envy is experienced, users are more likely to experience depression and decreased life satisfaction.[6] Being in the core of a network can also lead to increased role demands, and thus is likely to increase stress on the position holder. If a central node in the network is un-politically skilled, we would expect the stress inherent in their social positioning to eventually erode their coping ability and personal resources and ultimately lead to a deterioration of their social networks.

Some support for this notion is found in the work of Cullen and colleagues, who found that centrality in a communication network made it more likely that the position holder would experience greater overload in that role and less certainty over how to fulfill their obligations.[7] However, centrally positioned, politically skilled individuals experience less ambiguity and thus tend to thrive in these roles. This suggests that while the increased demands of being in the core of a communication network are deleterious for an employee's well-being, political skill increases their access to instrumental resources such that they have greater understanding of the workplace and experience less uncertainty about their role.

The dynamics of social isolation can lead to practical challenges for the growing number of employees who work remotely in some fashion. The number of people engaging in at least some remote work increased roughly 25 percent from 2003 to 2015. During this time frame, the percentage of employees who did some or all of their work from home on a given day rose from 19 percent to 24 percent. It is obvious that working remotely adds unique challenges to maintaining a work-related network. Remote employees work harder to impress their bosses and maintain their networks than less-remote colleagues, specifically engaging more frequently in ingratiatory behavior toward their supervisor and in behaviors to promote their accomplishments to others.[8]

Achieving greater centrality in a social network made it even more likely that employees would try to promote themselves to their bosses. Unfortunately, these types of behaviors were not likely to translate into higher supervisor performance ratings. This suggests that when you work remotely, supervisor-targeted and social network enhancing political behaviors are more important to your performance ratings than are efforts to make sure your supervisor understands your objective accomplishments.

Another work arrangement that highlights the importance and complexity of social networks exists when organizations arrange their processes into teams. Within a team context, one's centrality in an advice network has also been found to positively predict job performance. However, the same research found that negative team social interactions hurt team performance. We all have those people at work who make it hard to get our work done.[9] Now imagine that we could depict a social network that shows who is the most difficult person with whom to work—well, we can. This is called being central in a hindrance network and has been shown to be detrimental to job performance. Simply, when a team has more hinderers, team performance suffers.

Just as social networks are predictors of job performance, they also impact overall career success (i.e., promotions, satisfaction, and salary) through the ability to develop weak ties and to occupy positions within a network that connect two otherwise unconnected networks. When we have a large number of weak ties, we tend to have greater access to information and resources that, in turn, lead to career success. Connecting powerful groups tends to provide us a higher level of sponsorship for our career and, again, leads to career success. Taken together, this suggests that we should spend our time not only increasing the size of our networks but also focusing on "matchmaking": placing ourselves as a conduit between two unconnected but synergistic groups.

Political Skill and Social Networks

As scholars have sought to develop a more informed understanding of the linkages that explain how political skill affects work outcomes, some have suggested the importance of relationships and social networks. Indeed, researchers recently examined the importance of political dynamics in social networks, and a number of recent empirical investigations have reported on how work relationships, connections, and social networks can explain the relationships between political skill and a number of important work outcomes.[10]

Social networks are built through linkages between two nodes. These two-person linkages are the threads that weave together and create the social fabric of the workplace. Political skill facilitates an individual actor's ability to access and leverage these social networks. Politically skilled employees are better at developing strong relationships and enhancing their social network positioning.

The research on political skill and social networking activity is in its early stages but growing rapidly. The current state of this research in combination with the cumulative theoretical and empirical knowledge developed by researchers regarding political skill over the last two decades strongly suggests that political skill may be a key driver in developing and leveraging social networks in the workplace.

Conceptually, network building can be envisioned as a communication process between two members of a relational dyad. This process relies on political skill as an ability that allows for the two parties to recognize the value of each other's social networks and a regulatory mechanism to help effectively communicate and interpret behavioral motivations. Most simply, political skill should assist employees in two fundamental social networking processes: network recognition and network leveraging.

Network Recognition. Accuracy in perception of the social network means that the series of relationships and connections we see as representing not only our own network but the overlap of all networks in the organization closely resembles the actual network structure. It is obvious then that in order to make the correct decisions about where and how to invest our social capital, it is important that we are accurate in our understanding of the social: networking system. Political skill is a competency that assists us in correctly interpreting informal relationships in the workplace.

Individuals differ in their ability to accurately assess the social network within which they operate, and some research suggests that informal and formal power influences a person's perceptual accuracy. For example, laboratory results indicate that lower-power individuals are more accurate in their perceptions than those primed with higher power.[11] In field studies, the power inherent in the formal structure has also been shown to negatively impact cognitive accuracy. Employees who occupy higher levels in the organizational hierarchy actually are less accurate in their perceptions of the informal social structure.

Whereas these power- and structure-related components of the workplace have demonstrated their influence on employees' network perceptions, there are also distinctions related to personality characteristics. It appears that our motivations drive our success in interpreting networks that align with our internal drives. For instance, employees' need for achievement is positively related to their ability to interpret both friendship and advice networks, and their need for affiliation predicts accuracy in assessing friendship networks.[12]

There are many documented benefits to being of the disposition that the glass is half full. However, when it comes to the role of this positive affectivity in accurately understanding social networks, this outlook has some problematic results. It is true that this personality characteristic, labeled by researchers as positive affect, does lead an individual to properly assess the friendship ties of others in the workplace. However, these same upbeat individuals were less precise in predicting their personal advice networks.[13] This implies that while positive individuals are more likely to understand the broad political landscape in organizations, they are also less likely to evaluate their own social capital correctly, likely leading to political missteps when implementing influence strategies.

Understanding the nature of human ties and social network ties is a fundamental part of the characteristics of politically skilled people. Politically skilled employees are more socially astute than their less skilled counterparts. When operating in the social network context that means political skill makes it easier for employees to accurately perceive not only the connections inherent in a social network but also the value or power in those connections. This makes the actor more effective in recognizing opportunities to expand or exploit their networks.

Network Leveraging. The ability to recognize social networks accurately is a precursor to using network resources to advance a personal agenda. Once networks are recognized, political skill allows for their effective relational development. The mechanisms by which political skill aids relationship building in the network context are similar to other areas of organizational life. Indeed, political skill demonstrates its effectiveness in the workplace by allowing people to develop and maintain productive relationships at work. It is these productive relationships that can be leveraged to secure advantageous positions in work and social networks, which facilitate individuals' work performance and effectiveness.

When we accept that social networks are built on a series of dyadic relations, then we see that the self-regulatory and trust-building aspects of political skill are critically important for network expansion and utilization. Indeed, high-quality work relationships consist of a number of key dimensions, including trust, support, loyalty, affect, accountability, instrumentality, respect, and flexibility. Political skill tends to facilitate and drive the development of these dimensions.

Such facilitation is evident in research investigating leader-member relations, whether we are considering leader political skill or subordinate political skill. Leader political skill is an important predictor of subordinate perceptions of relational quality.[14] This research has shown that subordinate political skill enhances perceptions of high-quality relationships even when the supervisor and subordinate are demographically different. Taken together, this research supports the idea that political skill is crucial to developing strong leader-member relations and that to the degree both parties are skilled, the dyad will experience improved functioning.

Although the measurement of political skill has been shown to be consistent across several cultures, its most interesting cross-cultural findings relate to interpersonal relations in China. Within China, the idea of high-quality relationships is replaced by a culturally unique concept known as *guanxi*. Guanxi "refers to the concept of drawing on connections in order to secure favors in personal relations."[15] Luo suggests that guanxi is:

1. Transferable: One partner in a guanxi relationship connects the other to a person in their own network, through network matchmaking behavior.
2. Reciprocal: It links individuals, usually with different levels of power, in a transactional relationship from which the less powerful individual usually gains.
3. Intangible: The relationship is governed by norms and unwritten expectations that result in damaging the perpetrator's reputation when violated.
4. Utilitarian: The relationship operates solely through the exchange of favors rather than through an emotional bond between the parties.
5. Personal: All connections, whether the parties are representing organizations or groups, are between the two members of the dyad.

Much like other relational concepts, political skill can improve the success and career development of employees through cultivation of guanxi between supervisors and subordinates. Politically skilled subordinates have been found to use their political skill to engage in behaviors that build supervisor-subordinate guanxi, which advances their careers.[16] Political skill has also been found to improve salesperson-customer guanxi and ultimately increase salesperson performance.[17]

Whereas we suggest that guanxi is a dyadic building block of social networks, some scholars have argued that the concepts share more significant overlap. This overlap occurs on three dimensions. First, both concepts focus on the importance of information in defining the proper structure of interpersonal relations. Second, both stress the goal of change by focusing on trust and loyalty. Third, both theoretical approaches recognize the presence of chaos and order.

Although still underdeveloped, research on political skill and social networks is beginning to substantiate the theory discussed above. Initial investigations into political skill and social networks have uncovered several interesting relationships. Political skill seems to make it more likely that individuals will engage in networking behavior whether in their workplace or in their community. Treadway and colleagues found that highly politically skilled individuals were more likely to engage in networking behaviors in all spheres of their life.[18] Specifically, when a person felt they were in short-term relationships with their organization, they engaged in significantly more community networking behaviors. Similarly, when an employee held the perspective that they had a long period of time before they died, they invested their networking behaviors in work-related networking. This implies our networking behavior is driven by our context-specific motivations and by our understanding of our identity in any given point in time. Political skill can move beyond just dyadic relationship building and it can build broader work and social networks, allowing people to build increased network resources. Thus, people high in political skill can become resources for others who may lack such social competencies.

As stated earlier in this chapter, social networks can be

constructed for any number of concepts. With this in mind, we can turn to two novel usages of social network analysis. The first of these studies assessed the power network in an organization to identify informal power. This research discovered that when an individual is a high performer in an organization, they are not always capable of converting that resource into interpersonal power. In fact, only when high performers possessed elevated levels of political skill were they able to obtain advantageous positioning in the power network of the organization.[19]

Whereas the leadership research we have discussed so far has focused on defined, legitimate supervisor-subordinate relationships, informal leaders are more abundant in organizations. These informal leaders can be identified by evaluating the leadership networks within an organization. We know that when an individual is central in these networks, they are an informal leader within a group. What research has shown is that political motivations make it more likely someone will emerge as an informal leader, but political skill helps these leaders leverage their leadership position into personal performance.[20] Thus, political skill assists in leveraging informal leadership positions into personal performance advantages.

A final unique network with which political skill has been integrated is an abusive one. Using social network analysis we can identify workplace bullies. Envision an analysis that asks coworkers who they have seen engage in bullying behaviors in the the last three months. The answer to this question creates a network in which centrality reveals the most prevalent bully in the organization. What we know from our research is that when someone is centrally located in a bullying network, they will be able to achieve higher performance if they are politically skilled. Politically skilled bullies are able to strategically manipulate, coerce, and co-opt weaker individuals in the workplace and translate their resources into performance advantages for themselves.

The cumulative assessments presented in this chapter speak to the importance of political skill in effective networking and positive impacts on your career. Political skill allows for more accurate assessment of the informal networks in the organization by enhancing the actor's social astuteness. This characteristic also leads to elevated opportunity recognition. Once identified, interpersonal influence and authenticity increase the likelihood that the actor will be able to effectively leverage these network opportunities to achieve higher performance, enhanced reputation, and greater career growth. Most simply, politically skilled people are able to easily build effective friendships, alliances, and coalitions.

Conclusion

Politically skilled individuals are able to expand their business and social contacts within organizations. Specifically, those with political skill are able to build their social networks more easily. Developing social networks is much more than connecting with others on social platforms, such as counting the number of friends on Facebook and LinkedIn (although using social media can help build a network). Political skill can enhance individuals' ability to not only recognize those with whom to connect, but also to recognize how best to leverage and exploit their social networks for career success.

Research Highlight

Wei, L. Q., et al. (2012). "Developing and Utilizing Network Resources: Roles of Political Skill." *Journal of Management Studies*, 49(2), 381–402.

Although the empirical research on political skill and social networks is relatively new and somewhat limited in scope, one of the few studies that has been conducted in this area supports the overall arguments put forth in this chapter. More specifically, the researchers argued that political skill would increase employees' network resources, which would positively affect their job performance and career growth potential.

Using a two-wave sample of 281 supervisor-subordinate dyads from six firms, Wei and colleagues found that employees' political skill was positively related to their network resources at work, which included things like contacts at higher organizational levels and emotional support from colleagues. Additionally, network resources were positively related to both supervisor-rated job performance and career growth potential. Finally, results also indicated that political skill strengthened the relationship between network resources and both job performance and career growth potential.

In sum, despite the limited research in this area, early indications support the arguments that political skill enables success at work by facilitating social network development.

10

NEGOTIATING EFFECTIVELY

In 1976, the Southern African country of Rhodesia was popu-
lated by more than 6 million black citizens. Yet representatives
of the roughly 270,000 white citizens enjoyed a stranglehold on
the government, despite active international pressure for majority
rule. In 1965, Great Britain established a policy of not granting
independence for colonies until the white minority ceded control
to the majority, but Ian Smith, who had just assumed the premier-
ship, promptly and defiantly declared Rhodesian independence
and vowed to maintain white minority rule.

Over the next decade, no other government recognized
Rhodesian independence, and Great Britain repeatedly tried to
persuade Smith to adopt majority rule. In October 1966, British
Prime Minister Harold Wilson sat down with Smith aboard the
warship HMS *Tiger* for high-level negotiations. They failed.

In December 1968, Wilson again tried to negotiate with
Smith, this time aboard the HMS *Fearless*. Again, the talks failed
to advance majority rule in Rhodesia.

Smith was firm in his stance and by 1976 still did not seem
likely to acquiesce. On March 20, he stated: "I don't believe in
black majority rule ever in Rhodesia, not in a thousand years."[1]
The boldness of this assertion is impressive in isolation but

is magnified when considered in light of the ongoing war between Smith's government and two separate communist-backed Rhodesian black guerilla factions. Yet just three years later, in 1979, majority rule was a reality in the newly constituted government of Zimbabwe Rhodesia.

After years of repeated failure, what had changed? According to the in-depth analysis of James Sebenius, R. Nicholas Burns, and Robert Mnookin, Henry Kissinger got involved.

In their book, *Kissinger the Negotiator,* they detail how the ability to see the big picture, read counterparts, build relationships, and effectively deploy interpersonal tactics enabled Henry Kissinger to negotiate successfully where others had failed and to achieve what many had come to believe was likely impossible without a full-scale race war.[2] Considering this story in light of the preceding chapters, it should be evident that Kissinger's favorable result was due in large part to his political skill. Although many of us will not have the opportunity to lead a high-stakes, multiparty negotiation that results in dramatic shifts in the geopolitical landscape, we are regularly engaged in negotiations.

Think about it. There are a number of work-related scenarios that you might find familiar. You likely went through some sort of negotiation as part of landing your current job. You have probably had discussions with a coworker to move a deadline. Maybe you have haggled over details while trying to close a deal with a prospective client. For those of you in managerial positions, you might have had discussions with a subordinate about a transfer to another division. Or, for those at the top of their organizational hierarchy, perhaps you have had to negotiate the purchase or sale of a company division or to convince a board to pursue a merger with another firm. Regardless, the far-from-exhaustive list above should make it clear that negotiations are a common and integral part of life at work, whether you are brand new to the job or consider yourself a seasoned deal maker.

Although these examples vary in many ways, they share an important aspect. In fact, this commonality exists for the majority of negotiations, including the deal Kissinger facilitated in Southern Africa. The reality is that most successful negotiation outcomes are not achieved by imposing your will on the other party but rather by finding creative ways to make sure the interests of all parties involved are met. A common description of this aspect of negotiations refers to this as an ability to move away from a mind-set focused on dividing a fixed pie into small pieces and toward an approach that looks to expand the pie such that everyone is satisfied.

Like many things, especially those involving interpersonal interaction, this is easier said than done. However, consistent with our arguments throughout this book, we contend that it can be more easily done by the politically skilled. This chapter is devoted to explaining how more successful negotiation outcomes are facilitated by considering the role of networking ability, social astuteness, interpersonal influence, and apparent sincerity in light of common aspects of negotiations.

Preparation

More than likely, when someone talks about negotiation you probably picture two people haggling back and forth about the price of a good or service. Although this certainly is an aspect of negotiation, it's far from an all-encompassing characterization of the process. In fact, most negotiation experts agree it's not even the most important part of the process. That honor typically is reserved for planning and preparation. We won't detail all aspects of the planning process here, but given its role setting the stage for a successful negotiation, we feel compelled to describe how several aspects are enhanced by political skill.

Perspective-Taking

For example, one key task during preparation is to identify all of the relevant issues. This certainly makes sense, as it is difficult to come to an agreement if you haven't thought through all of the things that will be on the table. However, to successfully identify all of the issues in play, we often need to fight against our tendency to focus on ourselves and what we want to gain from the negotiation.

Instead, it is most helpful, if not critical, to consider what the other party or parties might want out of the deal. This exercise in perspective-taking can be difficult for those with limited ability to see "the big picture." However, political skill facilitates this, as social astuteness provides the ability to make connections among pieces of information from and about the other party, as well as observations we have made in interactions leading up to the current negotiation. This is especially true for a politically skilled person if they have negotiated with this party before. As we noted in chapter 2, political skill facilitates pattern recognition, such that we are able to connect the dots and, in the context of negotiation, better understand what the other party might be trying to achieve.

Beyond just identifying the issues in play, though, it is most helpful if we understand *why* these issues are "on the table." In negotiation parlance, these are referred to as "interests," and they are typically the key to unlocking and even creating value. Thus, to make the best deal possible, or sometimes even just a favorable deal, for all parties involved, it often is not enough just to know what the issues are. We need to know why everyone wants what they want—that is, their interests. Armed with this information, we can better construct packages, make offers, and justify claims that will satisfy the other party's interests and make them more likely to agree to our proposals.

Again, this requires the ability to see things from a different vantage point than our own. We need to be able to observe, process, and analyze this information in a way that helps us best make sense of the current situation. Political skill, particularly via social astuteness, facilitates this mental organization. As a result, politically skilled negotiators can recognize both what other parties want and why they want it, which makes it possible to maximize value during negotiations.

Gathering Information

In addition to, and in fact often to facilitate, perspective-taking to identify all issues and interests in play, negotiators often need to conduct research, gathering specific information to help them in their preparation. This research is critical to a negotiator's ability to construct offers that are advantageous to themselves and likely to be viewed favorably by the other party. For example, one of the biggest questions on a negotiator's mind is whether to make the first offer and, if they do, what that first offer should be.

Negotiation experts note that first offers need to be both aggressive and reasonable. They should be aggressive because the initial offer tends to "anchor" the negotiation. Consider a negotiation where the only issue is the price of an item. The seller is willing to accept as little as $500 and the buyer is willing to pay as much as $1,000. In this scenario, an initial offer nearer to either of those two numbers increases the likelihood of the final price being near that end of the possible spectrum of prices. Thus, an opening offer of $550 will "anchor" the discussion at that end of the range.

However, initial offers that are too aggressive are often labeled unreasonable. In the example above, where both parties would theoretically agree to a final price between $500 and $1,000, an initial request from the seller for $5,000 is likely to be judged as unreasonable. Although some might argue that because of the anchoring principle this aggressive offer should just ensure that the final price is toward the high end of the possible range of outcomes, such an extreme offer might backfire. Because it is so far above the maximum price the other party is willing to pay, they could simply walk away, unconvinced that a deal is possible. Even if the seller were to attempt to keep the buyer in the negotiation by lowering the price, they have likely lost credibility with the buyer, which can hinder a deal.

To construct aggressive yet reasonable offers, negotiators need a lot of information. Frequently, this information is not readily available, a fact amplified when the negotiator is not an expert in said area. It then becomes necessary to gather the requisite information to formulate a good opening offer. Although some basic research might yield beneficial results, particularly valuable information often comes from other people. But who should the negotiator contact and how willing will that person be to share the information?

Again, political skill aids in this endeavor. Because politically skilled individuals are socially astute, they are typically able to identify powerful and influential people. This description includes those with valuable information. Additionally, because politically skilled individuals are adept networkers, they often have made connections with these individuals and are in a position to call on them for input as they prepare for the negotiation. Further, if they haven't already established these connections their networking ability gives them the ability to do so, which gives them access to the information they need.

Strategy and Style

Another important thing to consider prior to engaging with the other party or parties is what strategy you will employ. This typically manifests in the use or implementation of a particular conflict resolution style. Scholars generally agree that these styles vary along two dimensions, assertiveness and cooperativeness, which result in five different styles.

- Avoiding: low assertiveness and low cooperativeness
- Accommodating: low assertiveness and high cooperativeness

- Compromising: moderate assertiveness and moderate cooperativeness
- Collaborating: high assertiveness and high cooperativeness
- Competing: high assertiveness and low cooperativeness

We can essentially ignore the avoiding approach, as employing this strategy would be akin to not negotiating. The accommodating approach is a style suited for those willing to give in on many issues for the sake of getting a deal. Compromising is a popular style as it occupies the middle ground. With this approach, negotiators attempt to reach an agreement by exchanging concessions such that each party gives up a little on some issues in order to get a little on other issues. A collaborating approach seeks to maximize the benefit for both parties by looking for ways to create value. Conversely, negotiators pursuing an aggressive, winner-take-all strategy are looking to claim as much value as possible for themselves.

It is tempting to look at the above styles and try to declare one approach better than the others. The reality is that the optimal selection of approach depends on several factors. One such factor is the negotiator's goals, which can vary depending on the situation. For example, at times it might be more or less important to consider the impact of the negotiation on the relationship with a counterpart. In a one-time negotiation, particularly one focused almost exclusively on a single issue like price, it is perfectly understandable to focus more on maximizing your own value than on the relationship with the other party. In such cases, you might rely more on a competing approach. However, if you are negotiating with someone you plan to do business with repeatedly in the future you might opt to be less competitive, even if it means sacrificing some value, in order to maintain a positive relationship and smooth the path for additional deals in the future.

This likely seems fairly straightforward, and to a degree it is. Just match the strategy to the situation. However, doing so is easier said than done. First, you need to be able to identify the elements of the situation and select the most appropriate style. Again, this takes a level of awareness provided by the social astuteness dimension of political skill. However, as it turns out, we tend to default to one of the five styles. So if you're naturally competitive, you'll tend to approach interactions in that frame. This means that in addition to being mindful of the situation, we need to be able to adjust our behavior to employ the appropriate style for a given situation. This degree of behavioral flexibility is a hallmark of politically skilled individuals, thanks to their interpersonal influence ability. Thus, when they recognize the style appropriate for the situation, they are able to calibrate their behavior accordingly and are less likely to revert to their "default" style during the interaction.

Power Dynamics

There are, of course, some limitations to the somewhat simplified strategy-situation analysis and matching we presented above. One limitation has to do with the power dynamics in the situation. Certainly, we recognize that negotiating with our boss differs from negotiating with a subordinate. Generally speaking, you'd be wise to be more accommodating in the former situation than in the latter. However, these power dynamics are somewhat obvious. Where this becomes more important is in situations where defined hierarchies are less obvious.

In every negotiation, each party has alternatives other than coming to an agreement. In the absence of an evident hierarchy, the relative power among the negotiating parties is determined by the strength of these alternatives. Consider a situation where one party has a very attractive alternative, but the other has an alternative they'd consider almost a worst-case scenario. Obviously, an aggressive, competitive style could benefit the party with a strong alternative, whereas the same approach might backfire on the other party, hindering an agreement and leaving them with their worst-case option.

Perceiving these differences in relative power and adjusting style/approach accordingly is critical to maximizing our chances of a beneficial agreement. Similar to many of the topics discussed above, this can (and should) be a part of the negotiation planning and preparation process. However, it is not always possible to determine the strength of the other party's alternative prior to engaging in the bargaining session (i.e., the trading of offers, etc.). In these instances, you have to rely on other information to determine the most appropriate strategy. But this does not mean that you should simply select a strategy and hope it works well.

Instead, you need to be able to read how things are unfolding during your interaction with the other party to get a sense of any potential power differences that are in play. Although some people will disclose their alternatives and see if you can match or beat the offer, not everyone will be so clear regarding their alternatives. In fact, at times, they might not even be able to articulate it. Thus, a great deal of social astuteness is required to determine the relative power among the parties during the negotiation, as it is often necessary to "read between the lines" provided through offers that are made and responses given to your offers.

Again, recognizing these differences is not enough. Should you realize that you are in a weaker position but have been employing an aggressive and competitive style, you will need to draw on interpersonal influence ability to adjust "on the fly." This can be extremely difficult to do in the middle of a negotiation, but it could be critical to your success maximizing value or even getting a deal. Even more important, making such an adjustment requires great skill and interpersonal savvy. An abrupt change in approach will send a clear signal to the other party that you have realized something is wrong. If they pick up on this, they might become more aggressive, akin to sharks sensing blood in the water. Instead, you need to be able to subtly shift your approach, assuring that you are managing the situation to your benefit.

Distributive versus Integrative Negotiations

Those of you familiar with some of the popular negotiation books available might have recognized that some of the above discussion touches on the differences between distributive and integrative negotiations. For those unfamiliar with these terms, distributive negotiation refers to when the process of reaching an agreement largely boils down to "dividing the pie," or determining how much of the available value each party will receive. Conversely, integrative negotiations are those in which it is essentially possible to come to an agreement that creates additional value, such that the "pie" is expanded.

Similar to our above arguments, political skill is beneficial to negotiators because it enables them to recognize whether the negotiation is distributive or integrative. Many negotiations contain multiple issues, some of which are distributive and others of which are integrative. Social astuteness enables negotiators to ask the appropriate questions to determine which issues fall into each category. Armed with this information, they can formulate offers that create additional value, which makes the other party more inclined to accept. Further, particularly politically skilled negotiators will be able to generate offers that create additional value *while* claiming more value for themselves. As a result, both parties walk away from the negotiation pleased with the outcome, even when one party might be viewed as having done better than the other.

Keeping Up Appearances

It is possible the suggestion that you can create additional value of which you then claim more seems somewhat manipulative, perhaps even unethical. That is a longer discussion than we have room for here, but we will note that such an outcome typically is more beneficial to your counterpart than if you had not created the additional value to be claimed. However, we also will admit that if it were apparent to your negotiating counterpart that this was transpiring, they probably wouldn't be quite as pleased as if they were kept in the dark about what you were up to. Thus, masking your true intentions, or at least part of them, could be critical to your success in both expanding the pie and claiming more of it.

To pull this off, however, requires political skill. More specifically, apparent sincerity enables politically skilled individuals to shroud any motives that could be construed as manipulative. As a result, when a politically skilled negotiator makes offers and claims that they are mutually beneficial, their counterparts find them genuine and believable, even if part of the intention in making the offer is to create more value to claim. The benefit of apparent sincerity in negotiations doesn't stop there, though.

Negotiations require great skill in projecting the appropriate image. As we discussed earlier, most of us have a more natural negotiating style to which we default during negotiations. Provided the negotiation in question calls for a strategy that matches our style, apparent sincerity might be considered less important (to a degree, but more on that in a moment). However, it is clear that we often will be presented with negotiation situations in which we need to employ a strategy counter to our natural tendency. In these instances, it is crucial that the strategy is executed in a believable manner. You can imagine what might transpire if someone who favors a more accommodating style and lacks political skill tries to negotiate with a competitive approach. Their aggressive plays and tactics won't be believable.

Instead of strength, the negotiator without political skill who attempts to operate with assertiveness runs the risk of signaling to their counterpart that they are feigning. This signal could prove disastrous. Even if they are operating from a position of strength and relative power advantage, their counterpart may be less inclined to yield. Instead, they might become more aggressive in an attempt to capitalize on a perceived weakness. In this scenario, at best we are likely to ultimately claim less value than we could have. At worst, however, we might entice such assertiveness from our counterpart that we prevent a deal from being made at all.

Finally, a large part of negotiations is building a rapport with counterparts and establishing a level of trust that facilitates sharing information. This flow of information is critical for developing creative solutions that expand value for those at the negotiating table. However, to get this information, you need to ask questions that uncover your counterpart's true interests—why they want what they want. And if they are to provide these answers, they will want to make sure that you can be trusted. Thus, even if you have pure and noble intentions, if your questions are delivered such that they aren't received this way, you are not likely to glean the information you need to reach an optimal agreement. Again, apparent sincerity can assure that things do not go awry, as the ability is not merely about masking but about the effective presentation of words and actions.

Keeping Your Cool

Earlier, we talked about the need for opening offers to be both aggressive and reasonable, as an initial offer too far outside the range of possible agreements runs the risk of pushing your counterpart away from the negotiating table. Now we'd like to consider the opposite side of that experience, where your counterpart makes a ridiculous first offer to you and how political skill can help you manage such a situation. Clearly, some people will be unfamiliar with the dangers this type of opening salvo creates. In fact, there are some cultures where such extreme offers are the norm. Thus, it's likely that you will be on the receiving end of an extreme, almost to the point of being offensive, opening offer or counteroffer at some point.

In such a situation, it can be tempting to believe that all hope for a deal is lost or that the goals you had set for the negotiation need to be tossed aside. And, if you are not careful, the feelings of panic or discouragement such an offer creates will be communicated via your facial expressions, body language, and tone. In some instances, such a strategic display of emotion could be beneficial by signaling to your counterpart that they are way off base. However, if not executed carefully, expressed emotions might instead signal that they have you "on the ropes" and embolden them in their aggressive approach. Similar to the instances we have outlined above, the combination of social astuteness, interpersonal influence, networking ability, and apparent sincerity enable the politically skilled negotiator to quickly recognize what is unfolding, calibrate their behavior accordingly, and display the behavior in a manner dictated by the situation.

Stress and emotions in negotiations extend beyond first offers, though. Indeed, certain topics and, unfortunately, certain people make negotiating very difficult. In these situations, things like the sensitivity of the issues in play or the abrasiveness of a counterpart can affect a negotiator in ways that limit their ability to maintain their composure. Beyond feelings of awkwardness and discomfort, these emotional tolls can derail agreements or, similar to overly aggressive offers, threaten to knock a negotiator off balance. Navigating these situations requires a great deal of self-regulation. Fortunately, research has shown that political skill acts as a buffer to stressors, such that their effect on politically skilled individuals is mitigated. Thus, in addition to enabling a negotiator to properly act in difficult situations and toward difficult people, political skill also helps to prevent these circumstances from getting "under their skin."

Multiparty and Team Negotiations

In discussing the ways in which political skill has beneficial impacts on negotiations, we have focused almost exclusively on one-on-one situations. However, it could be argued that political skill is even more important in multiparty and group negotiations.

Why? Well, none of the above is changed in a group negotiation. In fact, the importance of everything we have outlined thus far is typically only heightened with the addition of more people.

For example, in a multiparty situation the negotiator now has to consider the interests, potential strategies, and reactions, etc., of additional counterparts. Thus, heightened social astuteness becomes even more advantageous as the act of "connecting the dots" becomes more complex. Determining what could satisfy multiple parties as well as oneself is far more challenging than working out a deal between two people. Additionally, selecting a strategy can be more problematic as the power differential between you and one counterpart might suggest you employ an assertive style, while the relative power between you and another counterpart dictates that you be more accommodating. Balancing these competing demands requires a great deal of interpersonal savvy, which political skill provides.

Things are similarly complicated by group negotiations. Although you have a partner or partners to aid in the preparation and execution of a negotiation strategy, this often entails navigating interpersonal dynamics within a team so that you find yourself engaged in a "negotiation within the negotiation." As an example, consider the difficulty for President Kennedy during the Cuban Missile Crisis. Prior to actually negotiating with his Soviet counterpart, President Kennedy had to negotiate proposed solutions and strategies with his team. Reading the social dynamics of these situations is every bit as important as reading the dynamics in play with counterparts.

Further, additional challenges arise once you make it to the actual bargaining table. Although not always stated, there often is a hierarchy and power differential within the ranks of the counterpart group. Understanding if there is a "true" decision maker and what this person most values becomes key to obtaining an agreement and to unlocking the most value. Additionally, even though the other team is ostensibly on the same side, there could easily be (and often are) layered and competing interests among the group of counterparts. Because these aspects of the opposing group's dynamics are typically more difficult to uncover during preparation, it is critical to be able to decipher the differing statements and reactions within the counterpart group in order to best navigate the negotiation. Thus, as a social effectiveness construct, it is clear that political skill becomes even more important to ensure success when additional people are added to the already complex process of negotiating.

Conclusion

In sum, negotiation is a critical part of everyday life and a necessary aspect for a successful career. In fact, as we outlined in our opening example about Henry Kissinger, we argue that political skill can enable you to succeed where others have failed. Although you might never be called upon to negotiate peace and lasting change for a troubled region of the globe, we hope you will agree with us that political skill has value to you as a negotiator by enabling in you, like Kissinger, the ability to see the big picture, to read counterparts, to build relationships, and to effectively deploy behaviors so that you can both create additional value for all involved and—if and when you deem necessary—claim a little more of it for yourself as well.

Research Highlight

Solga, M., et al. (2015). "Political Skill in Job Negotiations: A Two-Study Constructive Replication." *International Journal of Conflict Management, 26*: 2–24.

Negotiations are a critical aspect of work life. This is certainly the case when initially joining a company, as negotiations determine things like starting pay. However, they also can be important when presented with relocation and job transfer opportunities within one's current company. Solga and colleagues examined both situations in a recent publication.

In the first study, they ran a laboratory-based simulation with college students, who were asked to negotiate the initial terms of a job. The researchers found that, regardless of the role the student played (i.e., employer or candidate), political skill was associated with better distributive negotiation outcomes. This indicates that politically skilled candidates will be more successful securing greater pay, while politically skilled employers will be more successful limiting the amount it costs to acquire new talent.

In the second study, the researchers examined a group of managers who had been nominated for a foreign assignment and given a chance to renegotiate their salary and benefit packages. The results of this study indicated that the more politically skilled managers were more likely to select a problem-solving approach as a negotiation strategy, which in turn was related to greater increases in annual salary and annual benefits. This suggests that politically skilled individuals know how to capitalize on negotiation opportunities by selecting a strategy that will generate objectively better outcomes.

In the second study, they replicated this finding and also found that negotiator political skill led to using a problem-solving negotiation strategy. Politically skilled individuals were more likely to choose problem solving as a negotiation strategy. The choice of problem solving was directly related to an increase of annual gross salary as well as to additional annual net benefits.

11

Influence through Digital Communications and Social Media

Technology continuously revises and shapes the way we conduct business. It is likely there are fewer handshakes closing business deals today than there were in the time before the internet made face-to-face communication unnecessary (but not necessarily less important). Take a moment to consider that. The handshake has always been, and still is, a symbol of agreement and trust between two parties. Yet we now find ourselves in a world where closing a deal with just a few mouse clicks and a digital signature is steadily becoming the norm. This substantial revision to business etiquette is possible because new technologies are so powerful that they somehow manage to warp the world, and the accompanying social norms, into their new ordering of society. The very idea of closing a business deal from a few hundred miles away, let alone from a different continent, and without some physical expression of agreement, would have been ludicrous just a short time ago—yet here we are.

Consider *smart*phones (or as they are now called once again: *phones*). It is easy to fall into the belief that the newest upgrades to this year's model of the iPhone are purely silicon, plastic, and glass. However, make no mistake, those upgrades being marketed to the masses also come in the shape of updated social norms, expectations, and altered (we hope, improved) human functioning. The evidence? Consider this: If you are not a digital native, it is likely that the only thing you carried out of your house on your first day of work was either a ring of keys and a wallet or perhaps a purse with basic sundries. Yesterday, however, when you left the house you carried a small, half-pound rectangular weight with you. Going to a meeting? Bring the phone. Going to sign papers in HR for a few minutes? Bring the phone. Going to the bathroom? Bring the phone. That is a profound change in our behavior, and it doesn't even consider the panic you feel upon finding out you left that half-pound chunk of plastic, metal, and glass at home.

Political skill was conceived purely as an interpersonal skill that could help us succeed in the workplace. It should be no surprise that this is still how we describe political skill. However, as the socially astute reader will undoubtedly have noticed, the advent of ubiquitous digital communications has affected the meaning, or at least broadened the scope, of what is considered *interpersonal.* Likewise, the rapid development of this new form of communication has generated ambiguity regarding the social norms governing how we interact in this new digital space. This means that those not actively seeking to understand the "new" rules of interaction are almost certainly sure to break them, most likely without even realizing their misstep.

Simon Sinek, author, speaker, and consultant, expresses this beautifully in a brief speech:

> When we show up to a meeting, or a lunch, or a dinner— with our colleagues, our clients, or our friends, or our families—and we put the phone on the table, we have announced to everyone in the room that they are not that important to us. And by the way, putting the phone upside down is not more polite.[1]

This is a new social norm. It is a simple rule: don't put your phone on the table. Note how many people do just that at your next dinner out with friends or colleagues. You may think this is being overblown and that it is not actually a norm. Certainly, it would be correct that this rule is not written in stone, and it has not been codified to the extent that social precepts like "Sneeze into your elbow," or "Look someone in the eye when talking to them." However, expect to see the next generation teaching their children to keep their phones off the table. Perhaps you already have seen this social norm in its earliest stages—being enforced upon adolescents—in the form of "No phones at the table." As phone users ourselves, we understand what it means to have that phone near us—we are either waiting for messages from friends, or we sit on that precipice where we are just a single notification away from tuning out of the current conversation. For these reasons, we tend to instinctively know that someone with a phone in their hands is less attentive and attuned to our current conversation.

In another striking illustration regarding how the mere presence of a phone can influence others, Simon Sinek acts out an exchange where he, the leader, is asked a question by an employee.[2] He first responds with a phone in his hand. He then repeats the exercise with his hands free. If you happen to have your phone handy (you know you do), take a moment to watch this in action and you will *feel* the difference between these two responses. However, the only variation is the presence of the phone. Sinek argues that the phone has a subconscious effect on us that makes those we speak to, while holding the phone, feel like they are *not* the most important thing to us in that moment. In this example, the only difference between making someone feel important and not important is a phone in our hands.

Think about this "rule" in relation to apparent sincerity. Even with extensive training, mentorship, and acting classes you may not be able to overcome the perceptions of insincerity that accompany a phone held in your hand. This may seem like an innocuous or even trivial example—who cares if you are holding a phone, right? However, it is important to realize that you might just be violating a new social more without even knowing it. With new technology come new norms, and successfully integrating them into our lives—including our social lives—is imperative.

This is the reason digital political skill is a necessary extension of the original concept. And it should be thought of just like that—not a replacement but an extension. It is a new set of rules that needs to be laid over top of the original game. The board is still the same and the basic moves operate as they always have; however, there are a few more rules and a few new pieces to keep track of, and this chapter will help you do just that.

The Expanded Rules

Chess is one of the most well-known games in the world. Its blend of deep strategic complexity mixed with an elegantly simple rule set makes chess a simple game to learn but a lifetime pursuit to master. The game itself was conceived over 1,000 years ago, likely around the sixth century. Surprisingly, the game played in 600 AD likely was very similar to the game we play today. Despite spreading across the globe by traders and conquering armies, the original version of chess remained remarkably stable over time. However, small revisions to the game, such as certain pieces acquiring new moves and thus opening up new strategies, substantially increased the complexity of the game and would give current players a strategic advantage over the old masters.

Let's examine two examples of these changes. First, in the original rules the pawn could only move forward one square. In contemporary chess the pawn can move forward two squares on its first move. This is a subtle change. Simply one additional square forward. However, consider how this changes the playing field. Both players can now advance their pawns forward more quickly, thus increasing the pace of the game and increasing the maneuverability of the back-line units. Similarly, the queen's move was very weak in chess's early conception, the rules only allowing her to step one space diagonally. Not until the fifteenth century did the queen gain the ability to wreak havoc across the board by moving in any direction for any number of spaces the player saw fit. In today's iteration of chess, players failing to capitalize on their queen's power are certain to be left behind or find themselves in a constant state of check.

We don't have the luxury of watching the rules of our game of office politics change over the course of a century. Even though we are firmly settled in the digital age, rules are still being tested and finalized *while* the game is being played. Don't fret about these changes—you are politically skilled; the same skills that brought you success in the past will aid you now and in the future.

It is important to consider the expanded "moves" available to us now that we are here, firmly set in the twenty-first century. At one point, influencing a group of people required several steps. Perhaps as a manager you had to communicate a meeting time to each member of your team, either in person, via phone calls, or by scheduling a standing meeting. Then, assuming everyone was available at the designated time, you would communicate your vision to them via speech and gesture. The time between conceiving your message and delivering it could be days, and at its fastest, hours (if you were lucky).

Today? That meeting can be scheduled and held within 20 minutes, thanks to the ubiquity of email (whether you should actually do this on a routine basis is another point entirely). Or, if you so choose, you could conceive of an idea and just send it out via email, no meeting required. Like the queen, where once you could only travel a short distance per move, now you can run the board in an instant. However, being able to move a queen farther than before meant that players needed to consider a great deal more vulnerabilities than if only a few squares were available. Similarly, the use of digital tools to influence others leaves you vulnerable in ways that were never quite as concerning in face-to-face interactions. Certainly, you *could* have spent too little time planning before a meeting in the past, but now planning can essentially be ignored before a meeting occurs because of the speed at which employees can be summoned.

Conveniently for the sake of this book, the original pieces in chess were divided into four divisions: infantry, cavalry, elephantry, and chariotry. Each of these represented what we now know as the pawn, knight, bishop, and rook—the names have changed, but they are generally the same. And so are our four dimensions of political skill; they remain the same in the digital realm as they do in all our other interpersonal interactions. However, they operate slightly differently in response to the new playing field.

Social Astuteness

The comedy duo known as Key & Peele hosted one of the most forward-thinking sketch comedy series of the 2000s. Their material covered a plethora of topics, but their most insightful work focused on social intersections. Their sharp and incisive wit brought to light issues facing society in a medium that was both humorous and insightful. In one telling sketch, two characters begin texting each other about meeting later that night at a bar.[3] However, both recipients grossly misunderstand the tone and meaning of the other's texts. It begins with simple misunderstandings, such as a friendly "whatever, I don't care [when we meet]," being interpreted as a flippant "WHATEVER, I don't care" (readers with teenaged children may be familiar with this expression). This quickly escalates to one character writing an angry text and his words being read instead as considerate and caring, quite the opposite of his intent. After misinterpreting a slew of texts, they eventually meet at the bar with wildly different interpretations of their earlier conversation. This sketch works so well because anyone who has texted others knows that misinterpreting someone's demeanor is all too common.

The most important nuance of this sketch is that the actors speak aloud both what they are writing to, and receiving from, each other. Thus, we get to see and hear Key angry and frustrated, literally spitting each word out as he types; Peele is soft-toned and relaxed, thinking that this is just a friendly conversation. The words on the text messages are identical, but it is the recipient who is imbuing the words with emotion. Herein lies the most important nuance of digital political skill.

In face-to-face communications, the responsibility of imbuing words with meaning is squarely on the shoulders of the speaker. True, the recipient's perceptions of those words matter, but the sender—through the use of apparent sincerity and genuineness—is responsible for ensuring the message is delivered with the appropriate tone.

In digital communications, the opposite tends to be true; the emotion and tone of the message are solely up to the recipient's perceptions, something that is all too often detached from the sender's original intent. Without hand gestures, facial expressions, and nuanced emphasis on words, the reader/recipient is left to interpret or ascribe meaning. Unfortunately, often we find ourselves searching for meaning where there is none.

Consider the following sentence:

Per my last email, I think we should consider addressing the problems in HR first.

Ah, yes, the dreaded "Per my last email." This might only be rivaled by "It has been brought to my attention," in all its euphemistic glory. It is possible that the sender of this email is not aware that writing "Per my last email" is usually read as a passive-aggressive way of saying *"Go back and read the last email, again."* Of course, the author of this email may have just wanted to save space by not rewriting an entire argument that has already been presented. It seems small, but consider how the otherwise innocuous words "We need to talk" take on quite a different meaning when received via email, text, or, as was more likely the case, on a folded sheet of notebook paper in middle school.

This likely has happened to you at some point. Perhaps it was in an email from a coworker or your boss. The text of the email evoked such a strong reaction that there was no other option than to immediately go and speak to that individual in person. When confronting the sender, you likely found that they were completely unaware of the tone underlying their email/text. Perhaps, in realizing your misinterpretation, you had to quickly cap your anger and think of a reason why you came to their office so as not to look sheepish.

Being socially astute means actively searching for clues to better understand the meaning of the communications you receive. If something seems off, that is your cue to take a step back and consider the entire situation. This could mean doing something as simple as rereading the text, determining if the writing is out of character for the sender, or a host of other tools that you would employ if you happened to be face-to-face with this person. We often find ourselves in situations where someone may come across as unintentionally harsh or hurtful. In those situations, we would do the same things: ask them to repeat themselves, determine if the words might have been taken out of context, or simply ask a follow-up question. Being socially astute will allow us to look past just the words on the screen and understand the context of the message.

Likewise, a socially astute sender recognizes the aforementioned problems and considers how to ensure their message is interpreted as intended. They do this by ensuring the patterns they create leave little room for their recipient to misunderstand the tone being set. This is best expressed through our choice of words and our phrasing, a facet of the interpersonal influence dimension of political skill.

Interpersonal Influence

Despite the physical distance between recipient and sender, it is possible to influence people via emails and texts. For example, have you ever received an email that unintentionally made you upset? Angry? If so, you are not alone. One interesting statistic is that 64 percent[4] of people have had a similar experience. It also means that you were influenced by the email and, thus, by the sender. To believe that text-based communications are a completely ineffective method of influencing others is to discount all forms of written communication. How many people have been stirred to action after reading insightful reporting about some wrongdoing? How many people have found solace and peace in the words of Thoreau? How many people extract lyrics from their favorite songs, sometimes completely leaving the music itself behind?

Words matter. Words have meaning. We should never discount the power of a new communication medium just because it is novel. However, many people do just that when it comes to email and text-based communications. It is likely that you have received a text from your boss that seemingly attempted to break every rule of grammar, spelling, punctuation, and presentation possible. It may have looked something like this:

hey janet – thanks for the update please submit your tps report by tues morning. -chuck

Whether the sender knows it or not, he has *influenced* the recipient. That influence may lead her to believe that the boss does not care that much, is slightly lazy (or terribly efficient maybe?), doesn't respect his subordinates, or a whole host of other potential thoughts. Again, as with social astuteness, when meaning is not clearly expressed, the recipient will conjure up the tone they think is appropriate. In this case, there are only a few clues that Chuck, the boss, leaves for his subordinate—mainly that his message was terse and haphazardly written. The lack of basic formatting suggests this is not a message he would have written to a superior, only to a subordinate. The simple fix is to follow the basic rules of grammar and style for communications.

Hey, Janet,

Thanks for the update! Please submit your TPS report by Tuesday morning.

Chuck

This is not a lesson in email etiquette. Instead, this is about recognizing that the way you address the recipient and present your message are going to affect how they are influenced by what you wrote. Clearly, this has a substantial tie-in with apparent sincerity, as we often need to not only choose the appropriate words but also the appropriate medium.

Apparent Sincerity

Consider the basic rules of etiquette that your parents likely taught you as you were growing up. One popular practice handed down through the generations is that we do not just say thank-you after receiving a gift, but we also send an aptly titled "thank-you note." This is a strange twist to a basic rule of social interaction that in-person, eye-to-eye communication is best. However, this is an instance in which writing a letter to our benevolent gift giver is a display of gratitude that goes above and beyond the personal thank-you.

This is not entirely surprising because writing is powerful. We convey some of our most important messages in writing: contracts, awards, and even love notes. Despite our penchant for using the pen to craft these staples of social life, we must consider how email and text messages have supplanted these other mediums. The time of writing letters to friends and family is nearly passed as email makes the process quick, easy, and instantly gratifying. Nonetheless, despite moving toward electronic communications, we still send wedding invitations in the mail—on physical, tangible, sheets of paper. Of course, this battle is not over. While wedding announcements have held strong, the graduation party invite has been offloaded to systems like Evite.com. Similarly, contracts for our jobs have retained their pen-and-paper roots (even if they are ultimately scanned and transferred electronically). The question is, how do we determine the appropriate medium to use when sending messages?

Apparent sincerity plays a substantial role in determining which occasions and agreements have held on to their physical roots, while others have gone the way of the Evite. For example, a wedding, by its very nature, centers around the idea of two people expressing a genuine love for each other. Also, it involves a couple asking sincerely that their friends and family participate in the event. It is likely that, because society is trained to expect physical copies of an invitation, an email invite would seem insincere or less formal. Contrast this with a graduation party invite: as opposed to a sincere request for your presence at a joyful yet solemn event, a graduation party invite is more akin to a sincere request for the presence of your wallet. The actual events and the sender's intents are different in substance and form. Now, let's bring this rule into the workplace.

Did you just decide to hire someone? Perhaps this candidate stood out among a pile of applicants and endured a grueling interview process that spanned multiple teams and levels in your organization. Do you send her an email saying "Congratulations"? Maybe. If you are a future colleague she just met during the interview process, this seems like the perfect medium to express your excitement about her joining the team. However, if you are a manager, it is likely that a phone call (one step closer to face-to-face interaction) would be more appropriate in this instance.

Similarly, if you are in the unenviable position of having to fire someone, do you do it via email? Unfortunately, people do get fired this way. If you are reading this and thinking that dismissing someone by email is absurd (as we are while writing it!), count yourself lucky to be a member of an organization (or, quite possibly, a generation) that would never consider such a callous, cold, impersonal act. We can imagine that, without a doubt, those emails likely include a version of the phrase "We are sorry to be giving you this news." Stating this in an email is simply not sincere. Genuine concern and real sincerity could be demonstrated by meeting with this person to deliver the news. We want to appear sincere and genuine in our communications, and firing someone via email is not going to allow us to express ourselves in this fashion. Whether this person is being let go because of a failure to perform or because of an unavoidable downsizing, email is not the way to appear sincere. Reprimanding via email makes the leader appear weak or, at best, passive and afraid of confrontation. Similarly, offering condolences because of the unavoidable layoffs seems thin and self-serving when communicated via a digital medium.

Thus, apparent sincerity revolves around the same ideas as it does in face-to-face interactions—expressing genuine emotions at the appropriate times and places. In the sphere of digital communications, we should not consider using digital communications to replace our basic face-to-face interactions. Even if it would seem easier—or, more likely, more comfortable—to address something via email, the urge must be resisted. Again, just because we can does not mean we should.

Networking Ability

As opposed to the other dimensions of digital political skill, networking ability in the digital age is more about knowing what *not to do*, instead of knowing what *to do*. Again, the ease with which technology allows us to connect has lowered the barrier to making connections to such a degree that we often take for granted connections in general. Whereas we once had to travel to meet someone at a sales conference or even something as simple as taking the elevator up to the next floor, we can now just send an email, connect with them through LinkedIn, or even friend them on Facebook. Although this is incredibly efficient, it likely reduces our follow-through (e.g., saving their business card, maintaining the relationship) and, thus, the strength of that relationship.

The bottom line is that adding another contact to LinkedIn does not count as networking. Instead, the skilled networker uses all of the digital networking tools available, like LinkedIn, to enhance their ability to forge strong relationships. In a previous chapter, Bill Clinton's Rolodex of business cards was discussed. He would pull out cards every night and make calls to maintain relationships. Now, instead of just blindly calling (although still not an awful strategy, just less efficient), we can use social media to determine when calls can be best placed. Did your contact just get a promotion? Was a child born or did their oldest just graduate high school? If you suffer from an inability to make small talk, networking in the digital age is an absolute gift as you can have all of your discussion topics planned out in advance.

Again, the basic rule of digital political skill applies here: *Just because I can, should I?* Yes, online social media sites essentially enable you to discard your Rolodex and your stack of business cards. Similarly, you can send "Happy Birthday!" messages once a year to give your connection a brief proof of life. But that's all it is—you are explicitly saying: "Hey, I still exist, too." Ten or more years ago, calling people on their birthday meant something—and it *still* means something today. Not only does it mean that you remembered their birthday, but that you made time to actually speak with them (this is why your mom calls you on your birthday...and why *you* should call her [*nudge*]). When we transition this type of relationship building to a few detached and soulless keystrokes, and especially after Facebook or LinkedIn explicitly warned you: TODAY IS XANDER'S BIRTHDAY, the intended sentiment is somewhat undermined. Sure, the message itself gets through, but the meaning that is associated with the time—your time—spent speaking together and catching up is completely lost.

Thus, it is best to still rely on many of the age-old techniques of forming and maintaining relationships while enhancing those practices with technology. Use these new technologies to make that process more efficient, not replace it.

On the flip side, many people wanting *to connect with you* will rely heavily upon social media because of its speed. Being less politically skilled, they will lean solely on digital networking to get the job done. Knowing this, it behooves the astute networker to ensure their online presence is representative of who they are as a person and that it matches how they would present themselves in person.

Have you recently been told you were getting a new boss? Did you google that person once you found out his or her name? This is becoming quite common practice because of the sheer amount of information available online. Each account we create, particularly social media accounts and blogs, can be found by anyone with just a few keystrokes and a few clicks of the mouse. One of the authors of this book did just this (with a group of other midlevel leaders) in 2010 when told the name of his incoming boss. On the first page of search results were a link to this leader's home page for their side job as a coach for a certain fitness-based multilevel marketing outfit that sells nutrition products. Included on this page was a series of shirtless before-and-after photos of the leader. The impression we walked away with was that here was a leader who was slightly narcissistic and most certainly going to try to hawk his wares to all of us. Thus, before this senior leader had even arrived for his first day of work, his first impression had *already* been made on many of his employees—and it was not flattering. (Author's note: As this leader progressed in the organization over the past decade, his fitness page was removed—mentors *are* a great thing).

The message here starts with an echo of that familiar warning: "Be careful what you post online." From a networking perspective, this matters because your *reputation* may start online. People who have never met you might be inclined to form impressions about you before ever meeting you because of what they find online. Networking in the digital age includes maintaining any online presences that you have created for yourself. More than just maintenance, it likely requires some form of cultivation or, at the very least, a serious review of the security options in place to ensure your profile remains as you desire, either private or public facing.

Good networkers will not shy away from having a presence online; instead they will leverage it to their advantage. Consider the fact that, barring your involvement in a high-level bank robbery that made the newspaper, you control much of what will show up on Google when people search for you. This is a unique advantage in terms of networking when compared to traditional conversation. Whereas in conversation you must give and take in terms of the direction the conversation, online profiles allow you to put everything you want others to know about you front and center. Is it likely that you will find any reason to discuss your love for Japanese garden design while speaking with a new subordinate? Probably not. That tidbit of information can be placed on your profile, or blog, or personal website, and if it interests your subordinate they might just bring it up. I once read that a potential leader in an organization I was interviewing loved performing magic for the children of his employees; that never would have come up in conversation, but I brought it up because it spoke to me about a leader who truly cares about his people and I wanted to know more.

Networking no longer starts with a handshake and a passing of business cards. It often starts days, weeks, or even months ahead of time. The politically skilled among us will ensure we are ready to start building connections at our new place of work before we even walk through the door.

Crossing Generations: Rules from the Bottom Up

The "rules" of society generally are taught from the top down. Parents teach their children not to cough without covering their mouths, to shake hands firmly, and to look people in the eye when speaking. Similarly, in organizations, we onboard new members of our team by teaching them the unspoken rules embedded in our organization's culture. The rules that we teach are simple and generally have existed for quite some time. Barring any major societal changes, or revisions to your organization's culture, your children will teach their own children to cover their mouths when coughing and those hired after you will teach new employees to smile when greeting clients.

This is not so in the digital space, as the "rules" governing email, text, and whatever the newest medium is have not been universally accepted or ingrained in the workplace. We are moving closer to accepting some universal principles on the "older" platforms like email, but even something so ubiquitous in today's workplace is rife with contradicting guidance. The inconsistency and lack of a coherent standard makes sense because these digital platforms have been simultaneously developed, introduced, and put to use almost immediately; we are building the plane while it is in flight. There has been little time to generate standards because the platforms themselves are created or updated faster than rules governing their use can be established.

Almost inevitably, by the time we adopt a new technology in the workplace, it has already been available as a personal tool for quite some time. Text messaging was once relegated to use only among friends and families. Now it is possible that you have texted coworkers, bosses, and subordinates. Are the rules the same? Almost certainly not. The platforms we use are changing, both in form (e.g., text messaging used to be cumbersome, with only nine keys available to type out a message) and social function (e.g., we use text for any number of social or work reasons now), so quickly that there often is little time to establish rules. Where once "Never text your subordinates" was good advice, now it is an accepted practice in many organizations. Thus, the speed at which the technology has been changing means the rule makers are those who have the most expertise with using these platforms in a social manner: the youngest members of our society.

For once, the rules are being pushed upward.

Consider texting. Perhaps you are a *seasoned* leader and when you began texting, your texts read much like the sentences in this book: complete sentences, correct grammar, accurate punctuation, and capitalized letters (*Thank you, editors, copy editors, and proofreaders!*). However, the texts you received from the younger people in your life looked quite different. Those messages may have arrived on your phone without any of basic grammatical features—particularly lacking capitalization and punctuation. You may have found the time to lament how <insert generation non grata here>'s writing skills have deteriorated to the point of no return. Instead of just telling your spouse about how your nephew can't write to save his life, the most socially astute among us will ask why we are receiving the error-laden texts. Is it *really* that bad out there in today's public schools?

Asking why is a reasonable question in many unfamiliar situations. If you were to walk into a business meeting in a foreign country marked by a culture quite distinct from your own, it is likely that you would be disoriented for a few moments (even if you are especially astute). It is unlikely that this disorientation would lead you to cast aside their cultural practices. Instead, you probably would attempt to adapt to their norms during your time working with them.

Consider the digital natives, or at least those who have been using a communication platform longer than you, to be a part of a culture somewhat foreign to your own. In doing so, give their practices some consideration. I am not suggesting that you stop writing in proper English when texting, but take a moment to consider that there may be a culture gap between you and them before casting their writing aside.

Let me give you an example. Many young users of text consider punctuation unnecessary. In fact, instead of using punctuation to delineate thoughts and ideas, they consider the use of punctuation as a way to emphasize a certain feeling or tone. Consider the period. If you happen to have a phone handy and access to messages from someone who is a digital native (or perhaps parents of a digital native), go back and read their texts. It is likely that no periods are there. Why? Digital natives consider periods to be an expression of anger. From our research (that is, discussing this issue with numerous digital natives), it is almost as if they actually read the punctuation mark as the word "period." Consider the differences below:

What you type: I don't want to go to the mall today.
What they read: I don't want to go to the mall today, *period.*

The tone of the message has changed quite a bit, right? There are employees in your organization, right now, who are operating under a set of digital rules (like the one above) that they take to be a *given.* It is likely that you are not aware of all of these rules and, as such, you might be violating them. Do you, as a leader, friend your employees on Facebook? That is a no-go. Are you following your subordinate's Instagram page? Probably not the best practice. Do you use text messaging in place of email, expecting employees to respond to work-related matters from their personal phone at a moment's notice? This tends to be considered unacceptable as well, though this is starting to change.

Violating these digital rules is not so much a faux pas as violating the social rules ingrained in our society because they are not clearly defined yet. But why not work toward learning the new rules? You can improve relations with your employees and gain a better understanding of the digital landscape. If you need an additional reason, it should be that if your employees are following these rules, so are your clients—and it makes sense to always make the best impression possible.

This is not an argument in favor of blindly accepting rules that are not compatible with your organization or your personal style as a leader. In my discussions with the digital natives it is clear that rules are being pushed up, then slightly revised, and finally pushed back down. Just a decade ago, as a junior member of your organization, it is unlikely that you would have ever considered texting a boss to be appropriate. Today, as a more senior leader in your organization, you may find yourself receiving texts from your subordinate. If the text looked something like, "hey – I am going to be late today – traffic is really bad sorry – jen," you might have been just a bit frustrated. Digital natives, for the most part, have learned that this lackadaisical, colloquial writing is generally an unacceptable business communication. However, they recognize that a text is a much more effective way to transmit time-sensitive information to someone when compared to email. In the confluence of these two competing demands (i.e., efficiency, professionalism), we find that digital natives in the workplace are doing their best to adapt their language to ours (again, this is because there are two prevailing cultures constantly crashing into each other in today's society).

Of course, digital natives are still employees, and they are not dumb. Whether it is because you instructed your subordinates that texts should still be sent in a professional manner, or because your subordinates want to play it safe, the texts you receive likely are going to meet your expectations. They will include capitalization, grammar, and correct spelling. They certainly will include periods (but only because they know you won't read it as "period"). Digital natives do this because they understand how to meld the rules, or they are at least willing to work toward a complete synthesis of the two. We should really laud them for this effort as we have *not* been as accommodating. Again, simply the idea of texting a supervisor likely is foreign to you. However, digital natives are pushing the issue a bit because they realize how efficient a means of communication it can be—in essence, they are not standing on ceremony.

Conclusion

The point of this? The socially astute among us will be seeking to understand the changes in the norms that govern digital communications. Not because they feel they have to oblige each new standard but so they can better understand their subordinates. This will ensure we can better shape our own personal messages directed toward our subordinates. It is vitally important to recognize that the rules are constantly changing. Digital platforms change quickly (consider how Facebook has slowly fallen out of favor with the youngest members of society), and new forms of communication undoubtedly will emerge in the next few years. One of those likely will become as ubiquitous as texting or Facebook—be ready to learn and recognize that those rules will be different than the ones that exist today.

Research Highlight

Momm, T., et al. (2010). "Political Skill and Emotional Cue Learning." *Personality and Individual Differences, 49*(5), 396–401.

Researchers have long examined how emotional expressions convey information about others' attitudes and intentions. Findings suggest that individuals vary in their ability to recognize emotions and that the context can influence how well others' cues are recognized. Like political skill, those with better emotion recognition ability experience greater effectiveness in the workplace. In their 2010 study, Momm and colleagues used this knowledge to test whether politically skilled individuals responded better to emotion recognition training than those who lacked political skill.

The authors found that politically skilled individuals were no better than others in recognizing emotional cues before the training. However, after completing the training, the politically skilled individuals outperformed the others. This suggests that politically skilled individuals are better able to adapt their skills to new domains and that they tend to be more socially perceptive.

Take these findings to heart. Recognizing and understanding the emotional cues of others is a critical social skill. This difficult task has only become more complex with the advent of online communication platforms that often remove most or all of the emotional expressive cues that are so prevalent in social interactions. No matter how skilled you believe you are in recognizing emotional cues in a face-to-face meeting, note that online communications are a new frontier. Take the time to learn how to recognize the new emotional cues and stay ahead of the game.

12

LEADERSHIP AND
TEAM PERFORMANCE

The concept of leadership has generated great interest for centuries, much of it devoted to a search for the characteristics of effective leaders. Even today, it is rare to pick up a newspaper or magazine and not read about leaders—presidents, military officers, corporate CEOs, coaches. And despite the variety of arenas where leadership manifests, most people seem to believe that the characteristics of effective leaders are constant—that the same qualities make for an effective five-star general, CEO of a major corporation in any line of business, or any other organization head.

But that's about where agreement ends. The qualities that really distinguish the most effective leaders—that specific set of characteristics—remain debatable.

We won't attempt a complete definition here, but we believe that political skill must be high on any useful characteristics list, because that is what makes it possible for a leader to effect critical and needed change. In this chapter, we discuss how political skill plays a central role in the leadership process, whether you are influencing another individual, leading a multibillion-dollar corporation, or coaching a football team.

The Main Ingredient in the Leadership Recipe

One constant element among definitions of leadership is *influence*: leaders define and interpret events, inspire, motivate, orchestrate, and coach as needed to achieve their goals. As President Harry S. Truman once said: "A leader...has the ability to get other people to do what they don't want to do and like it."[1]

If leadership is an influence process, then to be effective at it, you need at least two basic qualities. You need *political will*, that is, the desire, motivation, or propensity to exercise influence.[2] You also need *political skill*, the style and savvy to make the influence successful, which is a different matter entirely and crucial if you want to lead. Without the will to lead, political skill is an underutilized resource, smoothing your path in small ways. But without the skill to exercise influence effectively, political will is only an endless source of difficulty and disruption.

Political Skill and the Obscure Nature of Leader Style

Leader style is the manner in which leaders express particular behaviors, the way they do what they do that makes others perceive them as leaders and defer to them. Indeed, it has been suggested that the effectiveness of leaders is ultimately judged on the basis of their style, and that it is as much a matter of how they say things as of what they say. Leader style is another concept that has been discussed for years—again with no satisfactory consensus on its vital elements. The only conclusion reached by experts after years of examining leader style is that no one really knows exactly what it is or how it might affect leadership.

We suggest that leader style is basically encompassed in the concept of political skill. Like political skill, leader style involves the execution of behavior that contributes to effectiveness. But political skill also encompasses the necessary preconditions for effective behavior: the sound reading of a situation and astute understanding of what behavior is required—and of how to use that behavior to convey sincerity and concern for the common good. In addition, the networking component of political skill generates the social capital that is vital for success in group undertakings.

Leader Social Capital

Social capital is built by developing networks and their associated social connections and ties, which gives you access to resources you can use to advance your own aims. (This is not as manipulative as it sounds, of course, because leaders also make themselves available to others who are advancing goals that won't necessarily benefit the leader.) In general, the service is mutual; either simultaneously or over the long haul, everyone in a social network benefits from the connection. Politically skilled leaders accumulate extensive stores of social capital through their ability to embed themselves in diverse networks of talented and influential people. In one study, Fred Luthans and his associates (1988) identified networking as the activity successful managers engaged in most frequently, and it involved the use of political skill to gain competitive advantage.[3]

The alliances, coalitions, and friendship networks that leaders build inside and outside the organization contribute to a favorable reputation and significant positioning within the network, which allows for greater access to information, greater influence, and greater capacity to generate trust and cooperation. Politically skilled leaders are adept at the use of favors to inspire personal obligation and commitment from those around them. This all greatly increases their power and influence.

President Truman's definition—getting people to like doing what they don't want to do—is an appropriate way to think about leadership. It conjures up images of inspiration, motivation, coaching, and orchestration and facilitation of the effort of others to exercise influence in ways that maximize goal accomplishment. These behaviors reflect the style of politically skilled leaders. Interestingly, over the years, the question we have heard most often from managers in organizations (either in consulting projects or in seminars and classes) is, "How do you motivate employees?"

This perennial question brings to mind a variety of possible answers that relate to specific views on leadership. For some, motivating employees involves being very directive and almost dragging them in the right direction. For others, it involves reinforcing desired behaviors with rewards and extinguishing undesired behaviors by withholding rewards or applying sanctions and punishments. What these two views have in common is that they position the leader as making employees do things they really don't want to do.

However, Truman's mark of good leadership—to get people to do something they don't want to do *and to feel good about doing it*—seems to call for a different view. So, then, back to the question about how leaders motivate their people. Well, our best answer is—you don't. You can't do it by dragging or luring your team along; but you can create the conditions and circumstances whereby the team members will motivate themselves. How can you accomplish this? Political skill.

Leader style is encompassed in political skill, but exactly how does it play out in terms of leaders' efforts to use this style or political skill on others? In the next sections, we examine how politically skilled leaders make strategic use of rhetoric, language, and communication to accomplish their goals.

Political Skill and the Communication of Leadership

Leadership often involves defining and interpreting events for others. That makes the act of leadership, and even the very way we come to identify people as leaders, intertwine intricately with language, rhetoric, symbolism, and nonverbal communication, all of which are designed to convey certain images.

Louis Pondy captured a lot of truth when he called leadership a "language game"—an activity where meanings, not words, reflect what is being communicated.[4] For purposes of discussion, we separate leadership as communication into the three separate categories of language and rhetoric, symbolic behavior, and non-verbal behavior and strategic emotion communication. However, the influence process inherent in leadership is something that is brought to life by a strategic integration of all three.

Language and Rhetoric

Verbal language represents the most common way we commu-nicate with others in organizations and in everyday life and thus represents a strong basis of influence. The term *rhetoric* sums up both the process itself and the ambiguity people feel toward its deliberate use, as it denotes the effective use of words to persuade or influence others but further suggests an element of artificial eloquence and showy elaboration in the effort. Research in lead-ership has depicted charismatic leaders as strategically employing rhetoric to manage impressions and to influence, motivate, and persuade others.

Information that materializes through debate, conversation, and verbal interaction forms the basis for much of how people perceive their world, which makes language a potent form of social influence. Furthermore, it is through language that people experience the political realities of organizations, and this hap-pens largely through the efforts of leaders to interpret what goes on in the organization and make it meaningful—which is a major aspect of political skill.

Strategic communication—that is, interaction designed to accomplish specific goals and objectives—often deliber-ately employs ambiguity and confusion rather than clarity.

Counterintuitive though it may seem, strategic ambiguity in communication can be a way to manage meaning and thereby exercise influence by capitalizing on a lack of agreement concerning the meaning of activities and events in the organization. It is a matter of stock humor that politicians and top managers use intentional equivocation and vagueness in strategic efforts to protect their positions—but they do it in real life, too, and it often works—partly as a result of their political skill and partly as a result of their followers' lack of skill.

Conceptually, the core of political skill and communication is built on each party, leader and follower signaling their intent through strategic communication.[5] This communication is used to accomplish a variety of goals in organizations, only one of which may be clarity. Managers generally perceive one of their key roles as providing clarity, definition, and direction for employees, and this role is diminished if things are too clear. Therefore, in a situation where goals, procedures, and so forth are clear, managers with low to moderate political skill might actively engineer increased ambiguity so they could then provide solutions to clarify it. Managers with greater political skill, in contrast, might instead negotiate new roles that take advantage of existing clarity to provide hitherto unfeasible benefits to the organization.

Symbolic Behavior

Communication in organizations does far more than impart knowledge and information. It can be symbolic, intended to convey meanings and exercise influence. *Symbolic behavior* is concerned with how individuals create or participate in their environments by creating shared meanings and understandings. Jeffrey Pfeffer points out that it "operates fundamentally on the principle of illusion, in that using political language, settings, and ceremonies effectively elicits powerful emotions in people, and these emotions interfere with or becloud rational analysis."[6]

Symbolic behavior is an important part of how reputations

are created and maintained, and business leaders and politicians alike work hard at manipulating symbols to create the perception that they are powerful. Their resulting power is based less on reality than on appearance—but perception is reality in many cases, especially where suggestions and implied desires can be taken as commands. Symbolic communication is thus probably most effective in ambiguous working environments, which put most emphasis on the leaders' interpretations of events.

Through language, communication, and symbolic behavior, managers can switch the focus of their performance evaluation from outcomes to behaviors or simply render outcomes and behaviors indistinguishable. We argue that people tend to judge others by their goals, by what they are trying to do, and not by what they accomplish. If this is so, then leaders can orchestrate situations to their advantage through the strategic use of symbolism, language, and rhetoric. This led Jeffrey Pfeffer to conclude that political language is often effective because people are judged by their intent, by the outcome they are seeking, rather than by what they are actually doing.

Nonverbal Communication and Strategic Emotion

In addition to what you say, the way you say it—your facial expressions, nonverbal behavior, and the emotions you choose to demonstrate—can represent important and influential mechanisms of influence. Of the several processes that constitute strategic nonverbal influence, impression management is the most relevant, and nonverbal behavior plays a key role in forming impressions. Politically skilled individuals are the most successful at the effective execution of nonverbal communication because they present it in the most genuine and convincing manner.

The use of expressed emotion as a source of strategic influence is an important part of everyday life, particularly so on the job. You laugh at the boss's jokes whether or not you find them amusing; you sometimes feign anger with a coworker or sadness with a subordinate to strategically convey a certain image that will influence the reactions you receive. When things go wrong, you might act more distressed than you feel—even crying if it would be socially acceptable for you to do so—to divert wrath, thus making a strategic display of emotion designed to temper the response.

The content of displayed emotion is apparent in language, gestures, facial expressions, and tones of voice—displays Erving Goffman summed up as "control moves."[7] The use of emotion to control others or a situation is important, but it depends on *displayed* emotions. These are not necessarily the same as *experienced* emotions, and it is often counterproductive to allow genuine feelings to show. If your boss makes a comment that angers you, displaying anger openly based on what you are experiencing might conceivably cut through the problem and clear the air—but chances are it will only make things worse. Politically skilled individuals understand their emotions and express them in constructive ways.

Some jobs (airline flight attendant, for example) have formal rules that specify the proper emotions to express. It is simply part of the job to treat passengers in a friendly, smiling manner, and the flight attendant need not experience friendship to express good cheer. Although most workplaces don't have such explicit rules, most develop conventions as to when and to what extent emotions can or should be displayed.

Politically skilled individuals are able to control their emotional displays effectively and convincingly, and they have the ability to express emotions over an extended period of time, reflecting "emotional stamina." Indeed, politically skilled employees show lower levels of emotional labor in general than those without political skill.[8] Most simply, some leaders know just how and when to display emotion strategically, perhaps to show a softer side, such as when discussing a tragic event.

For example, as president, Bill Clinton was a master at the combination of rhetoric, nonverbal behavior, and strategic emotion to convey points he wished to make forcefully and, above all, convincingly. He is a living illustration of the relationship between political skill and communication. His supporters and detractors alike marveled at his ability to position himself in ways that ensured success and allowed him to emerge from the depths of adversity unscathed. Televised speeches, interviews, and press conferences constantly showed Clinton's strategic use of pauses for effect, nonverbal behavior, and control of his emotions to convey powerful and believable images. Clinton accomplished his reputational sleight of hand with his amazing level of political skill. Indeed, this reinforces the importance of spin, where reality is nonexistent and interpretations are manipulated through image management.

Applying Spin

Language, rhetoric, symbolic behavior, nonverbal communication, and the calculated demonstration of emotion can all help you exert social influence toward the people around you, whether an individual or a group. Where do you learn such behavior? Given the focus on rhetoric and symbolism through various communication media as characterizing what leaders do, perhaps business schools and in-house training departments should reconsider the most appropriate types of training to prepare future managers to fulfill their various roles. Because so much of managerial and leadership work focuses on symbols, images, and interpretation, we argue that the appropriate role for the manager may be closer to a motivational speaker than an accountant. The importance of language in the development and use of power and influence has led us to recommend acting and/or English classes to aspiring leaders.

If leaders can be compared to stage and screen actors, it should be no surprise that acting and drama classes seem to be catching on as management and leadership development, as we discussed in chapter 3. Numerous business schools seem to be taking stock of such demands on managers, offering courses in dealing with the media as useful vehicles for managing your career and enhancing the image of your company. Of course, the real key is not to learn just to *play* the role, however convincingly, but to *become* the person in the role, which will contribute to increased perceptions of authenticity; such authenticity is best carried out by people high in political skill.

Charisma and Political Skill

The characteristic we see associated with leadership probably more than any other is *charisma*, that special quality that tends to inspire people to follow a vision or course of action. Nonetheless, until a couple of decades ago, the leaders of large corporations were routinely selected on the basis of their performance track record, as though charisma either was unimportant or implied by their track record in lower management positions. That approach no longer works. Rakesh Khurana, who conducted one of the largest studies of CEO selection ever made, confirms that you can't just be a "competent manager" today and be selected to run a Fortune 500 company; you must be seen as a "charismatic leader."[9] He argues that this change in selection trend dates back to 1979, when Lee Iacocca took over the Chrysler Corporation and orchestrated its amazing turnaround, taking the corporation from ashes to success. In the process, he catapulted himself into celebrity status. Indeed, Khurana aptly notes, CEOs have become the equivalent of rock stars, and, promoted aggressively by the media, they regularly grace the covers of major magazines. The scandals at corporations such as Enron, Theranos, and WeWork, and the top executives involved, may be driven by creatures created, at least partially, by the national media.

Leader charisma has indeed been a topic of intense interest. However, if the ability to inspire people to action generally is what we mean by charisma, then it would seem to be encompassed in political skill. That is, politically skilled leaders are effective because they astutely read contexts and adjust, adapt, and calibrate their behavior to create the desired image; use their social capital to further reinforce their image; and do all this in a sincere, authentic, and convincing way. Thus viewed, charisma becomes simply part of the competency set we call political skill. We argue that leaders engage in active efforts to manage impressions of their charisma, and we maintain that it is political skill that allows such efforts to succeed.

Adding validation to the link between political skill and charisma is recent research that investigates followers' perceptions of leader charisma. Blickle and his colleagues found leader charisma to be an important component of followers' beliefs that their leader was effective.[10] Specifically, leaders who possessed the personality trait of inquisitiveness were seen as charismatic when they also possessed higher levels of political skill. This supports the idea that personal creativity benefits leaders when they also possess the political skill necessary to craft a vision in a manner that engages their followers.

When this vision is solidified in the eyes of followers, leaders are likely to be seen as transformational leaders. Transformational leadership occurs when people engage with others in such a way that leaders and followers raise each other to higher levels of motivation, ethics, and morality. More simply, the charisma of transformational leaders likely stimulates their followers' intellect, inspires their followers to act, and becomes a source of pride for their followers. Leaders' political skill has been found to positively predict transformational leadership. When looking at the relationships more closely, research has found that the social astuteness of the leader was more broadly associated with the characteristics of transformational leadership; specifically, charisma, individualized consideration, and intellectual stimulation. In contrast, the leader's interpersonal influence ability more likely increased only perceptions of charisma and intellectual stimulation.[11] While this directly shows political skill's importance in developing transformational leadership capabilities, it also shows that the mechanisms that predict this relationship are more nuanced and lend themselves to specific leadership development programs.

Political Skill and Top Executives

As we noted at the outset, organizations are political arenas. The practice of politics at work is a fact of life, and it only increases as you go up the corporate hierarchy. For top executives, political skill is not just beneficial for success and effectiveness, it is essential.

Much of what top executives do is symbolic in nature—and thus susceptible to image creation and manipulation. This observation is far from new; as Cyril Sofer pointed out:

> The would-be successful executive learns when to simulate enthusiasm, compassion, interest, concern, modesty, confidence, and mastery, when to smile, with whom to laugh, and how intimate to be with others. If the operation succeeds, he will have fabricated a personality in harmony with his environment.[12]

Successful managers learn to calibrate appropriate behaviors to fit situations, get to know all the right people, and develop the subtleties of the art of self-promotion. That is, managers and executives must consciously manage the image they project, and do so to perfection, with political skill. The social astuteness and interpersonal influence facets of political skill play key roles here, and, of course, none of this works if not done convincingly, that is, in an apparently sincere and genuine way.

And networking ability also is critical to managerial effectiveness. Effective managers spend much of their time on networking activities, much more than they devote to what would be considered traditional managerial activities. Leadership involves goal accomplishment with and through others, and the social capital that accrues to those with political skill is what makes it possible for leaders to be effective—thus further illustrating the critical role such skill plays in organizational life.

Accountability and Reputation

Political skill, accountability, trust, and reputation come together to enhance leader effectiveness. In chapter 7, we discussed the role of political skill in the development and maintenance of reputations, and the same observations apply here to leadership because of the immense role reputation plays in leaders' ability to be effective.

That is, political skill influences the formation of leader reputation and causes others to trust leaders more; also, those with greater trust tend to give leaders more leeway. So politically skilled leaders have the freedom to go beyond normal restrictions on behavior because their people expect them to do only things that benefit them and the organization. Unfortunately, that works only as long as it works; when the expectations are based on reality and leaders do engage only in beneficial behaviors, all is well, but leaders sometimes buy into the view that anything they do is by definition right. At that point, they easily slip into behaviors that help themselves but not the organization.

In fact, this is one way we can make sense of the corporate scandals at Enron, Theranos, and WeWork. For example, was Tyco CEO Dennis Kozlowski given more leeway to do what he wanted and held less accountable for the results because of his reputation, political skill, and the trust that they produced? It certainly seems so. He apparently felt no duty to his employer when he looted Tyco of millions of dollars in personal vacations, paintings, furnishings, and more.

Consider also the case of football coach Mike Price. Based on his winning record, Price was hired as head coach at the University of Alabama—which had been one of the most prestigious coaching jobs in the country since legendary coach Paul "Bear" Bryant built the team into a perennial college football powerhouse. But Price was fired before he ever coached a game at Alabama. His personal indiscretions before the season began reflected the behavior of someone who let his celebrity status go to his head; he seemed to believe he was not accountable for his actions. Maybe he thought he was going to be accountable only for how many games he won and not for his behavior off the field, even though he was a highly visible representative of the university. He may have thought of himself as following Bryant, who'd been cut a lot of slack concerning off-field behavior precisely because he did win a lot of football games—but Price hadn't won anything for Alabama yet, and he was operating in a social climate that had changed since Bryant's day.

To depict reputation simply, we can say it includes two components: performance and integrity. Today both are needed, whereas years ago, if leaders were very successful at producing the results they were measured by (profitability for executives, won-lost record for coaches, and the like), they could behave in just about any way they wanted and it was tolerated or even hushed up. Those leaders didn't have to be discreet, they just needed to post high performance records. High status and a good reputation still entice some leaders to engage in unethical, immoral, or illegal behavior, but nowadays leaders with true political skill are too astute to fall into the celebrity trap.

Celebrity CEOs are those who garner media attention for their current or past actions. Their effectiveness is ultimately measured in terms of their ability to translate their celebrity into long-term profitability and/or corporate reputation. One might point to Bill Gates as effective in turning his philanthropy and wealth into added value for his company. However, just as many celebrity CEOs are enticed by the glamour and fame of celebrity and experience the moral failings that accompany extreme hubris. Look no further than Harvey Weinstein, former CEO of the Weinstein Company, whose alleged sexual abuse of dozens of women occurred within his formal and informal duties as CEO of one of the most successful film production companies in the world.

Trust

Trust is another outcome of political skill that helps leaders be viewed favorably, even in cases where they fall short of a goal or demonstrate questionable behavior. Politically skilled leaders tend to engender trust, so if they do something wrong, people's initial reaction is to attribute the behavior to failed positive intentions, just bad luck, or someone else's doing. Leaders low in political skill, who might not be trusted or viewed as good people, find the public is quicker to attribute poor performance or questionable behavior to self-serving intentions.

The motives or intentions attributed to behavior affect people's reactions to it. The public might howl for punishment for someone who behaved immorally if they thought the misdeed was intentional but not if they thought it was caused by someone or something else. It is natural to like—as well as trust and believe in—politically skilled people, so when they do something wrong, the first instinct is to look for reasons it was not their fault.

The Martha Stewart case is an interesting one. Although she gained recognition as a television celebrity and a successful businesswoman, Stewart initially did not appear to have much political skill. It seems clear from the unsympathetic public reaction to the prison sentence she received after being found guilty of lying to federal investigators about a 2001 stock trade. They didn't seem to like, trust, or believe in her, and that reaction might have a lot to do with the media posturing Stewart engaged in throughout the legal proceedings, showing little if any remorse and no humility. She seemed to position herself as above the law, unapologetic, and indignant in her claims of innocence.

However, Stewart's experience in prison and fall from grace have appeared to humble her and provided her the basis from which to reclaim her popularity. We can now see Martha Stewart's ability to turn her public failings into resurgence as a smaller player in the media world by poking fun at her own "stuffy" image on shows like *Martha and Snoops Potluck Dinner Party* indicates she has seen the benefit, at least personally, from exercising humility in the media. This makes her appear more genuine and authentic.

While anecdotal evidence of the importance of trust in everyday relations abounds, examples, like the ones shared here, can lend themselves to ambiguous interpretation. Adding clarity to these links, however, is research supporting the underlying connection between political skill and trust. Treadway and his colleagues found that leader political skill increased the trust of their followers and ultimately reduced follower cynicism and improved employee commitment.[13] In environments already rife with distrust, politically skilled subordinates should also be more committed, less dissatisfied, and have their job performance impacted less than their skill-deficient colleagues'.

Political Skill of Elected Officials

Partisan politics has always been an arena for influence, whether it be face-to-face persuasion or coalition, or network building designed to muster sufficient support to push through, or block, legislation. Political skill is obviously important in politics, and it may well be the most important characteristic that distinguishes truly effective political leaders. Politicians operate in a world of image creation and management, where there is more interpretation of fact than reality, and their (or their advisors') ability to promote ideas with the proper spin is critical to success or even survival. Thus, politics provides an arena not that different from the way influence is exercised in organizations or life in general. Political skill is critically important in all these contexts; it is simply more widely recognized among those who compete for office.

For example, what characteristics do people look for in a US president? Obviously, there are about as many answers to this question as there are people to ask, but some interesting similarities appear across media polls. The American public seems to want a president who looks and acts presidential, which includes style, temperament, likability, and authenticity.

If candidates are perceived as phony, the public won't like them or vote for them; if candidates are perceived as charismatic, people tend to like them and will probably vote for them. So, liking candidates is important because people will probably trust them more and have more of a comfort level with them. Politically skilled candidates understand this well and are skillful at managing impressions that lead to favorable outcomes. Because politicians have a reputation for phoniness, the candidates who succeed appear sincere, genuine, and authentic—that is, the what-you-see-is-what-you-get sort of people. This is a key competency of the politically skilled, and it can make the difference in an election.

In *The Presidential Difference: Leadership Style from FDR to George W. Bush* (2004), Fred Greenstein evaluates our recent presidents on the important qualities of organizational capacity, vision, emotional intelligence, public communication, political skill, and cognitive style.[14] Particularly noteworthy for our purposes here are the latter three qualities.

Public communication involves masterful use of rhetoric, language, and symbolic behavior (as we discussed earlier in this chapter) to convey ideas. Franklin D. Roosevelt, John F. Kennedy, Ronald Reagan, and Bill Clinton were at their best as effective public communicators, according to Greenstein.

Greenstein refers to political skill as the assertive use of power to build support for policies and establish a reputation among others in the political arena for understanding and being able to work the political system to one's advantage. Lyndon Johnson is Greenstein's pick as the "master of political skill," with Roosevelt, Reagan, and Clinton also highly developed in this area. Harry S. Truman is not usually regarded as particularly noteworthy for political skill, but he did seem to perfect the art of persuasion. Greenstein points out that Truman developed "the art of getting along with others," and he quotes Truman as acknowledging that aspect of political skill: "Because of my efforts to get along with my associates I usually was able to get what I wanted."

Greenstein suggested that Roosevelt and Reagan provide excellent examples of how limitations in intelligence, or cognitive style, did not limit their presidential effectiveness, which was carried mostly by their excellent communication ability and political skill. Clinton's political skill was exceptional as well, but he was also known for his high level of intelligence.

Jo Silvester and her colleagues have engaged in an intriguing line of research confirming the importance of political skill for elected officials. Most interestingly, they (Silvester, Wyatt, and Randall, 2014) discovered that political skill was positively correlated to followers' perceptions of resilience and analytical skills.[15] That is, they were better able to handle the competing demands and complex problems their elected role challenged them with.

Political Skill in Higher Education

Increasingly, we see similarities between the arena of partisan and electoral politics and the arena of higher education at the top levels, where the skills and competencies required of university presidents involve more and more political adeptness. What used to get someone placed on the short list by search committees for university president positions was an impeccable set of academic credentials: a doctorate from a prestigious university followed by a distinguished record of accomplishment as a scholar in that field of study. Such credentials were believed to be necessary (and desirable) because they would command the respect and acceptance of the reputable scholars who served on the faculty of the university in question.

However, in recent years, particularly at public universities that depend on the state legislature for a portion of their budgets, university presidents are spending more of their time in the state capitals lobbying for increased budgets for faculty and staff salaries, adding or improving facilities, and the like. Influence ability, networks, connections, coalition building, and familiarity with the legislative process are real assets that can distinguish effective university presidents.

When Florida State University (FSU) hired Dr. T. K. Wetherell as its new president in 2002, it chose a community college president out of an impressive list of qualified candidates that included the president of Ohio State University and others of similarly high academic credentials. What made the difference? The time Wetherell had spent in the Florida state legislature, where he'd served for several years as the speaker of the house.

The local newspaper article that reported on the selection noted,

> A university president's political skills—knowing where to find the money, which legislators to see about new programs—mean more than academic credentials.... Connections were at least equally important in his selection....He has the ability to get people to trust him.... Wetherell has a good combination of intelligence, persuasiveness, and toughness....T. K. has a giant reputation.[16]

In an interview with T. K. Wetherell, we asked him to define political skill. He replied, "I think political skill is getting people to do things they would not normally try to do—get them to believe they can do the work." He added, "I am the weakest link in the chain—everyone else does the hard work. I simply know how to get them to do the work." When asked about leaders he regarded as having political skill, he mentioned both Clinton and Reagan and added, "I met Bill Clinton five times, and he is both charismatic and brilliant. When one combines charisma with ability, that is a powerful combination. When I spoke with Clinton, even in a room with fifty other people, he always made me feel that I was the most important and interesting person in the room. I met Reagan one time and he had that same presence about him. It's hard to define political skill, but people know it when they see it."

Political Skill and Team Leadership Performance

The word *leadership*, of course, raises the implicit question: Leadership of what? Leadership implies team, group, or unit performance. The dynamic changes in our global environment suggest that the role of leaders is changing. A leader, once described as an overseer or gatekeeper, is better described today as a coach or facilitator and a motivator. Instead of ensuring that employees are adhering to rigid, top-down bureaucratic rules, today's successful leaders are eliminating barriers—including structural impediments in the organization—and facilitating and orchestrating the efforts of employees toward collective goals. These changes inherently require managers to possess a different set of skills than their predecessors needed.

Without doubt, effective leaders in organizations today and in the future will need to focus their energies toward interpersonal activities such as coaching, coordination, and orchestration. This is especially true in team-based organizational settings, which are becoming more and more prevalent these days, where leader behavior plays a critical role in influencing team performance.

The type of participation that leaders foster among team members makes a big difference in overall performance. Teams with substantive participation (that is, the ones whose leaders relinquish some measure of control to subordinates) generally outperform teams where subordinate input is limited to consultation. Substantive participation means less direct control and new risk for the leader. Because of this, it might be that political skill can be used to constrain autonomous subordinates, so it is used as a subtle means of accomplishing influence aimed at goal achievement. The intuitive ability of politically skilled leaders to read their followers needs and not exhibit the same style toward every subordinate makes them particularly well-suited for leading in the team environment.

The relationship between leader political skill and team performance goes beyond the theoretical. One study examined the possibility that leader political skill might influence followers by making them feel greater support from the leader and the organization, which in turn would lead to greater trust in the leader and subsequently increased commitment to the organization. The researchers found that leader political skill did increase followers' perceptions of support, which led to trust, which subsequently affected follower commitment to the organization, all of which was believed to make the followers more attached and productive.[17]

Effective leadership is often defined in terms of the performance of the team being led, and politically skilled leaders can facilitate interaction, orchestrate action, inspire effort, and coach followers to perform better as a team. We extend those observations now to coaches who have led successful sports teams and to how they use political skill to increase team performance. We could select any of a number of sports and find successful coaches in each, but because of its tremendous popularity, we will focus on college football.

Certainly, college football history is rich in successful coaches, including such legends as Knute Rockne of Notre Dame and Paul "Bear" Bryant of Alabama, as well as famous more recent coaches such as Joe Paterno of Penn State and Bobby Bowden of Florida State. We do not have the space to examine the political skill of each of these men, but we believe that in Bobby Bowden we have a wonderful example, borne out by his account of his life. Indeed, Bowden is one of the winningest coaches in the history of Division I college football, and we argue he has been so successful because he both understands the game of football very well and is very politically skilled.

Just what are the necessary qualities of successful football coaches, and how do those qualities and characteristics get translated into their teams' actual performance? Bobby Bowden seems to possess many of the very same qualities we've described in politically skilled and effective corporate executives, politicians, and presidents. You don't have to spend much time with Bowden to find that he lives by a set of strong principles from which he does not stray. He is self-confident but never arrogant—in fact, he believes strongly in the importance of humility. Also, he is a person of integrity, enthusiasm, and loyalty, and he leads by example.

As Bowden admits, an important part of what he did as a football coach was to persuade and influence people who played for him, both in the recruitment process and in day-to-day coaching. He had to apply his political skill to ensure team effectiveness. He had to be able to size up athletes and be able to adjust his coaching style a bit to the unique needs and character of each player, and he had to do this with his assistant coaches as well. That is, he articulated a general philosophy that covered the whole team but adjusted within that general philosophy to the particular needs of different players and assistant coaches.

Bowden spent most of his career at the top of his profession, and it is not just because of his winning record. Reputations involve two broad categories of qualities. One is that you have to produce results, and Bowden clearly did that well. However, reputation is also made up of character, as outlined in chapter 7. Throughout his career Bowden also was considered a role model in this area. In sum, Bobby Bowden has extensive political skill, and he employed it quite effectively in dealing with the various constituents with whom he had to interact, including the players and coaches he led, the university presidents and athletic directors for whom he worked, and the boosters, the fans, and the local and national media. He is socially astute, interpersonally influential, and well positioned in his extensive network, and he always deals with people in genuine, sincere, and authentic ways, inspiring trust, confidence, and liking; a politically skilled person, indeed.

Conclusion

The skills needed to ensure leader effectiveness and subsequent group success have changed to emphasize factors such as social acuity and interpersonal astuteness, or what we call political skill. If you assume that one critical job of a leader is to eliminate barriers that might hinder team effectiveness, then some degree of political skill is essential. Leaders do not have to be intellectual geniuses to succeed, but they do need to have the "right stuff." We believe that political skill represents a critical element of the right stuff.

Research Highlight

Ahearn, K. K., et al. (2004). "Leader Political Skill and Team Performance." *Journal of Management, 30*(3): 309–27.

Much of our book has been about how political skill can help the individuals who possess it. However, as we close with a chapter on leadership, we want to highlight that being a politically skilled leader is beneficial for others as well.

For example, in a study of casework leaders in a large state child welfare system, leaders' political skill was a significant predictor of team performance, measured in terms of placement of children in legally final living arrangements. This relationship held even after controlling for the influences of leader experience, team member experience, average number of team placements, average age of children served, and average caseload of teams.[18]

Although the casework study was interesting and important, it provided no understanding of just how or why leader political skill influenced team performance.

This study was the first to empirically evaluate the link between leader political skill and follower performance. The results demonstrate that political skill is valuable when trying to lead a team. The authors suggested that it was the ability of these leaders to effectively manage relationships with their followers and fulfill the relation-based duties of leadership: attending to follower needs and encouraging participation. Each of these leadership duties requires the leader to exert less direct control over their employees and use indirect forms of influence to achieve team goals.

Epilogue

We hope you have enjoyed this guided tour through what we believe to be the fascinating world of political skill. You learned that part of political skill probably is something with which you are born, but part of it can be trained and developed, often and perhaps most effectively with the help of mentors or coaches. We encourage senior executive mentors and executive coaches to train and develop managers to increase their political skill. We think this will not only help individuals to be more effective but also will help organizations operate more efficiently and effectively.

We started this book by talking a little about organizational politics and how this term frequently, if not mostly, has been regarded as negative. Thus, it might have been natural to consider the term *political skill* also as being negative. However, our intention in over a quarter-century of work in this area has always been to characterize political skill as a positive set of competencies that can be used to make good things happen for both employees and organizations. Indeed, at its root, political skill simply is about influence at work (both in work settings and in terms of its operation). To realize success in your job and career, and for organizations to operate effectively, it is often necessary to influence others to see things your way and do what you want; that is, you need to manage shared meaning of things, so others see things the way you do or you want them to. When you develop the ability to do this well, you ensure effective influence over others because they do not perceive they are being influenced—rather, they believe they are doing the right thing because they see it as their own viewpoint.

A final issue we address here is whether political skill is inherently good and is only used to make good things happen, or if it also could be used to make bad things happen. Unfortunately, the answer is not exclusively one or the other but both. We wish the politically skilled would influence others to do only good things, but there are some with personal agendas who influence others to do bad things—sometimes very bad things. So, much like charisma, which we like to regard as a good quality or characteristic but can be used for good or bad, political skill also can be used for good or bad. As you develop your political skill, we hope you will use it for good.

NOTES

Chapter 1

1. Pfeffer, J. (1981). *Power in Organizations.* Boston: Pitman. Mintzberg, H. (1983). *Power in and Around Organizations.* Englewood Cliffs, NJ: Prentice Hall.
2. Goleman, D. (1995). *Emotional Intelligence.* New York: Bantam Books. Goleman, D. (1998). *Working with Emotional Intelligence.* New York: Bantam Books.
3. Hedlund, J., and Sternberg, R. J. (2000). "Too Many Intelligences? Integrating Social, Emotional, and Practical Intelligence." In R. Bar-On and J. Parker (eds.), *The Handbook of Emotional Intelligence.* San Francisco: Jossey-Bass, pp. 136–67.
4. Ferris, G. R., Treadway, D. C., Kolodinsky, R. W., Hochwarter, W. A., Kacmar, C. J., Douglas, C., and Frink, D. D. (2005). "Development and Validation of the Political Skill Inventory." *Journal of Management*, 31(1): 126–152.
5. Bacharach, S. B., and Lawler, E. J. (1980). *Power and Politics in Organizations.* San Francisco: Jossey-Bass.
6. Pfeffer, J. (1992). *Managing with Power: Politics and Influence in Organizations.* Boston: Harvard Business School Press.
7. Watkins, M. D. and Bazerman, M. H. (March 2003). "Predictable Surprises: The Disasters You Should Have Seen Coming." *Harvard Business Review*, pp. 72–80.
8. Carnegie, D., (1936). *How to Win Friends and Influence People.* New York: Simon & Schuster.

9. Ferris, G. R., et al. (2005). "Development and Validation of the Political Skill Inventory." *Journal of Management, 31*: 126–52.

Chapter 2

1. Rosch, E. H. (1973). "On the Internal Structure of Perceptual and Semantic Categories." *Cognitive Development and Acquisition of Language*, Elsevier, pp. 111–44.
2. McAllister, C. P., Ellen, B. P., and Ferris, G. R. (2018). "Social Influence Opportunity Recognition, Evaluation, and Capitalization: Increased Theoretical Specification through Political Skill's Dimensional Dynamics." *Journal of Management*, 44(5): 1926–52.

Chapter 3

1. A young Ivanka Trump appeared on the cover of the May 1997 edition of *Seventeen* magazine.
2. *Born Rich* is a 2003 documentary film about the experience of growing up in wealthy families.
3. Anett Grant and other experts provide additional insight into Ivanka Trump's speaking style at https://www.refinery29.com/en-us/2018/07/203710/ivanka-trump-voice-body-language-changes.
4. The 10,000-hour rule was popularized in Malcolm Gladwell's 2008 book *Outliers*. Note that in the ensuing years, researchers such as Anders Ericsson have taken issue with this statement as a too succinct summation of their research.
5. Quote taken from the King James version of the Bible, 1 Timothy 6:10.
6. *Poets & Quants* quote from poetsandquants.com/2018/07/22/inside-touchy-feely-stanfords-iconic-mba-course/.
7. Stanford's Most Famous Elective: gsb.stanford.edu/experience/learning/leadership/interpersonal-dynamics.
8. Stanford GSB's "Touchy Feely" course, more officially known as OB 374: Interpersonal Dynamics, focuses on the idea that forging relations is integral to successful management; poetsandquants.com/2018/07/22/inside-touchy-feely-stanfords-iconic-mba-course/.
9. The Influence Line: gsb.stanford.edu/experience/news-history/where-would-you-put-yourself-influence-line.
10. MacNamara, B. N., Hambrick, D. Z., and Oswald, F. L. (2014). "Deliberate Practice and Performance in Music, Games, Sports, Education, and Professions: A Meta-Analysis." *Psychological Science, 25*: 1608–18.

11. Mueller, B., and Shepherd, D. A. (2012). "Learning from Failure: How Entrepreneurial Failure Aids in the Development of Opportunity Recognition Expertise." *Frontiers of Entrepreneurship Research, 32*: 1–14.
12. Ozgen, E., and Baron, R. A. (2007). "Social Sources of Information in Opportunity Recognition: Effects of Mentors, Industry Networks, and Professional Forums." *Journal of Business Venturing, 22*(2):174–92.
13. Lombardo, M. M., Ruderman, M. N., and McCauley, C. D. (1988). "Explanations of Success and Derailment in Upper-Level Management Positions." *Journal of Business and Psychology, 2*(3): 199–216.
14. *Sherlock*, "The Hounds of Baskerville." Series 2, Episode 2. Directed by Paul McGuigan. Written by Mark Gatiss. BBC, January 8, 2012.
15. Annie Murphy Paul's (2012) article in *Time* magazine, "How to Increase Your Powers of Observation," is a succinct and helpful review of how to get started making observations in the workplace.
16. Michael Simmons's five-hour rule; entrepreneur.com/article/317602.
17. Bandura, A. (1977). *Social Learning Theory*. Upper Saddle River, NJ: Prentice-Hall; Burke, M. J., and Day, R. R. (1986). "A Cumulative Study of the Effectiveness of Managerial Training." *Journal of Applied Psychology, 71*(2): 232–45; Harrison, J. K. (1992). "Individual and Combined Effects of Behavior Modeling and the Cultural Assimilator in Cross-Cultural Management Training." *Journal of Applied Psychology, 77*(6): 952–62.
18. Ferrazzi, K. (2001). *Never Eat Alone*. New York: Crown Business, p. 40.
19. Drake, G. (February 10, 1987). "Acting Classes for the Political World." *New York Times*, p. 22.

Chapter 4

1. Gallup (2017). Presidential approval ratings—Barack Obama. Retrieved from news.gallup.com/poll.
2. Kpundeh, S. J. (1998). "Political Will in Fighting Corruption." In S. Kpundeh and I. Hors (eds.), *Corruption and Integrity Improvement Initiatives in Developing Countries* (pp. 91–110), United Nations Development Programme.
3. Post, L. A., Raile, A. N. W., and Raile, E. D. (2010). "Defining Political Will." *Politics and Policy, 38*: 653–76.
4. Treadway, D. C. (2012). "Political Will in Organizations." In G. R. Ferris and D. C. Treadway (eds.), *Politics in Organizations: Theory and Research Considerations*. New York: Routledge, p. 533.
5. Kapoutsis, I., et al. (2017). "Political Will in Organizations: Theoretical Construct Development and Empirical Validation." *Journal of Management 43*: 2252–80.

6. Hammergren, L. (1998). *Political Will, Constituency Building, and Public Support in Rule of Law Programs.* Center for Democracy Governance; Bureau for Global Programs, Field Support and Research, US Agency for International Development, PN-ACD-023.
7. Shaughnessy, B. A., et al. (2017). "An Integrative Social Network—Political Conceptualization of Informal Leadership: Performance Consequences of Need for Power, Informal Leadership, and Political Skill in a Mediated Moderation Model." *Journal of Leadership and Organizational Studies, 24*(1): 83–94.
8. House, R. J., and Howell, J. M. (1992). "Personality and Charismatic Leadership." *The Leadership Quarterly, 3*(2): 81–108.
9. Christie, R. C. (1970). "Scale Construction." In R. Christie and F. L. Geis (eds.), *Studies in Machiavellianism.* San Diego, CA: Academic Press, pp. 10–34.

Chapter 5

1. Higgins, C. A., Judge, T. A., and Ferris, G. R. (2003). "Influence Tactics and Work Outcomes: A Meta-Analysis." *Journal of Organizational Behavior, 24*: 89–106.
2. Hugo Münsterberg was a German American psychologist. He was one of the pioneers in applied psychology, extending his research and theories to industrial/organizational, legal, medical, clinical, educational, and business settings.
3. Gilmore, D. C., et al. (1999). "Impression Management Tactics." In R. W. Eder and M. M. Harris (eds.), *The Employment Interview Handbook.* Thousand Oaks, CA: Sage Publications, pp. 321–36.
4. Higgins, C. A. (2000). "The Effect of Applicant Influence Tactics on Recruiter Perceptions of Fit." Unpublished doctoral dissertation, Department of Management and Organizations, University of Iowa.
5. Gilmore, D. C., and Ferris, G. R. (1989). "The Effects of Applicant Impression Management Tactics on Interviewer Judgments." *Journal of Management, 15*: 557–64.
6. Treadway, D. C., et al. (2014). "The Roles of Recruiter Political Skill and Performance Resource Leveraging in NCAA Football Recruitment Effectiveness." *Journal of Management, 40*(6): 1607–26.
7. Marchica, J. (2004). *The Accountable Organization.* Palo Alto: Davies Black, p, 73.
8. Kaplan, D. M. (2008). "Political Choices: The Role of Political Skill in Occupational Choice." *The Career Development International, 13*(1): 46–55.
9. Breland, J. W., et al. (2017). "The Effect of Applicant Political Skill on the Race Dissimilarity-Recruiter Recommendations Relationship. *Human Resource Management Journal, 27*(3): 350–65.

10. Huang, L., Frideger, M., and Pearce, J. L. (2013). "Political Skill: Explaining the Effects of Nonnative Accent on Managerial Hiring and Entrepreneurial Investment Decisions. *Journal of Applied Psychology, 98*(6): 1005–17.
11. Shaughnessy, B. A., et al. (2011). "Influence and Promotability: The Importance of Female Political Skill." *Journal of Managerial Psychology,* 26(7): 584–603.

Chapter 6

1. Frink, D. D., and Ferris, G.R. (1998). "Accountability, Impression Management, and Goal Setting in the Performance Evaluation Process." *Human Relations, 51*: 1259–83.
2. Ferris, G. R., et al. (1994). "Subordinate Influence and the Performance Evaluation Process: Test of a Model." *Organizational Behavior and Human Decision Processes, 58*: 101–35.
3. Treadway, D. C., et al. (2007). "The Moderating Role of Subordinate Political Skill on Supervisors' Impressions of Subordinate Ingratiation and Ratings of Subordinate Interpersonal Facilitation." *Journal of Applied Psychology, 92*(3): 848–55.
4. Fang, R., Chi, L., Chen, M., and Baron, R.A. (2014). "Bringing Political Skill into Social Networks: Findings from a Field Study of Entrepreneurs." *Journal of Management Studies, 52*(2): 175–212.
5. Spence, A. M. (1974). *Market Signaling: Informational Transfer in Hiring and Related Screening Processes.* Cambridge, MA: Harvard University Press.
6. Wright, J. P. (1979). *On a Clear Day You Can See General Motors.* New York: Avon Books.
7. Gould, S., and Penley, L. E. (1984). "Career Strategies and Salary Progression: A Study of Their Relationship in a Municipal Bureaucracy." *Organizational Behavior and Human Performance, 34*: 244–65.
8. Kipnis, D., and Schmidt, S. M. (1988). "Upward Influence Styles: Relationships with Performance Evaluations, Salary, and Stress." *Administrative Science Quarterly, 33*: 528–42.
9. Bartol, K. M., and Martin, D. C. (1990). "When Politics Pays: Factors Influencing Managerial Compensation Decisions." *Personnel Psychology, 43*: 599–614.
10. "Up and Out: Rude Awakenings Come Early." *Chicago Tribune,* November 10, 1995, Section 4, p. 3.
11. "Job Security: Collect Those Brownie Points." *Chicago Tribune,* March 4, 1996, Section 3, p. 3.

Chapter 7

1. Merriam-Webster. merriam-webster.com/dictionary/reputation.
2. Seibert, S. E., Kraimer, M. L., and Liden, R. C. (2001). "A Social Capital Theory of Career Success." *Academy of Management Journal*, 44(2): 219–37.
3. Wihler, A., Blickle, G., Ellen III, B. P., Hochwarter, W. A., & Ferris, G. R. (2017). Personal initiative and job performance evaluations: Role of political skill in opportunity recognition and capitalization. *Journal of Management*, 43(5), 1388–1420.
4. Goffman, E. (1959). *The Presentation of Self in Everyday Life*. New York: Doubleday.
5. Spence, M. (1973). "Job Market Signaling." *Quarterly Journal of Economics*, 87(3): 355–74.
6. Wihler, A., et al. (2017). "Personal Initiative and Job Performance Evaluations: Role of Political Skill in Opportunity Recognition and Capitalization." *Journal of Management*, 43(5): 1388–1420.
7. Logan, D. A. (2001). "Libel Law in the Trenches: Reflections on Current Data on Libel Litigation." *Virginia Law Review*, 8: 503–29.
8. Fombrun, C. J. (1996). *Reputation: Realizing Value from the Corporate Image*. Cambridge, MA: Harvard Business School Press.

Chapter 8

1. Fortnite closes in on 250 million players: pcgamesn.com/fortnite/fortnite-battle-royale-player-numbers.
2. Fortnite usage and revenue statistics: businessofapps.com/data/fortnite-statistics/.
3. Polygon's report on the working conditions at Epic provided the basis for the introduction to this chapter: polygon.com/2019/4/23/18507750/fortnite-work-crunch-epic-games.
4. American Institute of Stress, 2019, stress.org/workplace-stress.
5. The long-term effects of stress in the workplace are well reported by the *Atlantic*: theatlantic.com/business/archive/2015/02/the-alarming-long-term-consequences-of-workplace-stress/385397/.
6. Sifferlin, Alexandra. "Why stress makes it harder to kick the common cold." *Time*, April 3, 2012. http://healthland.time.com/2012/04/03/why-stress-makes-it-harder-to-kick-the-common-cold/.
7. On the virtues of adaptability: hbr.org/2011/07/adaptability-the-new-competitive-advantage.
8. Seligman, M. E. P., and Campbell, B. A. (1965). "Effect of Intensity and Duration of Punishment on Extinction of an Avoidance Response." *Journal of Comparative and Physiological Psychology*, 59(2): 295–97.

Chapter 9

1. Hill, R. A., and Dunbar, R. I. M. (2003). "Social Network Size in Humans." *Human Nature, 14*: 53–72.
2. Flap, H., and Volker, B. (2001). "Goal Specific Social Capital and Job Satisfaction: Effects of Different Types of Networks on Instrumental and Social Aspects of Work." *Social Networks, 23*: 297–320.
3. Leana, C. R., and Pil, F. K. (2006). "Social Capital and Organizational Performance: Evidence from Urban Public Schools." *Organization Science, 17*(3): 313–416.
4. Fang, R., et al. (2015). "Integrating Personality and Social Networks: A Meta-Analysis of Personality, Network Position, and Work Outcomes in Organizations." *Organization Science, 26*: 1243–60.
5. Mulki, J. P., et al. (2008). "Workplace Isolation, Salesperson Commitment, and Job Performance." *Journal of Personal Selling & Sales Management, 28*: 67–78.
6. Tandoc, E. C., Ferrucci, P., and Duffy, M. (2015). "Facebook Use, Envy, and Depression among College Students: Is Facebooking Depressing?" *Computers in Human Behavior, 43*: 139–46; Krasnova, H., et al. (2013). *"Envy on Facebook: A Hidden Threat to Users' Life Satisfaction?" Proceedings of the 11th International Conference on Wirtschaftsinformatik (WI2013)*, Universität Leipzig, Germany.
7. Cullen, K. L., Gerbasi, A., and Chrobot-Mason, D. (2018). "Thriving in Central Positions: The Role of Political Skill." *Journal of Management, 44*: 682–706.
8. American Time Use Survey, 2015; bls.gov/tus/.
9. Sparrowe, R., et al. (2001)." Social Networks and the Performance of Individuals and Groups." *Academy of Management Journal, 44*: 316–25.
10. Brass, D. J., and Krackhardt, D. M. (2012). "Power, Politics, and Social Networks in Organizations." In G. R. Ferris and D. C. Treadway (eds.), *Politics in Organizations: Theory and Research Considerations* (SIOP Frontier Series volume). New York: Routledge/Taylor and Francis, pp. 355–75.
11. Simpson, B., Markovsky, B., and Steketee, M. (2011). "Power and the Perception of Social Networks," *Social Networks, 33*: 166–71.
12. Casciaro, T. (1998). "Seeing Things Clearly: Social Structure, Personality, and Accuracy in Social Network Perception." *Social Networks, 20*: 331–51.
13. Casciaro, T., Carley, K. M., and Krackhardt, D. (1999). "Positive Affectivity and Accuracy in Social Network Perception." *Motivation and Emotion, 23*(4): 285–306.

14. Brouer, R. L., et al. (2009). "The Moderating Effect of Political Skill on the Demographic Dissimilarity–Leader Member Exchange Quality Relationship." *The Leadership Quarterly, 20*: 61–9.
15. Luo, Y. (1997). "Guanxi: Principles, Philosophies, and Implications." *Human Systems Management, 16*: 43–52.
16. Wei, L. Q., et al. (2010). "Political Skill, Supervisor-Subordinate Guanxi and Career Prospects in Chinese Firms." *Journal of Management Studies, 47*: 437–54.
17. Li, J., Sun, G., and Cheng, Z. (2017). *Journal of Business Ethics, 41*: 551–62.
18. Treadway, D. C., et al. (2010). "The Interactive Effects of Political Skill and Future Time Perspective on Career and Community Networking Behavior." *Social Networks, 32*: 138–47.
19. Treadway, D. C., et al. (2013). "Social Influence and Interpersonal Power in Organizations: Roles of Performance and Political Skill in Two Studies." *Journal of Management, 39*(6): 1529–53.
20. Shaughnessy, B. A., et al. (2017). "Informal Leadership Status and Individual Performance: The Roles of Political Skill and Political Will." *Journal of Leadership & Organizational Studies*, pp. 83–94.

Chapter 10

1. Ian Douglas Smith (April 8, 1919–November 20, 2007) served as prime minister of Rhodesia (now Zimbabwe) from 1964 to 1979. He believed that Rhodesia should continue to be ruled by its European-descended minority, but he was forced to concede a power-sharing government when support from South Africa and Portugal ended.
2. Sebenius, James K., R. Nicholas Burns, and Robert H. Mnookin (with a forward by Henry A. Kissinger). *Kissinger the Negotiator: Lessons from Dealmaking at the Highest Level.* New York: HarperCollins, 2018.

Chapter 11

1. Speech by Simon Sinek given on October 17, 2016, at the Data Marketing & Analytics (DMA) "&Then" conference in Los Angeles, CA; https://www.youtube.com/watch?v=g5MduPwLT5U.
2. This is illustrated in the same speech referenced above.
3. This is a brilliant sketch by Key & Peele (note that it is not-safe-for-work or the ears of little ones): https://www.youtube.com/watch?v=naleynXS7yo.
4. The data for this infographic was provided by CPP (creators of the Myers-Briggs personality indicator) and Sendmail: ragan.com/infographic-how-and-why-emails-get-misinterpreted/.

Chapter 12

1. Matthews, C. (1988). *Hardball: How Politics Is Played Told by One Who Knows the Game.* New York: Harper & Row, p. 195.
2. Mintzberg, H. (1983). *Power in and Around Organizations.* Englewood Cliffs, NJ: Prentice-Hall.
3. Luthans, F., Hodgetts, R. M., and Rosenkrantz, S. A. (1988). *Real Managers.* Cambridge, MA: Ballinger Publishing.
4. Pondy, L. R. (1978). "Leadership as a Language Game." In M. W. McCall and M. M. Lombardo (eds.), *Leadership: Where Else Can We Go?* Durham, NC: Duke University Press, pp. 87–99.
5. Treadway, D. C., et al. (2008). "The Role of Politics and Political Behavior in the Development and Performance of LMX Relationships: A Multi-Level Approach." In G. B. Graen and J. A. Graen (eds.), *Knowledge-Driven Corporation: Complex Creative Destruction.* Charlotte, NC: Information Age Publishing, pp. 145–80.
6. Pfeffer, J. (1992). *Managing with Power: Politics and Influence in Organizations.* Boston: Harvard Business School Press, p. 279.
7. Goffman, E. (1959). *The Presentation of Self in Everyday Life.* Garden City, NY: Doubleday.
8. Liu, Y., et al. (2004). "Dispositional Antecedents and Consequences of Emotional Labor at Work." *Journal of Leadership and Organizational Studies,* 10(4): 12–25.
9. Khurana, R. (2002). *Searching for a Corporate Savior: The Irrational Quest for Charismatic CEOs.* Princeton, NJ: Princeton University Press.
10. Blickle, G., et al. (2014). "Inquisitiveness, Political Skill, Charisma, and Effectiveness." *International Journal of Selection and Assessment,* 22: 272–85.
11. Brouer, R., Chiu, C., and Wang, L. (2016). "Political Skill Dimensions and Transformational Leadership in China," *Journal of Managerial Psychology,* 31(6): 1040–56.
12. Sofer, C. (1970). *Men in Mid-Career: A Study of British Managers and Technical Specialties.* Cambridge, England: Cambridge University Press, p. 61.
13. Treadway, D. C., et al. (2004). "Leader Political Skill and Employee Reactions." *The Leadership Quarterly,* 15: 493–513.
14. Greenstein, F. I. (2004). *The presidential difference: Leadership style from FDR to George W. Bush.* Princeton, NJ: Princeton University Press, p. 40.
15. Silvester, J., Wyatt, M., and Randall, R. (2013). "Politician Personality, Machiavellianism, and Political Skill as Predictors of Performance Ratings in Political Roles." *Journal of Occupational and Organizational Psychology,* 87(2): 258–79.

16. Cotterell, B. (December 19, 2002). "Political Skills Important for Job." *Tallahassee Democrat*, 4A.
17. Ahearn, K. K., et al. (2004). "Leader Political Skill and Team Performance." *Journal of Management*, *30*: 309–27.
18. Treadway, D. C., et al. (2004). "Leader Political Skill and Employee Reactions." *The Leadership Quarterly*, *15*: 493–513.

INDEX

employment interview: fit and,
100–101; implicit rules of
engagement in, 121; impression
management in, 102;
interpersonal influence in, 102;
political skill and, 104–106;
research on, 104–106
Ericsson, Anders, 53
executive coaching, 58–60
executive derailment, 59
experience, 31
experienced emotions, 230
expressed emotions, 199, 229

F
feedback, 49–50, 53–58, 60, 68, 76;
executive coaching and, 60; filmed
role-playing with, 63–64; social
astuteness and, 63–66; videotape,
60, 64
feedback sessions, 63
fit: of CEOs, 106–107; employment
interview and, 100–101; in
interviewing context, 108–110;
nature of, 100; political skill
and, 101–103; potential *vs*, 123;
selection-based on, 99–100; of
university professors, 107–108
flexibility, 11, 60, 124, 135, 180;
adaptation and, 156–157;
behavioral, 66–67, 75, 120, 126,
194
Fortnite, 149–150
Fortune 500 firms, characteristics of,
124
friendships, 10, 33, 48, 103, 184

G
Gandhi, Mahatma, 85
Gates, Bill, 236
genuineness, 12, 209; developing of,
72–76
Gerstner, Lou, 106

Gladwell, Malcolm, 52
goal assessment, 36–38
goal setting, 117–118
Goffman, Erving, 141, 230
Goleman, Daniel, 7
Gore, Al, 13–14
Grant, Anett, 49
Greenberg, Julia, 163
Greenstein, Fred, 239–240
Grunick, Tom, 14

H
Harris, K. J., 130–131
Hayward, Tony, 73
Helyar, John, xviii
higher education, 240–241
higher-quality relationships, 77, 148
high political skill, 67, 73, 85, 88, 90
hiring process. *see also* employment
interview: based on fit, 99–103;
CEOs, 106–107; psychology in,
98–99; university professors,
107–108
Hitler, Adolf, 82, 85
Hobel, Mara, 75
Holmes, Elizabeth, xviii, 135, 145,
160
Holmes, Sherlock, xix
Hugo, Victor, 133
human capital, 135–136, 139–144

I
Iacocca, Lee, 106, 232
impression management, 102,
130–131, 139, 229
induction, 61
influencers, 91
informal networks, 184
informed learning, 57–58
ingratiation, 102, 109, 119–121,
125–126, 131
integrative negotiations, 196
integrity, 12, 107, 124, 138, 236, 244